Social Movements in Malaysia

This volume describes and analyses several of the most important social movements in contemporary Malaysia. Contemporary Malaysian non-governmental organisations (NGOs) have evolved over the years into significant actors in Malaysian politics and society. The Reformasi movement that began in the late 1990s proved the potency of some of these movements, as civil society came to play a more critical political role. Shifts in the organisational manifestations of social movements have reflected Malaysians' changing perceptions of the place, nature and function of civil society in the polity.

Included in this collection of essays are discussions of Malaysian movements organised around women's rights, the environment, human rights, global peace, Islam and the rights of indigenous peoples. The contributors trace the historical roots of the movements as well as of the legal framework in which they operate. These groups face particular constraints posed by Malaysia's political and economic environment as well as organisational weaknesses. However, it is argued that they have still managed to find innovative ways to network and lobby for shared goals and have had a real impact on a range of government policies and popular attitudes.

Contents
Meredith L. Weiss: Malaysian NGOs: history, legal framework and characteristics
Lai Suat Yan: The women's movement in peninsular Malaysia, 1900–99: a historical analysis
Patricia A. Martinez: Complex configurations: the Women's Agenda for Change and the Women's Candidacy Initiative
Saliha Hassan: Islamic non-governmental organisations
Sundari Ramakrishna: The environmental movement in Malaysia
Meredith L. Weiss: The Malaysian human rights movement
Fadzilah Majid Cooke: Non-governmental organisations in Sarawak
Fan Tew Teng: The peace movement and Malaysian foreign and domestic policy

Social Movements in Malaysia
From moral communities to NGOs

Edited by Meredith L. Weiss
and Saliha Hassan

LONDON AND NEW YORK

First published 2003
by RoutledgeCurzon
2 Park Square, Milton Park, Abingdon, Oxfordshire OX14 4RN

Simultaneously published in the USA and Canada
by Routledge/Curzon
711 Third Avenue, New York, NY 10017

Routledge is an imprint of the Taylor and Francis Group, an informa business

First issued in paperback 2015

© 2003 Meredith L. Weiss and Saliha Hassan; individual chapters © the individual contributors

Typeset in Times by
M Rules

All rights reserved. No part of this book may be reprinted or reproduced or utilised in any form or by any electronic, mechanical, or other means, now known or hereafter invented, including photocopying and recording, or in any information storage or retrieval system, without permission in writing from the publishers.

British Library Cataloguing in Publication Data
A catalogue record for this book is available from the British Library

Library of Congress Cataloging in Publication Data
A catalog record for this book has been requested

ISBN 978-0-7007-1646-3 (hbk)
ISBN 978-1-138-87903-4 (pbk)

Contents

Preface		vii
List of contributors		x
Introduction: from moral communities to NGOs		1
MEREDITH L. WEISS AND SALIHA HASSAN		
1	**Malaysian NGOs: history, legal framework and characteristics**	17
	MEREDITH L. WEISS	
2	**The women's movement in peninsular Malaysia, 1900–99: a historical analysis**	45
	LAI SUAT YAN	
3	**Complex configurations: the Women's Agenda for Change and the Women's Candidacy Initiative**	75
	PATRICIA A. MARTINEZ	
4	**Islamic non-governmental organisations**	97
	SALIHA HASSAN	
5	**The environmental movement in Malaysia**	115
	SUNDARI RAMAKRISHNA	
6	**The Malaysian human rights movement**	140
	MEREDITH L. WEISS	

vi *Contents*

7 **Non-governmental organisations in Sarawak** 165
   FADZILAH MAJID COOKE

8 **The peace movement and Malaysian foreign and domestic policy** 181
   FAN YEW TENG

   Notes 196
   References 207
   Index 220

Preface

This volume on *Social Movements in Malaysia* grew out of a perceived serious lack in the literature. While non-governmental organisations (NGOs) associated with various social movements have proliferated over the past two decades in Malaysia, with interest in these bodies growing apace, few texts critically assess what these movements are and how they have fared. The aim of this book is thus twofold. First, the volume will provide a starting point for interested individuals – researchers, prospective volunteers and others – regarding the state of civil society and social movements in Malaysia, providing very specific information about the principal movements. Second, the volume will offer contributors and readers who are themselves activists a chance to evaluate how much their efforts have achieved and how movement strategies could be improved.

This book took shape during a particularly tumultuous time for Malaysian civil society. The Reformasi movement engaged the time and attention of activists and analysts, including most of our contributors. While this movement perhaps slowed progress on this volume, it made the book ever more critical, as awareness of civil society and especially NGOs – their range and their potential – skyrocketed throughout Malaysian society. Some movements have remained relatively unchanged in their aims and strategies since the onset of the Reformasi movement in late 1998. Others, such as the human rights and women's movements, have been irrevocably changed and revitalised, adopting more aggressive strategies and attracting a broader, more highly committed base.

Contributors to the volume are either social movement activists or academics concerned with civil society and the non-governmental sector, or both. Perhaps reflecting demographic trends both among social activists and among the academics who study them, most of the contributors to this volume are women. We asked that each contributor survey a particular movement rather than just a particular NGO or campaign.[1] Authors were asked to provide an overview of the history, progress and composition of the relevant social movement (defined as a network of NGOs focused on a particular issue area), including networking, collaboration and future prospects. We specified also that authors were to be critical in their assessment of how the movement in question has succeeded and failed, its strengths and shortcomings, and its position within the wider array of social movements in Malaysia. Movements covered in this volume include the environmental movement, the women's movement, the human rights movement, the peace movement, Islamic-oriented NGOs and Sarawak NGOs.

However, partly because the pressures of activism kept many too busy to write and partly due to other exigencies, there are serious gaps in the volume. This book does not include chapters on the consumers' movement (though some activities involving affiliated NGOs are covered in other chapters), on movements in support of the urban poor or *peneroka bandar* (urban pioneers or 'squatters'), on activism by and for *orang asli* or *orang asal* (indigenous peoples of peninsular Malaysia, Sabah and Sarawak), on movements promoting alternative models of development, on the Chinese education movement, on groups focusing on estate- or factory-workers, on church-based groups or other non-Islamic religious-based activism, or on NGOs dealing with HIV/AIDS and sexuality. There is a chapter on Sarawak but none on Sabah, and the rest of the chapters are primarily concerned with peninsular activism. There also is no chapter on foreign NGOs having some interest and activities in Malaysia. In other words, there is enough left out to fill another volume at the least.

At the same time, we do hope that this book serves its purpose, providing information and sparking interest in these energetic, important organisations, as well as promoting critical and productive reflection on what civil society has accomplished in Malaysia and where it should go from here. We are grateful to all our contributors for their thoughtful – even if not always timely – reflections and their hard work. We would also like to thank the Malaysian Social Science Association (PSSM) for their consistent support of this endeavour, particularly current president Abdul Rahman Embong and past president Jomo K. S. Were it not for the PSSM's moral support and assurance that publication would be possible, we probably would not have pursued this project so confidently, if at all. Moreover, several contributors participated in a related panel on NGOs at the PSSM's Second Malaysian Studies International Conference in Kuala Lumpur in August 1999.

Overall, then, what this book cannot accomplish, especially in terms of breadth of scope and more theoretical analysis, we hope it will stimulate. Clearly there is a need for more work in this field – this volume is intended as an introduction rather than the last word.

Contributors

Fan Yew Teng is a former teacher and former Member of Parliament. He has been tried and convicted for sedition and also been detained under the Internal Security Act. He is one of the founders of SUARAM, a human rights NGO, and has been the co-ordinator of both the Malaysian Action Front, a coalition of more than 30 NGOs, and the Burma Solidarity Group Malaysia. He was also Executive Director of the Center for Peace Initiatives (CENPEACE) between 1994 and early 1997. He is the author of about a dozen books, including *The UMNO Drama* and *Anwar Saga: Malaysia on Trial*.

Lai Suat Yan is currently a lecturer in the Gender Studies Programme of the University of Malaya and is also a volunteer with the All Women's Action Society (AWAM). Prior to joining the university she worked full-time in the National Council of Women's Organisations (NCWO) followed by SUARAM, a human rights NGO. Her research interests are in gender violence and related issues of sexuality and health. She has published articles on rape and domestic violence.

Fadzilah Majid Cooke is a research fellow at the Research School of Pacific and Asian Studies. After being awarded her Ph.D. from Griffith University in Brisbane in 1996, she taught for several years at the University of Wollongong. Her Ph.D. dissertation was on forest resource policy in Malaysia, 1970 to 1995, based on fieldwork in Pahang and Sarawak. Her Master's thesis, submitted to the University of the Philippines, Diliman, was on the issue of Australian–Filipino cross-cultural marriages in the 1980s. In 1999, she published the book, *The Challenge of Sustainable Forests: Forest Resource Policy in Malaysia 1970 to 1995*. Her interest in the Philippines is a continuing one. Fadzilah's current work takes her to

Contributors xi

Sarawak as well as Papua New Guinea, where her interest lies in community approaches to forest resource management. She has published in Southeast Asia, Europe, Papua New Guinea and Australia.

Patricia A. Martinez is a Malaysian whose Ph.D. is in the field of religion. Her specialisation is Islam. Together with being trained in the traditional study of Islam and fluent in Arabic, she works at the intersection of postcolonial studies and postmodern philosophy (especially on identity, power and race) as well as feminist theory. She has presented and published her research on theorising in postcolonial premise; the politics of location in feminist work in religion; the racialisation of Islam and Islamisation in Malaysia; and various aspects of Muslim women's engagement with the state and with modernity.

Sundari Ramakrishna received a B.Sc. in botany from the University of Punjab, India; a Diploma in Education from the University of London; and a Ph.D. in marine microbiology from the University of Malaya. She has worked as a lecturer for thirteen years in both Methodist College and Sunway College, teaching biology and mathematics. Since 1997, she has been working with Wetlands International – Asia Pacific in the areas of conservation of wetlands areas, conducting surveys to identify critical wetlands habitats and the species that live in them, and development of wetland education tools. She is currently the Director for Malaysia Country Programme at Wetlands International, which involves co-ordinating and overseeing all projects under the programme. Her hobbies include playing the piano, jungle trekking and jogging.

Saliha Hassan is a lecturer in the Department of Political Science, Universiti Kebangsaan Malaysia. Her main research interest is non-governmental organisations (NGOs) in the Malaysian political system as well as related issues within the domestic and international milieus. She has been a member of the GESEAS-IKMAS research group on 'Discourses and Practices of Democracy in Southeast Asia: NGOs in Malaysia' (1997–8) and 'Globalisation at International, National and Local Levels in Southeast Asia: A Transforming Civil Society in Malaysia' (1999–2003). She has presented her research findings at both local and international seminars and conferences. Her publications include 'Peranan badan bukan kerajaan dalam pembentukan masyarakat madani' ('NGOs in the Formation of a Madani Society in Malaysia', 1998) and 'NGO, masyarakat sivil dan demokrasi' ('NGOs, Civil Society and Democracy in Malaysia', 2000).

Meredith L. Weiss is currently a lecturer in political science at Yale University. She has spent several years in Malaysia and Singapore, conducting research on civil society, political change and related issues. Recent and forthcoming publications on Malaysia include articles and book chapters on non-governmental organisations (NGOs), the 1999 general elections, the Reformasi movement, the changing nature of ethnicity and communalism, and the role of civil society in opposition politics. She has also written on NGOs, particularly women's groups, in Singapore.

Introduction
From moral communities to NGOs

Meredith L. Weiss and Saliha Hassan

The remarkable global expansion in the number and scope of non-governmental organisations (NGOs) since the 1970s has given rise to a flurry of studies on the roles and impact of civil society. These groups tend to be taken as a new phenomenon. However, while the specific shape of many contemporary NGOs may be new, they often build upon a long history of social networks and associations. Such is the case in Malaysia, where today's increasingly vibrant NGO community has evolved from an array of associations stretching back to the colonial era. Those early organisations were usually oriented around the ethnic or religious community, often linked with mosques, churches, clan networks and the like. They were concerned primarily with the socioeconomic and moral welfare of their communities. Since then, a subset of NGOs has come to focus much more on politics, including issues of both distribution and rights. Their roots in those early associations, however, are still apparent in NGOs' membership, moral authority and place within the polity. This volume is inspired by an interest in placing today's social movements in perspective, understanding their positions in and contributions to Malaysian state and society.

Malaysia's civil society shares important features with those of other states, particularly its fellow post-colonial, developmentalist regimes. Wary of challenges and determined to streamline policy-making as much as possible, the state leaves relatively little space for informal or oppositional political activity. Moreover, the regime may draw upon a regulatory framework bequeathed by the British colonial administration to curtail perceived threats to its authority. All the same, civil society retains an important niche in the polity. A brief overview of key debates concerning civil society helps to put its contributions in context. Then, an introduction to the primary social movements in contemporary Malaysia will suggest the varied ways Malaysian citizens participate in the nation's political life and social development.

The shape of civil society

Fascination with the nature and potential of civil society has burgeoned worldwide since Poland's Solidarity and its counterparts toppled the communist order in the late 1980s. Reformers elsewhere have searched for clues of how they, too, might have such an impact, while scholars have traced the minutiae of civil societal organisations and activities to specify more precisely how this sphere links up with others. The concept of civil society was developed in the West, however, to refer to an essential part of liberal democratic regimes. Most of the polities in which civil society is now so anxiously watched and nurtured are far from liberal; nor do many aspire to such status.

Civil society both provides for needs not met by the state and helps transform states in line with citizens' preferences. Adrian Leftwich (1993) defines civil society as consisting of those cultural, political or economic areas of social life that are organised by private or voluntary arrangements between individuals outside the direct control of the state. Within it are mechanisms that function in conflict resolution and in building trust and networks to link citizens. By their collaborative activities, civil societal associations thus foster not only opportunities for individuals to further their specific interests but also societal and institutional linkages to enable community building (Yamamoto 1995). Implicit within the notion of civil society is a principle of civic virtue and an emphasis on rational, co-operative and moral interactions both among the members of a society and between them and their government (De Lue 1997).

Iris Marion Young specifies a niche for civil society by contrasting voluntary associational life with the state and economy, based on how each co-ordinates action and its relative control of systematic power. In her formulation, the state co-ordinates action through the medium of authorised power, the economy through money, and civil society through communicative interaction. These are not three spatially distinct spheres, but different kinds of activity or levels of association among which citizens may move freely (Young 1999: 144–5). As she describes:

> civic associations and public spheres outside state and economy allow self-organization for the purposes of identity support, the invention of new practices, and the provision of some goods and services. Perhaps even more important, public spheres thriving in civil society often limit state and economic power and make their exercise more accountable to citizens.
>
> (Young 1999: 141)

To perform these roles, civil society depends on a variety of mechanisms, including the proliferation and advocacy initiatives of NGOs. By presenting their vision of a better society and striving to be 'catalytic agents for change' through their public involvement, NGOs help keep the state in line with citizens' preferences and interests (Yamamoto 1995: 7). Still, the chances for NGOs to achieve their demands depends largely on how open and susceptible the state and society are to such pressure. For their part, governments may define state interests as the general good and deny influence to the 'special interests' represented by societal associations. By at least attempting to mediate between the legitimate rights of the state and citizens' moral and civic rights, NGOs serve as a 'third sector' between these two spheres (Korten 1990; Lim 1995; Marcussen 1996).

Rulers and ruled may have divergent conceptions of the rights and responsibilities of each towards the other, but the state is at an advantage based on its access to power. Corbyn elucidates the place of civil society with regard to protection of individuals' rights vis-à-vis the state:

> Rights were developed as claims made by people organising outside the structures of government. The rights secured required the government to defend its citizens both against abuse of economic power, and against the abuse of constitutional power by the State itself. Today, it remains the case that these rights can only be defended by a vibrant, well-resourced and well-organised civic culture, which can monitor the activities of the State and business, and allow the people to organise and represent their claims upon them.
> (Corbyn 1996: 56)

Still, not all civil societies or organisations are effective. Some may be too small, too enervated, or too closely linked with traditional (such as tribal or village) social cleavages to accomplish much in the way of co-ordinating or advocating for broader interests (Ibrahim 1995).

It is for its potential as a buffer between citizens and state that 'a rich and pluralistic civil society' is so often deemed a condition for democratic politics (Leftwich 1993: 615). What is civil society's place, though, in non-democratic or semi-democratic politics? The composition of civil society in its 'ideal' form, for instance, is hardly what is found in most developing states. Social networks are 'supposed' to cross societal cleavages, uniting citizens without regard to ascriptive identities. This ideal is seldom realised – but civil society is not necessarily any less significant for the fact that specific organisations within it are constituted on ethnic, religious or even familial bases.

Those organisations are loosely categorised here as 'NGOs'. Regardless of the terminology chosen to refer to them, the organisations in question may be defined as groups of citizens engaged in collective action for self-help or issue advocacy outside the aegis of the state. They are social organisations 'formed voluntarily for common objectives and collectively engaged in economic activities or public affairs' (Yamamoto 1995: 6). A number have achieved some degree of clout in the formation of public policies while others are more influential in society than vis-à-vis the state. Such groups may also be termed 'action groups' (Haynes 2000)[1] or subsumed under the category of (new) social movements (Klandermans 1989; Diani 1992; Habermas 1981).[2]

Initially, literature on NGOs in the developing world focused primarily on groups involved with economic development (credit schemes, collectives, skills training and so on). This focus reflected governments' treatment of NGOs as 'mere subsidiaries of government agencies' (Yamamoto 1995: 5).[4] Attention has shifted particularly since the 1990s, though, towards advocacy-oriented NGOs such as human rights and women's groups, most of which have a distinctly political bent. The bulk of voluntary associations in the developing world focused initially on charitable work and social services, often oriented around organised religion; then more on community development; and now increasingly on politicised issues such as the environment and civil liberties.

Many associations in Malaysia and elsewhere are far from the sorts of grassroots-based, internally democratic groups privileged by the literature on civil society and NGOs. Even comparatively hierarchical or authoritarian voluntary associations can foster self-determination and self-development by facilitating identity and voice (especially for usually excluded or marginalised groups), innovation and provision of goods and services (Young 1999: 149–50). Indeed, as Judith Adler Hellman bluntly advises, 'the assumption that movements are automatically more democratic seems as ill-founded as the assumption that they inevitably promote democratization simply because they make demands on the system' (1994: 133–5).

All the same, even Hellman finds that popular movements may help with the formation of new identities, the expansion of civil society, the search for new ways of doing politics, and the mobilisation of new sectors of society. For instance, in Malaysia, constituencies such as urban squatters, indigenous peoples and women have been empowered through associational activity to discover new strategies for further mobilisation and to magnify the force of their demands. Of course, not just 'good' interests find their voice in civil society. As Thomas Carothers (1999–2000: 19) clarifies, 'civil society is a broader concept, encompassing all the organisations and associations that exist outside of the state (including political parties) and the market'. Included in civil society are not just politically progressive groups, but also apolitical associations concerned with social welfare, culture and sports as well as right-wing militia groups and other not-so-civil organisations.

What allows non-governmental actors to have such political import is their generation of social capital. Social capital consists of the resources for collective action accumulated by past experience of engaging in associations, and also refers to the attributes of people that favour their civil engagement. Robert Putnam brought the concept of social capital into vogue with his studies of Italy (1993) and the United States (2000). He explains that secular, horizontally organised associations 'make democracy work' by fostering social trust from networks of reciprocity and civic engagement. The generation of social capital among civic-minded citizens enables better policy performance and more satisfied, happy citizens. In less politically liberal contexts, the accumulation of social capital also facilitates citizens' organising to protect their interests against the predations of the state. Hence, civil society may play a role in expanding political participation and fostering political change, regardless of whether the state conceives of itself as democratic or welcomes citizens' political engagement.

State and civil society in Malaysia

Malaysia is in many ways typical of a developmental, semi-authoritarian, ethnically plural polity. The state makes no pretense of practising or aspiring towards liberal democracy. As Prime Minister Mahathir describes, Malaysia practises 'realistic democracy':

> Malaysia is not over-zealous about the democratic system to the point where we accept without question everything that is done in the name of democracy. If the people and the country benefit, then we will accept practices, which are said to be democratic. If the people and the nation get only the worst from any practice that is said to be democratic, we will give priority to what is good for the country and the people, and put aside the questions of whether or not it is democratic . . . What is important in a system of governance is the people and the nation's well-being.
> (*Sunday Mail*, 5 December 1996: 2)

At the same time, Malaysian citizens do have some space to organise to complement or even to oppose the regime. As elsewhere, the government has an implicit bargain with its citizens: in exchange for a degree of compliance and quiescence, including leaving 'politics' to politicians, the state will provide socioeconomic development and security, and meet most welfare needs. However, when the economy declines, elite factionalism complicates patronage arrangements, or some other imbalance disrupts the state in its developmental mission, Malaysian citizens tend to consider this social contract invalid and speak out against the regime. The state has at its disposal a range of harsh regulations to keep activists in check at such moments.[5] Still, as in other developing or recently developed states, the spread of mass education, mass communications and globalised discourses of human rights, as well as the increasingly secure middle-class status of an ever-greater proportion of the populace have fostered a rise in critical engagement with the state, sometimes through opposition parties but often through advocacy-oriented social movements.

Malaysia is a constitutional monarchy. Regular, reasonably free elections for federal and state legislatures have been held since before independence in 1957. Nonetheless, the same coalition has held power without interruption since 1955. Called the Perikatan (Alliance) until 1969 and Barisan Nasional (National Front, BN) since resumption of parliamentary government after nearly two years of rule by emergency decree, this coalition is comprised primarily of communal parties representing Malaysia's major ethnic groups, Malays, Chinese and Indians. The BN has been dominated from the outset by its chief Malay component, the United Malays' National Organisation (UMNO), led since 1981 by Prime Minister Mahathir Mohamad.[5] Government under the BN combines democratic elements with significant restrictions on individuals' political and civil rights and liberties, justified in the name of stability, social harmony and consistency for continued economic development. As Mahathir describes, 'the duty of government is ensuring peace and harmony through political stability which also creates a conducive environment for economic prosperity' (*Sun*, 18 April 1997: 2).[6]

Malaysia has maintained a course of regime-led, intense economic development since the 1970s with a view towards becoming a fully industrialised state by the year 2020.[7] Malaysian society has changed as a result. In particular, the enhancement of affirmative action policies since 1970 has promoted the growth of a new Malay middle class, particularly in the professional/technical and administrative/managerial categories. These individuals are generally dependent upon and hence supportive of the regime and Malay political dominance. Their political conservatism has left the emergent middle class largely demobilised and loath to be too involved in activities that might challenge the smooth implementation of development plans. Despite offering critiques and recommendations of more sustainable, socially just or environmentally wise development strategies, civil society has taken a back seat in Malaysia's economic development since the regime has generally faced little pressure to heed these calls.

The state does tolerate a set of opposition parties and has even allowed them to control state legislatures. Nonetheless, opposition challenges have been met at times with crackdowns and more consistently with gerrymandering and other means of skewing electoral outcomes to benefit the incumbent regime. Indeed, disputing arguments from civil society that his regime has stunted citizens' rights and political growth, Mahathir maintains that it is sometimes necessary to limit civil and political rights in order to provide for the material needs of the populace. He insists, 'freedom from poverty and the wish to develop are also essential elements of human rights' – and it is upon these rights that the state prefers to focus (Mahathir 2000: 74). While he acknowledges that some pressure groups may actually be useful to the state, Mahathir decries others as concerned with special interests to the detriment of the majority, the rule of law and political stability (Mahathir 1986: chap. 9).

In combination with opposition parties, NGOs have indeed posed a threat at times to the political order Mahathir is so keen to maintain. Probably the strongest challenge to the regime to date came with the 1999 elections, when the far-reaching Reformasi movement galvanised the main peninsular opposition parties to unite in the Barisan Alternatif (Alternative Front, BA) with the support of an array of civil society organisations and activists. This challenge came in the wake of a marked trend towards executive centralisation under Mahathir and of the Asian economic crisis, which seriously impacted the Malaysian economy in the late 1990s.

The development and place of Malaysian civil society

As outlined in the following chapter, then described in detail in subsequent contributions, the social movements active in Malaysia today developed out of welfare, religious, commercial and communal progress and self-help bodies active since the early twentieth century. Some of these groups have maintained a distinctly political flavour since their inception, but most began with more of a focus on service delivery then evolved towards issue advocacy. Particularly since the 1970s, these organisations have come to populate a civil society that looks increasingly like what is described in the literature. However, their right to participate as democratic actors remains contested. The state considers a much higher level of social control necessary than do NGOs. Thus, one of the fundamental issues uniting and mobilising civil society in Malaysia has been the attempt to carve out legitimate space for political engagement outside political parties and the state.

Anthony Milner (1991) suggests that the invention of 'politics' in Malaysia was a relatively recent development. Prior to about the 1920s, Malayans[8] saw themselves as powerless subjects, not as active citizens with the authority to legitimate the rule of their sultan. Once citizens took it upon themselves to evaluate the policies passed down by sultans (or colonial or Islamic leaders) and voice their own preferences, those officials found themselves obliged to justify their choices and perspectives in terms designed to appeal to their popular base. In other words, a public sphere developed where previously there had been none. Since that time, a wide array of political parties and NGOs have evolved to represent specific perspectives and interests. Still, scholars paid relatively little heed to Malaysian associational life until 'social welfare bodies' had given way to more political NGOs by the 1980s.

Even today, studies of Malaysian civil society are few and tend to be rather lax about terminology and scope. For instance, Makmor Tumin explains that nowadays, 'the term NGO is used widely and readily for all bodies in Malaysia except political parties, labour unions, freemasons, cooperatives, military organizations, government bodies and private organizations including several other small bodies' (1998: 62). He himself refers to all officially registered societies as NGOs, excluding only political parties and adding in comparable groups registered as different sorts of entity (Makmor 1998). In one of the best works available on Malaysian NGOs, Tan Boon Kean and Bishan Singh (1994) are far more precise in discriminating between advocacy-oriented NGOs and other sorts of association, such as government-organised NGOs (GONGOs). As they acknowledge, though, the fungible identities and shifting foci of Malaysian associations mandate just a simple classification scheme. Even their dichotomy of welfare-oriented and issue-oriented NGOs, though, may not hold up at all times, since seemingly apolitical welfare groups have been known to adopt a political stance at critical moments.

Indeed, Malaysian NGOs diverge in various respects from what the traditional NGO literature predicts for developing states. To begin with, relatively few groups concentrate on areas such as agricultural extension activities, skills development and credit provision. The Malaysian state has itself taken the lead in rural development, provision of social services and the like, rather than leaving a vacuum for developmental and politically engaged NGOs to fill. Moreover, Malaysia's reluctance to accept assistance from agencies such as the International Monetary Fund has limited external pressure to involve NGOs in development projects, which would have legitimated and strengthened these groups. Still, the 'old politics' of struggles over economic growth, distribution and security, rather than contests over identity and symbols, remains highly germane in Malaysia. In consequence, the primary target for Malaysian social movements is not society or business but the state.

Just as importantly, contra academic distinctions, groups formed around ascriptive identities constitute a vital part of Malaysian civil society. For instance, groups representing the demands of ethnic Chinese for equal rights in language, education and culture have long been among the largest, most significant associations in multiracial Malaysia. Religious groups, especially Islamic ones, are even more problematic for theorists, though constituting the most politically potent sector of civil society in contemporary Malaysia. Ernest Gellner (1994), for instance, denies that an Islamic society (presumably including Malaysia) could support a civil society, given the attention Islam gives to the *ummah*, or faith-based community, rather than that defined by territory and polity, and the anti-democratic tendencies inherent in theocracy.

Indeed, while not denying the relevance of a civil society construct, Muslim intellectuals in Malaysia and Indonesia have recognised the need to define more clearly how well their conception of Islam accords with democratic norms and practices. Out of these efforts has come the concept of *masyarakat madani*, or a society modelled on that of the Prophet Mohammad's era and guided by Islamic precepts and values. As first enunciated by former Malaysian deputy prime minister Anwar Ibrahim,[9] a *masyarakat madani* is a caring society built upon Islamic principles of communal interdependence. As a project, it represents a way to make Malaysians more self-sufficient, civically conscious and engaged in sociopolitical discourse on democracy, pluralism, social justice, accountability and good governance. Rulers and ruled would be held to the same moral (as opposed to performance-based) standard. More than simply a political concept, though, *masyarakat madani* refers to an all-encompassing system of social organisation, much as Islamists promote Islam as *ad-deen*, or a complete way of life.[10]

While clearly akin to civil society, a *masyarakat madani* might be more aptly termed a 'civic society' based on constructive rather than adversarial interaction and informed by Islamic history. The principles at the root of the order are morality, justice, fairness, civility and consultation rather than majoritarianism. In practice, however, the terms 'civil society' and *masyarakat madani*, together with other variants/translations such as *masyarakat wargaan* (citizenship society), *masyarakat sipil* (civil society), and *masyarakat beradab* (civilised society), tend to be elided by both activists and academics. Even Anwar himself defined *masyarakat madani* as '*civil society* with democratic characteristics' (Anwar 1997: 9, emphasis in original) while Indonesian scholar Syamsurizal Panggabean scoffs that *masyarakat madani* is simply 'Arabic for *civil society*' (Syamsurizal 2000: 92, emphasis in original).

The failure of these alternative constructs really to take root suggests the structural and ideational similarities between Malaysian associational life and that elsewhere. While comprised also of elements from 'peripheral' groups, the old middle class and communities defined by ascriptive characteristics, Malaysian social movements, like new social movements in other states, are rooted in the new middle class and imbued with a sense of their own agency to bring about sociopolitical change. The politics of this class fragment 'is typically a politics *of* a class but not *on behalf of* a class' (Offe 1985: 833, emphasis in original). While issues of redistribution and economic justice may be significant, the demands expressed are not class-specific and activism involves broad, cross-class alliances. Moreover, activists may work at different times through institutional or non-institutional channels – that is, through political parties and state institutions or NGOs. Their determination of outlets and methods depends on both strategic calculations and ideological preferences.

Mahathir draws upon rhetoric of 'Asian values' to lambaste open contestation or dissent, especially from outside political parties, as inappropriate and 'western'. Francis Fukuyama credits Mahathir and the former prime minister of Singapore, Lee Kuan Yew, for having started the debate on Asian values at the end of the 1980s. He attributes ambiguities in the debate to the fact that it 'was propelled by actors with highly political motives, who were less interested in uncovering the real nature of value differences across societies than in scoring political points or legitimising their own policies' (quoted in Hitchcock 1997: vii). Among 'some of the values which Asians hold dear', Mahathir points to having an orderly society, societal harmony, accountability of public officials, openness to new ideas, freedom of expression and respect for authority (Mahathir 2000: 15). Portraying 'The West' as culturally decadent, amoral and destructive of the national culture and ways of life, the government assigns to itself the role of protecting local values, traditions and norms. The regime thus discredits initiatives from civil society, particularly those which legitimate themselves by universalist human rights, environmentalist or other norms, by alleging that local NGOs are aping 'The West' and being used by western agents jealous of Malaysia's success and keen to destabilise and impoverish the nation.

Implicit in the state's position is the assumption that social and economic well-being are prerequisites to the enjoyment of civil and political rights. In contrast, politicised NGOs insist that the causality is reversed: that in order to ensure social and economic well-being, citizens and their organisations must have the freedom to exercise their civil and political rights and to contest the state if necessary for the sake of citizens' interests. Different segments of Malaysian civil society draw upon distinct discourses to support their position, though the predominant strains are Islamic conceptions of justice and morality on the one hand and secular, universalist definitions of human rights on the other. Over the years, activists have come to emphasise what is common to these perspectives, enabling the formation of broad-based coalitions to advocate for issues of general concern.

Constraints notwithstanding, Malaysia boasts a myriad of NGOs promoting wide-ranging social, economic, cultural and political causes, interests and agendas. The relationship of these groups with the government ranges from collaborative to confrontational and may change with the specific issue or moment. For instance, many NGOs focused on welfare or recreation complement the government by providing social services. These groups tend to work closely with, for example, the Ministry of National Unity and Social Development (Johari 1993). More critical groups, on the other hand, challenge government policies that they see as incongruent with their ideals of social justice. Such groups may attempt to engage the state to negotiate on perspectives and aims, to empower the grassroots to enable citizens to raise their concerns with the government, or to work directly with the government to improve specific public policies. Examples of such critical NGOs can be found among groups advocating the expansion of democratic space or promoting alternative ideologies to the state's, such as the banned Islamic group Darul Arqam (see Chapter 4).

The Malaysian government has traditionally been more wary than friendly towards political NGOs. It tends to consider these groups as aligned with opposition politics. Indeed, the critiques of the government offered by political NGOs and opposition political parties tend to converge in matters such as the narrow space and limited freedom allowed for alternative political discourses and activism, the need for greater consideration for human rights, and the significance of promoting a viable civil society to further Malaysia's political development. Also, NGOs and opposition parties alike are affected by government regulations on publications, the expression of partisan political viewpoints and free interaction with the grassroots. These constraints are perceived to impact upon party and non-party activists' fundamental liberties and the promotion of more democratic, accountable governance. The government's response to this criticism is that opposition forces, including particular NGOs, have tended to misuse civil liberties in order to incite dissatisfaction, opposition and even hatred for the long-standing BN government.

Such debates have gained added significance since the late 1990s. Although political NGOs have been fairly visible since the 1970s, the sacking of Deputy Prime Minister Anwar Ibrahim from his positions in the government and UMNO in September 1998 launched the massive Reformasi movement that brought unprecedented numbers of Malaysians on to the streets and into opposition parties and NGOs.[11] All of a sudden, the issue of people's right to participate in political activities became a top priority even in generally apathetic sections of society. Moreover, the terms of pro-democratic civil society – judicial independence, executive interference, administrative transparency, freedom of information, freedom of expression, responsible media, civil liberties and human rights – quickly became household words. NGOs that had previously eschewed politics, women who had been relatively invisible in the public sphere and young people who had been indifferent to politics were drawn to the Reformasi front lines and seem unlikely to accept a return to the status quo ante.

Even this popular upsurge, however, does not represent a fundamental discontinuity with the past. First, NGOs remain constrained by legal restrictions, the still generally passive and conservative mass political culture, and ideological and strategic differences hindering deeper co-operation across civil society. As the chapters that follow describe, the strategies and constituencies of Malaysian social movements have altered somewhat over time – some more than others – but their fundamental characteristics are slow to change. Moreover, a focus on what civil society has accomplished in concrete and cultural terms tends to obfuscate the still overwhelming dominance of the state. Contemporary Malaysian social movements play a vital role in the polity and, as such, are well worth studying. All the same, at the end of the day, they occupy space granted, however grudgingly, by the state; are in many cases beholden to the state for financial resources and policy access; and still choose non-confrontational methods and an incremental approach more often than not. Furthermore, while the state probably could not quash all activism and oppositional ideas at this point – and certainly not without seriously dampening its own legitimacy – it could significantly damage NGOs by a crackdown.

Overview of the volume

This volume is far from comprehensive in its coverage of Malaysian social movements. Absent are NGOs dealing with Chinese education, the urban poor, indigenous peoples' rights, Christianity, labour, public health and more. Still, although this volume cannot cover all major movements in Malaysia today, those it covers are among the most important. Moreover, many of the insights offered in these chapters regarding the challenges faced by activists, the position of NGOs vis-à-vis the government and the opposition, strategies for popular education and mobilisation, and means of engagement with state and society apply to other movements as well. Finally, the sense of mission apparent in the NGOs described here, which motivates activists to risk censure and more, spurs on advocates for other causes, too.

Meredith Weiss sets the stage with her discussion of the background and character of Malaysian NGOs and the context in which they operate. As mentioned above, contemporary NGOs are the progeny of early twentieth-century organisations representing usually ethnic or religious interests. That legacy at least partly explains the continuing communal tendencies of many NGOs and their combination of welfare-related activities with more political advocacy initiatives. The regulatory framework in effect today also has its roots in the colonial era, particularly in the efforts of the British authorities to control Chinese secret societies, though the various laws have been augmented and refined since then. Weiss is cautiously optimistic in her evaluation of the relative strengths and prospects of Malaysian NGOs. While they face critical hurdles in the form of regulations, resource constraints and a public not terribly inclined towards active political engagement, they have helped foster greater democratic consciousness and have achieved some real successes in terms of policies.

Next, in Chapter 2, Lai Suat Yan describes the historical evolution of the women's movement in peninsular Malaysia, a discussion continued by Patricia Martinez in the following chapter. Lai begins by defining the parameters of women's activism in Malaysia, introducing key theories behind women's movements and considering how Malaysian activists situate themselves with regard to feminism and gender politics. As Lai explains, women have been active in campaigning for 'women's issues' since before independence; the women's movement is among Malaysia's oldest social movements. Women have worked variously through NGOs, political parties and trade unions, pursuing different aims by different means in each. However, having evolved from an earlier preoccupation with welfare services, NGOs seem firmly ascendant relative to parties and unions today as vehicles for women's pursuit of their interests.

Indeed, Malaysian women's groups have been forging a new course for political engagement among NGOs and activists. As Martinez elucidates, the Women's Agenda for Change and the Women's Candidacy Initiative, both launched in 1999, represent a genuine shift in the nature and direction of women's political activism. Martinez puts these initiatives in the context of prior efforts and concludes that women are renegotiating their conceptions of power and their place within the polity and society. Furthermore, while both these initiatives represent important steps for the evolution of the women's movement, they also suggest a new phase for NGO activism more broadly. Under these initiatives, women have surmounted social cleavages and set aside the distinction between civil society and political society to further a set of concrete aims and progressive norms by the most effective means available.

In Chapter 4, Saliha Hassan introduces Malaysia's hugely important Islamic NGOs. Saliha explains that the Malaysian state feels obliged to grant at least some ground to these groups, given their stature within Malaysia's dominant Muslim community and the popularity and scope of Islamist activism. Together with related political parties, Islamist *dakwah* organisations have pushed state and society towards new perspectives and priorities. Especially with the general rise in oppositional political activism since the late 1990s, Saliha sees Islamic NGOs and civil society more broadly as ever more significant to the Malaysian polity. She describes their varied roles and constituencies, as well as the broader political context, to investigate why it is that Islamic NGOs are so socially and politically significant today.

Sundari Ramakrishna then addresses what is perhaps the best-known movement in Malaysia, the environmental movement. She finds that this movement, too, can boast some genuine successes. As she describes, environmental groups target both state and society. While they seek environmentally sound policies, they also encourage citizens to appreciate nature and support efforts at conservation. Combining expertise, gumption and commitment, Malaysian environmental groups enjoy real clout in planning for and managing forests, wetlands, wildlife refuges and environmental policies more broadly, working either in collaboration with or in opposition to the federal and state governments. Still, environmental NGOs could increase their potency by networking more effectively with one another and with the community and by assuming a more aggressive posture at times.

In Chapter 6, Meredith Weiss turns to the human rights movement,

Introduction: from moral communities to NGOs   15

a movement that has been active since the 1970s but has grown immensely in size and significance over the past several years. As Weiss explains, the human rights movement is particularly amorphous in shape, as all sorts of groups and activists join in specific campaigns that fall under the rubric of human rights. However, NGOs devoted specifically to the promotion and preservation of human rights in Malaysia and elsewhere have taken shape over the last three decades, pressing both state and society for greater adherence to human rights conventions and perspectives. Despite pressures placed on human rights groups and activists by state repression and the difficulties of such broad-based collaboration, the movement has come to assume particular salience as a platform from which to critique the regime and recommend reforms. Still, the government's particular resentment of rights-related challenges and the movement's lack of strategic vision and sustained organisational development have so far hindered the human rights movement from having a more substantial impact.

The chapters to this point all focus primarily on peninsular Malaysian activism. As Fadzilah Majid Cooke explains in her contribution on NGOs in Sarawak, both the issues and the strategies facing citizens outside the peninsula tend to be different. In particular, Majid Cooke stresses the impact of state incursions on local communities' space and rights. NGOs' responses to such predations impact upon popular identities and foster the motivation to uphold the rights of the community apropos government authorities. In addition to describing the issues of land, livelihood and environmental protection in northern Sarawak, Majid Cooke suggests that NGOs may not have the option of scaling up their efforts to engage with the state and bureaucracy, so pick the most relevant and appropriate avenues for public education and activism. Even if these NGOs have had minimal impact on government policies so far, they have shifted public awareness of civil liberties and environmental priorities, as well as empowering the masses to stand up to the state.

Finally, in Chaper 8, Fan Yew Teng links several strands introduced earlier in the volume with his overview of the peace movement. Motivated by concern for human rights and in some cases religion, this movement targets both foreign affairs and domestic rights. Fan describes the efforts of Islamic and other groups to influence Malaysian foreign policy priorities and strategies, particularly in light of the Gulf War. These same sorts of groups are also active on the domestic front, promoting accountability, challenging police brutality and otherwise promoting rights and reform at home as well as abroad. Having traced moments at which NGOs worked in agreement with the state as well as against it, Fan cautions against too-facile a conception of NGO activism as oppositional, or, for that matter, as completely divorced from political parties and other institutions, even if it is a junior partner in such collaborative efforts. However, he concludes with a note of optimism echoed elsewhere in the volume, suggesting that the constraints of operating in a semi-authoritarian polity are not enough to keep Malaysian NGOs from forging on with their efforts at advocacy, education, mobilisation and reform.

Taken together, these chapters suggest that Malaysian social movements do play a meaningful part in both politics and society. NGOs grant citizens an additional, generally non-partisan outlet for political participation; encourage them to think critically about the polity and their position in it; and forge links both across sectors of civil society and between Malaysians and activists abroad. However, civil society in Malaysia is an evolving sphere. Not only the aims and shape of social movements, but their constituencies, reception by the state and comparative levels of success are still subject to change. All the same, it is clear that even if the regime or particular NGOs change, Malaysian social movements will continue their efforts to install a more sustainable, equitable, progressive, and moral social, political, cultural and economic order.

1 Malaysian NGOs
History, legal framework and characteristics

Meredith L. Weiss

Introduction

Though it is only relatively recently that the terminology of non-governmental organisations (NGOs) has been adopted in Malaysia and that issue-based advocacy groups have gained prominence, various sorts of civil society organisations have long played a role in the country. Contemporary Malaysian NGOs have their roots in a range of organisations, including Chinese secret societies, Indian nationalist associations and Malay-Muslim progress organisations. Moreover, the laws governing NGO activities date back to the colonial era, though they have been refined since then. The longevity of these strictures is testament to the ongoing tensions between state and civil society in Malaysia and the desire of both the colonial and independent state to control societal organisations. Today's advocacy-oriented NGOs are heterogeneous in structure, membership and ideology. Still developing as a political and social force, many of these NGOs remain constrained not only by the restrictive political environment, but also by personalistic structures, a shortage of funds, difficulties in rousing an often disengaged mass public, and ethnic and religious divisions. Regardless, Malaysian NGOs have made important contributions to fostering a democratically inclined and socially aware citizenry, bringing key issues to public prominence and nurturing a significant core group within civil society able to rally mass opinion at crucial junctures in support of political, social and economic reforms.

Little has been written about NGOs and civil society in Malaysia, even amidst the burgeoning interest in these topics in neighbouring countries. The government does not encourage such research by either local or foreign scholars and NGOs themselves have limited resources for critical analysis of their own or other groups' efforts. Most of the studies that have been done are either relatively superficial overviews of particular movements, funding agencies' evaluations of the groups they sponsor, or a handful of more empirical than analytical works on specific sectors such as environmental activism. A few more critical works are available, though each still covering only certain sectors. These include Khong Kim Hoong (1988–9) on the reasons for the development of Malaysian public interest groups, their characteristics, and their relationship with the government; Sheila Nair (1995 and 1999) on the nature of hegemony and resistance through new social movements, particularly the environmental, human rights and Islamic movements; Saliha Hassan (1998) on relations between the state and political NGOs; and Tan Boon Lean and Bishan Singh (1994), which presents an analytical framework, an overview of state–NGO relations, and case studies of recent rape law reform and anti-logging campaigns.

More country-specific studies would be helpful both as practical evaluations of what NGOs have accomplished and how they could be more effective as well as for theory building and comparative research. Context is particularly significant since much of the existing literature on NGOs, civil society and related topics just does not really apply to Malaysia. The restrictive legal environment and semi-authoritarian regime make studies of new social movements (NSMs) and NGOs premised on a liberal democratic setting not all that relevant. Also, the Malaysian state has itself taken the lead in rural development, provision of social services and the like, rather than leaving a vacuum for developmental (and politically engaged) NGOs to fill, so much of the literature on the roles of NGOs as partners in development is also not really applicable.[1]

The analysis here will focus only upon advocacy-oriented or political NGOs. While both advocacy-oriented groups and voluntary welfare organisations are often lumped under the rubric of 'NGO', the former are more politically relevant and contentious in contemporary Malaysia. Saliha Hassan (1998: 17–18) offers a useful definition: 'political NGOs are those that engage in public debates and dissemination of information relating to civil liberties, democratic rights, good governance, accountability of the government to the people, people oriented leadership – all of which relate to the central issue of democratic participation'. These NGOs centre around the question of good governance and present themselves as 'the conscience of the state' and as channels for the democratic participation of citizens in the polity, but are 'eager to distance themselves from the ethnic pre-occupation of the Malaysian political parties'.

Historical antecedents

While advocacy-oriented NGOs are a relatively new phenomenon, having developed in Malaysia only in the past two decades, these groups build on a long tradition of societal organisations. The primary historical antecedents to contemporary Malaysian NGOs are Chinese associations, especially secret societies; reformist Indian associations; and Malay nationalist and/or Islamic organisations prior to independence. While lacking the same issue basis of advocacy NGOs, these early organisations are significant for having prompted the development of the legal codes that still govern and constrain NGOs, for presaging the composition of NGOs generally along ethnic lines, and for moving beyond welfare and cultural functions to more critical political perspectives and activities.

Chinese organisations

A wide range of Chinese organisations developed in colonial Malaya, including:

- secret or Triad societies;
- clan organisations – mutual benefit societies representing a particular county, clan or dialect group;
- commercial and industrial organisations – associations for dispute mediation and the community's economic development, including chambers of commerce, commercial societies, unions and professional organisations;
- cultural organisations – book and newspaper reading societies, associations for the development of arts and language, university and school alumni associations and entertainment organisations;
- anti-Japanese organisations; and
- hundreds of privately established, privately funded Chinese schools (see Hicks 1996: 76–90).

Leadership within the Malayan Chinese community was drawn mostly from successful merchant-entrepreneurs involved with the mining, plantation agriculture, small-scale manufacturing, and retail and distribution sectors. Eventually in the pre-war years, clan and regional associations grew and consolidated into larger groupings. Starting around the turn of the century, these associations were gradually politicised, particularly in response to nationalist and revolutionary political upheavals in China prior to the establishment of the People's Republic of China in 1949, with both the Kuomintang and the Communists rallying support in Malaysia (Tan 1983: 115–53; Heng 1996: 34). Indeed, though 'essentially social and community welfare agencies' (Tan 1983: 113), many Chinese societies, especially secret societies, 'bordered on the political even if this political aspect was vague and not so explicitly and systematically laid out' (Lee 1985: 131).[2]

It was the secret societies that were seen as most violent and dangerous, inciting the colonial government more closely to regulate associational life. Chinese secret societies existed both in China (especially the political Triad Brotherhood, active since the seventeenth century) and among Chinese communities elsewhere. Brought overseas by early Chinese immigrants, hundreds of secret societies persist to this day in Singapore and Malaysia, despite successive governments' surveillance and suppression. A local Chinese secret society is 'a group composed of and operated by people of Chinese origin in the Straits Settlements and/or Singapore and Peninsular Malaysia, and which has a set of well-defined norms, secret rituals, and an oath that are intended subjectively to bind the members not to reveal the group's affairs' (Mak 1981: 8). The groups may have included members of only one or several dialect groups, and some even included non-ethnic Chinese members. Some societies had eligibility criteria related to place of residence or type of employment (Blythe 1969: 1). The societies operated on a range of fronts – political, social-welfare and criminal – and developed a mystique based on secrecy and ceremony, as well as fear of the violent methods used by the groups. Secret societies claimed enormous influence and membership; as of 1888, eleven secret societies in Singapore were reported to have 62,376 members, while Penang had five secret societies with 92,581 members (Hicks 1996: 91).[3] No central organisation controlled relations among all the various secret societies, so economic and other rivalries, manifested in murders, assaults, extortion and the like, did occur at times.

Secret societies offered ethnic Chinese a comfortable community of people with similar customs and language, as well as protection, authority and ordering rituals in a foreign, unfamiliar land. More specifically, Chinese secret societies were fostered and sustained by inadequacies in the legal protection system, with improvements in legal protection effecting a decline in the activity of Chinese secret societies. In other words, the strength of secret societies' conflict-reduction mechanisms may be what kept them alive (Mak 1981: 17–19, 21). Colonial police control was inadequate given language barriers hampering investigations, the protection each secret society afforded its members, and the groups' resentment of outside interference. Colonial authorities attempted both to reach a *modus vivendi* with leaders of the societies to get them to control their own members and to reach agreement by arbitration or conciliation. Upon transfer of the Straits Settlements to the control of the Colonial Office in 1867, the government also designed legislation to augment the powers of the Governor and other authorities in case of a disturbance. In particular, after a vicious secret society riot in Penang in 1867, in December 1869 the colonial government enacted a law requiring the registration of all societies of ten or more members (except Freemasons). Any registered society with illegal objects or likely to be a threat to the public peace was liable to be called upon to provide details of members, ceremonies and rules, and accounts, with fines and compensation charged to societies participating in riots. Though intended as a temporary measure, this law became permanent in 1872 (Blythe 1969: 2–5).

Despite the government's increased powers, disturbances continued within the Chinese community, whether linked with secret society action or in response to those very restrictions. Secret societies were considered too strong to ban outright, but given the bloody civil wars between Chinese factions, after 1874 'it was made plain in each of the States which came under British influence that secret societies were prohibited, and though the natural result of this policy was that the societies continued to exist clandestinely', it paved the way for strong action by the authorities against organisers or officials of such societies (Blythe 1969: 6). In the Straits Settlements, a new Societies Ordinance, predecessor to the contemporary Societies Act, came into force on 1 January 1890 and remained the basic law in effect until the Japanese occupation. This law also required all societies of ten or more persons to register. Any group could be denied registration or forced to dissolve in the interest of public safety and order, and participation in unlawful societies was punishable with fines and imprisonment. The law also specifically outlawed societies using a Triad ritual and criminalised possession of Triad documents or paraphernalia. In addition, a Banishment Ordinance allowed any person other than a British subject to be banished at any time in the interests of the public peace and welfare. Similar legislation was successively adopted throughout the Malay states, concluding with Johor in 1916. In addition, the British extended the Chinese Protectorate system – first introduced in Singapore in 1872 to advise the government on Chinese affairs and facilitate communication between the Chinese and the government – throughout Malaya, providing 'a poor man's tribunal to which all Chinese had access'. Regardless, secret societies remained, however unlawful, supplemented or replaced by gangs in some areas and, in the early twentieth century, by societies reflecting political movements in China (Blythe 1969: 5–7).

Though hundreds of secret society members were executed under Japanese rule during the Second World War, others fled to join resistance groups in the jungle (mostly linked with the Malayan Communist Party, MCP) and some became informers to the Japanese, secret societies still persisted (Blythe 1969: 8). When the British returned, societies of all kinds proliferated throughout Malaya. For five months, the colonial officials did not implement the Societies and Banishment Ordinances; during this time, Triad societies flourished until they posed a challenge to the government, especially in Penang. Gradually, the colonial authorities clamped down on Triad societies with the Societies Ordinance, though allowing all other associations so long as they applied for registration. The government's use of special emergency powers to crack down on communists and known or suspected secret society members weakened the secret societies somewhat.

The police used their powers of detention 'to ensure that the advent of independence in 1957 did not lead to increased society activity on the pretext that once the British had left the societies would provide protection for the Chinese community against a Malay-majority government'. Indeed, secret society personnel were active in the formation and campaigns of political parties, while the Singapore government was unsuccessfully pressed to consent to a potentially very politically powerful umbrella organisation open to Triad members (Blythe 1969: 9–10). Despite the defeat of the communist revolt and the withdrawal of emergency regulations, powers of arrest and detention, with double penalties for known secret society members, remained, having been incorporated into the permanent law in the interest of internal security. Secret societies have since declined in significance, though contemporary gangsters may use the same symbolism and, even beyond independence, Triad societies served their members 'as a source of unemployment relief, in providing welfare services and mediating in disputes' (Comber 1961: X–XI).

Indian societies

Indian migrants also formed organisations in colonial Malaysia, again along ethnic lines and paralleling to some extent movements in the home country. In particular, Indian associations in Malaya were closely linked with the contemporaneous independence movement in India. The urban–rural dichotomy among Indians in Malaya, particularly in the pre-war period, generally followed caste, linguistic, economic and educational divisions, without any homogeneous view of cultural identity or sense of belonging, complicating mass associations. Moreover, a western-educated, professional minority has maintained prominence as the elite of the community in terms of income and access to power since the 1920s. While caste formed the base of many Indian associations in peninsular Malaya in the 1920s, in line with the reform movement in India, others in the pre-war period were concerned with reforming and correcting abuses of the caste system, implying reform in Hinduism, as well (Tham 1971: 105–9; Rajoo 1985: 149–54).

Most Indian associations are religious organisations, followed by youth organisations, social organisations, and guilds. While early Malayan Indian organisations simply provided formal organisational structures and fostered *esprit de corps*, these organisations began to take on a more political character over time (Tham 1971: 107–9).[4] Indians were also among the first to establish modern, western-style trade unions in Malaya. Since many Indians were employed by large European estates and government departments, pre-war Indian organisations' activities were often identified with improving conditions of work for the community. While the quest for independence in India spurred concern for the plight of Indian workers in Malaysia, radical journalists also played a significant role in politicising Indian workers, both through their writing and through direct mobilisation (INSAN 1989: 51).

The multiplicity of Indian organisations all working separately, tending to stress in-group identity and highlight differences across sub-communities (not least the Muslim Indian community's tendency to associate itself with Muslim Malays rather than with Hindu Indians), precluded real unity (Rajoo 1985: 155). The first political body claiming to represent all Indians was the Central Indian Association of Malaya (CIAM), formed only after a long struggle, including a 1937 visit by Nehru to Malaya, during which he reportedly chided middle-class Indians for their indifference to the community and called for communal unity. CIAM activists – still mainly western-educated intellectuals – were influenced by and identified with the Indian Nationalist Movement in India and were supported by the Indian government. Though a few made statements regarding the British treatment of Indians in Malaya, these radical ideas had little impact (Rajoo 1985: 155, 170–2).

Post-independence, the organisation effecting the highest level of unity among Indians as a whole has been the Malaysian Indian Congress (MIC) – a political party rather than an NGO – and its predecessor, the Malayan Indian Association (MIA). The MIA was formed in 1936 among local-born Indians but was never very influential since its western-trained, elitist, urban leadership failed to penetrate the

Indian masses in estates and rural areas. Even the MIC, though, is not terribly representative, monolithic or potent as a partner in the Alliance (now Barisan Nasional) governing coalition. Also, it is most strongly pressed by other Indian associations mainly just to preserve and promote Indian language, culture and education (Tham 1977: 118–21). Among the difficulties in promoting stronger organisations among Indians, particularly the mass of Indian poor in estates and factories, continue to be poverty (and the reluctance of the middle class to get involved in the affairs of the poor), residual caste stratification, poor resources, the authoritarian culture among Tamil schools (especially plantation schools), and the predominance of paternalistic rather than grassroots, co-operative institutions in estates (INSAN 1989: 26–34).

While early Chinese associations determined the shape of legislation governing societies, the experience of Indian activism suggests not only the salience of ethnicity in organising, but also the drift in the pre-independence period towards politicisation of associations, then relative deradicalization or disempowerment with the entrenchment of Malay-dominated formal state structures. However, some of this legacy seems to be fading with the rise since the 1970s of issue-based advocacy associations, organised around sociopolitical issues not inherently limited to any one race. Nonetheless, the primary Indian organisations remain oriented largely around either religion or labour issues.

Malay societies

Pre-independence Malay societies played a crucial role in the development of both civil and political society, highlighting the shift of issues from the societal to the political sphere as activists became politicians. Divisions between the aristocracy and the agrarian masses, perpetuated by the British despite the advent of land titles for farmers, mass education and a capitalistic economy, rendered Malay social organisations slow to emerge. The only exceptions were long-standing, unstructured institutions for individual and communal benefit rather than articulation of interests, such as *gotong-royong* (co-operative efforts, in which a village jointly participated in tasks for the maintenance and welfare of the entire village community) and *tolong menolong* (mutual help, both in urban and rural areas).[5] Moreover, both tradition and British policy encouraged Malays to see the government as responsible for protecting their interests, stunting the rise of Malay organisations well into the post-independence era.

Though the majority of Malays remained in rural areas and occupations throughout the colonial period, economic and social changes

Malaysian NGOs: history, legal framework and characteristics 25

under capitalism, including increased urbanisation and social differentiation, encouraged a shift in associational life among Malays. Among urbanised Malays, as William Roff (1994: 178) explains, 'The circumstances of urban life – its heterogeneity, competitiveness, and relative freedom from customary sanctions and authority – produced for individuals both an often confusing sense of personal insecurity and a newly defined group awareness.' From the advent of colonialism until the late nineteenth century, the need for social identification was largely met in Singapore, Penang and Malacca by the formation of urban *kampung* (villages) of Malays from the same place of origin, often coinciding with specialisation of economic function. As urban life grew more complex and intense, however, these patterns of residence and occupation became more diversified and confused, and the significance of traditional structures for prestige and status waned (Roff 1994: 178–80).

New associational forms emerged around the turn of the century, mainly literary, social, religious and political. Initially, these associations were led by Malayo-Muslims (Arabs, Muslim Indians and Peranakans) rather than Malays, since the former were more involved in administration and affected by economic competition from the Chinese. This leadership appealed to linguistic and religious loyalties rather than old-style communal allegiances and emulated organisational forms from the West, including modern community organisations for unification, solidarity and social exchange along linguistic and religious lines. In particular, voluntary, membership-based clubs, whether for study and recreation or for sports, proliferated, though the various clubs tended to be divided along economic and educational lines. However limited their objectives, these associations did perform a socially integrative function (Roff 1994: 181–2; Tham 1977: 25–8). In towns and larger *kampung*, in the meantime, similar clubs and societies sprang up beginning from at least 1910, especially sports and social clubs, but also cultural and progress associations 'created in response to a growing awareness among urban and economically competitive Malays of the need to find new vehicles for personal and social self-improvement' (Roff 1994: 184–5).

Gradually, social change encouraged Malays to appeal to their community to pursue economic development and cultural revival. As Roff describes,

> Perhaps the most notable feature of the cultural welfare and progress associations was the way in which, despite their almost invariably local origins and circumscribed membership and their

lack of direct contact with each other, they all practically without exception recognized the larger Malay society of which they were a part and spoke in holistic (if not necessarily nationalistic) terms of the task of improving the educational and economic status of the Malays within the plural society.

(Roff 1994: 185)

Modern, educated Malays (teachers, government servants, small-scale businessmen, and journalists) took the lead in early twentieth-century 'progress associations'. Among these associations were the Persekutuan Keharapan Belia (New Hope Society, Johor Bahru, 1916), Persekutuan Indra Kayangan (Heavenly Land Society, Alor Star, 1918), Persekutuan Perbahathan Orang-orang Islam (Muslim Debating Society, Muar, 1919), and the first of the Persekutuan Guru-guru Melayu and Persekutuan Guru-guru Islam (Malay and Islamic Teachers' Associations, early 1920s). These groups discussed the problems of living as Malays in the modern world and worked to develop self-help and educational programmes to contribute to Malay advancement. Other associations of the era focused on more economic issues. Until the mid-1920s, Malay and Malayo-Muslim organisations in the Straits Settlements and the peninsular states were social, cultural and economic, but not political, even though some occasionally made representations to the government on relevant matters (Tham 1977: 25–8; Roff 1994: 185–7).

Malay quasi-political and literary associations developed through the 1930s. More overtly political organisations were less successful. The first of these was the nationalistic Kesatuan Melayu Singapura (Singapore Malay Union) in 1926, which aimed to raise political awareness and promote economic and educational development among Malays,[6] followed by others such as the left-wing, Indonesian-influenced nationalist Kesatuan Melayu Muda (Young Malay Union, 1938). These groups were spearheaded by young, English- or vernacular-educated Malays, along with a few traditional secular and religious authorities, rather than Malayo-Muslims as before. However, despite two congresses on the role of associations in the Malay community in 1939 and 1940 and some growing awareness of Malay rights and interests, the impact of these groups was limited since they had few members (and these from limited strata) and also there was popular uncertainty regarding political inclinations, persistent state (rather than national) parochialism among Malays, limited economic resources and squabbling over the definition of 'Malay'.[7] Moreover, thanks to British policies favouring the traditional aristocracy in economic and administrative positions, a comparable new middle class and reformist political awareness did not develop outside the urban Straits Settlements (Tham 1977: 25–8; Roff 1994).

Literary associations were more broadly successful. Starting in the inter-war period, the proliferation of Malay journals, especially from the late 1920s through the 1930s:

> assisted the newly emerging elites to educate the masses politically, as well as to challenge, gradually, the traditional social and political structure. At the same time, more forthrightly, they reminded their readers of the increasing economic dominance and demographic growth of the immigrant races.
>
> (Firdaus 1985: 58–9)

These literary efforts thus spurred the spread of radical nationalist sentiment, encouraged further by the increasing political access and assertiveness of Chinese and Indians. Many among the literary elite were also active in radical political parties, with journalists, essayists and writers of political fiction and poetry playing an enormous role in the development of Malay nationalism. Indeed, the 102 Malay nationalist newspapers and journals in existence between 1930 and 1941 'afforded the new intelligentsia an opportunity to voice criticisms of varying form and style against the prevailing social and political order' (Firdaus 1985: 62–3). At least two of these journals played a special role in forming and sustaining the first two country-wide Malay organisations (transcending state boundaries) – prime forerunners to present-day political NGOs – the Persaudaraan Sahabat Pena Malaya (Malayan Association of Pen Pals, 1934), initiated by the Penang-based newspaper Saudara, and the Kesatuan Melayu Muda (Young Malay Union), involving the Kuala Lumpur-based Majlis. The former association, though self-consciously non-political, was the first truly pan-Malayan Malay organisation, unifying a larger number of geographically and socially diverse Malays than any previous organisation. For its part, the latter group constituted 'the first organisational embodiment of radical ideas among the Malays' (Firdaus 1985: 63–4; also Tham 1977: 25–8; Roff 1994: 212–21). Even prior political organisations, which were state-based, conservative, pro-British and led by traditional aristocratic elites, were largely prompted by newspaper polemics (Firdaus 1985: 64).[8]

The basic characteristics of Malay associations persisted into the post-war period. Most were social, recreational or welfare-oriented, though a significant cohort of literary and quasi-political or political associations took up nationalist objectives. By the 1950s, two elite groups had emerged among Malays, one mostly government servants or bureaucrats (many of them also aristocrats), and the other comprised of teachers, journalists and others educated in the native schools.[9] The former group concentrated on political associations and the latter on literary and cultural associations, though both sets of organisations sought to protect the Malay community against 'the encroachment of alien influences, institutions and interests', whether through 'practical politics' or political socialisation (Tham 1977: 28–32).

Through the 1960s and 1970s, more economic associations were formed among Malays, including provident (welfare) associations and chambers of commerce or guilds for various trades and professions, some of them with an Islamic perspective. At the same time, social, youth and farmers' associations declined in the early 1970s, their activities largely supplanted by government programmes and projects (Tham 1977: 33–8). Economic associations among Malays and non-Malays pose an interesting contrast. Tham finds that the motivational basis of the Malay associations is 'to put pressure on the relevant ministry to obtain special privileges and financial assistance in respect of advancing the economic interest pursued', while non-Malay (especially Chinese) associations reflect 'the desire of their members to protect their specific occupational interests by preventing or discouraging governmental intervention in the operation of their activities', since government intervention 'usually leads to the lessening of their range of options' (Tham 1977: 63). He concludes:

> Associational development among the Malays in the post-war period is a reflection of the political changes in the Malay community. The quasi-political associations of the pre-war colonial period became replaced by registered political parties . . . The emergence of such political parties effectively transferred the function of ameliorating the economic and educational problems of the Malays to the political parties.
> (Tham 1977: 32–3)[10]

Women's organisations

Concomitant to these other pre- and post-war developments, women, especially Malays, began to play increasingly political roles, organising not just around traditional welfare services, but also around nationalist aims and to promote female education, one of the key issues for early politicised women's associations. The first of these formal women's organisations was the Malay Women Teachers' Union (Johor, 1929), followed

Malaysian NGOs: history, legal framework and characteristics 29

by a similar union founded in Malacca in 1938. The Kesatuan Melayu Singapura had a women's section by 1940, with other groups focusing not only on cooking and handicrafts but also adult literacy forming around the same time. Among these groups were numerous associations known as kumpulan kaum ibu (mothers' groups); these confederated at the state level in 1947, then united in 1949 as Pergerakan Kaum Ibu UMNO (UMNO Mothers' Movement), the women's wing of the United Malays National Organisation (UMNO), renamed Wanita UMNO (UMNO Women) in 1971. Though it had little real authority within the party, Kaum Ibu took a strong stance against the British Malayan Union plan and raised political awareness among both rural Malay women and the wives of prominent political and community leaders (Chapter 2 in this volume; Khadijah n.d.: 7–9; Manderson 1980: 50–5).

During the Japanese occupation, although most existing associations lapsed, the Japanese established new ones, also recruiting women into paid and unpaid labour corps. Through wartime women's associations such as the Malayan Reconstruction Co-operative Association (1944) and the Malayan Welfare Association (1944), which took part in rallies and public lectures, many women gained their first exposure to mass political activity. Indeed, as early as October 1942, the Japanese encouraged women to increase their involvement in public life and in both the commercial and production sectors of the economy. Food shortages, continuing illiteracy and the hardships of life under Japanese occupation highlighted women's disadvantaged status, stimulating both rural and urban women to press for change in the post-war period (Manderson 1980: 51–2).

Throughout Malaya, women's groups of the 1940s and 1950s were almost all communal in nature,[11] with many actually the women's section of new political parties, such as Kaum Ibu or the nationalistic Angkatan Wanita Sedar (Movement of Aware Women), the women's section of the Malay Nationalist Party (1945). Only Malay women's associations were predominantly political. Among Chinese, women's associations were mostly non-political, though some were involved with the communist insurgency – aided by Chinese schools, which spread communist teachings to girls as well as boys – or the nascent Malayan Chinese Association (MCA). Though some Indian women were active in the Indian Independence Movement and others were members of voluntary associations and trade unions (including at least one Indian Women's Association formed by 1946), overall they played a minimal role. Even the women's auxiliary of the MIC was only established in 1975, though women had been encouraged to take a more active part in the party as early as 1946 (Khadijah n.d.: 7–15; Manderson 1980: 53–5).

A partial exception to the communal norm was the Women's Union (Johor, 1945), one of the first women's associations formed after the war, with branches in various states. Though predominantly Chinese in membership, the Union's goals were non-racial and included labour-related, educational and political issues. Also, though most of its members were Chinese, too, the All-Malaya Women's Federation (1946) joined with the Malayan Democratic Union, the Malayan Democratic League, the MIC, the Malayan People's Anti-Japanese Ex-Service Comrades Association, and the Pan-Malayan Federation of Trade Unions to form the multiracial All-Malaya Council for Joint Action, seeking democratic self-government for a United Malaya (including Singapore) and liberal citizenship rights (Manderson 1980: 53–4).

Among early Malaysian associations, therefore, the structure, functions, and issue orientation of different groups varied partly with ethnicity and attendant socioeconomic traits and partly with time, as both political awareness and legal strictures evolved through the pre-independence period. Modern advocacy-oriented NGOs have developed only since the 1970s,[12] with new and old welfare- or service-oriented groups flourishing alongside. As Gerard Clarke explains, the activities of all NGOs[13] are inherently political: even welfare-oriented groups provide legitimacy for the state and bolster elites, while groups engaged in local development projects can prevent macroeconomic or political change and mobilise local communities as political participants (Clarke 1998: 195–6). However, it is newer issue-oriented NGOs – organised around women's rights, human rights, the environment or other causes – that have consistently attracted the ire of the Malaysian government and that are both self-consciously and popularly perceived to be political. Despite the evolution of these new NGOs, though, the basic traits of associational life inherited from pre-independence Chinese secret societies, Malay progress associations and other groups have remained relatively constant. The legal framework for societal organisations has been refined rather than overhauled, NGOs remain largely racially segregated in membership, only a small proportion of formal organisations are oriented around sectors or issues rather than communities, and tension persists regarding whether NGOs or only political parties should assume openly political roles.[14]

Legal framework and political environment

The most significant factor inhibiting the development of advocacy-oriented NGOs is Malaysia's regulatory environment. Article 10 of the

Malaysian NGOs: history, legal framework and characteristics

Federal Constitution of Malaysia guarantees freedom of speech, expression, peaceful assembly and association, though all may be limited in the interests of safety or public order. However, a range of laws curtail NGOs and discourage would-be supporters. Moreover, ubiquitous government rhetoric emphasises that NGOs represent 'special interests' and are thus anti-national, highlights the substantial successes of the regime in meeting people's needs (so those who criticise are 'ungrateful'), and challenges those who would oppose government policies to do so through political parties rather than through NGOs.

The legal framework governing NGOs is the legacy of the British campaign against Chinese secret societies, complemented by relics of colonial and post-colonial anti-communist measures. The main legal instruments related to NGOs are the Societies Act, the Police Act and a range of laws restricting speech, the press and assembly. Altogether, these laws determine not only which NGOs may exist as legal entities, what funding they may seek and accept, and what they may do, but also how NGOs make their case to the public and who may join.

The Societies Act

The Societies Act (1966) is the direct descendant of the late nineteenth-century colonial Societies Ordinance, implemented largely in response to the threat to the public order posed by Chinese secret societies.[15] The act covers all groups of seven or more people except those covered by other legislation, such as trade unions and co-operatives. All societies must not only register initially, but also obtain the approval of the Registrar of Societies for any subsequent change in name, venues of business, or constitution. The Registrar may deregister any society, with appeal possible only to the Minister of Home Affairs, and has the power to enter and search any society's premises. Societies have no legal standing in the courts; legal action may be taken only in the names of individuals. The Registrar may require a society to ensure that all its office-bearers are Malaysian citizens or prohibit connections with foreign societies.[16] Each society must submit yearly returns to the Registrar within 28 days of its annual general meeting, including audited accounts, constitutional amendments and details of office-bearers. Penalties for violations of the Societies Act include fines and imprisonment (Gurmit 1984: 1–5).

The Societies Act has been amended several times, most controversially in 1981 and 1983. The amendments of 1981, passed rapidly and with little consultation, defined a 'political society' to include any society that issued public statements (others were implied to be 'friendly') and required all existing political societies to register as such within three months or be denoted thus by the Registrar at any time. Political societies were sharply constrained as to permissible office-bearers and members as well as in foreign affiliations or sponsorship. Moreover, the Registrar could cancel the registration of any society that opposed or denigrated any matter under the federal and state constitutions, and gained increased powers to amend a group's rules or constitution. The amendments also increased all the fines stipulated for violations of the act (Gurmit 1984: 6–8). After an energetic campaign by a coalition of over a hundred NGOs under the Societies Act Co-ordinating Committee (SACC), later reorganised as the Secretariat for the Conference of Societies (SCS), the 1981 amendments were modified, with a new set of amendments passed by Parliament in May 1983.[17]

Under the revised amendments, the definition of 'political society' was removed, though the definition of political parties was extended to include societies that endorse candidates for state or federal legislatures. Any society may be deregistered if it shows disregard for the state or federal constitutions, especially certain sensitive issues; the minister declares it prejudicial to public security, order or morality; there was a mistake, misrepresentation or fraud in its registration; it has deviated from its registered objectives; or it has failed to comply with any of its own or the Societies Act's rules. Moreover, there is no time limit for when a decision of registration must be made and the penalty for organising activities while registration is pending was doubled. Both current and former office-bearers must respond to queries from the Registrar and even office-bearers who did not participate in a particular offence are liable for punishment on behalf of the society. Moreover, offences related to unlawful or deregistered societies as well as Triad societies may be registered as criminal. In investigating suspected violations, not only the Registrar and Assistant Registrar for Societies, but also registration officers, may search the premises and examine all documents of a society. Finally, decisions by the minister are final and may not be challenged in court (Gurmit 1984).

As of 31 December 1996, there were 28,219 organisations registered under the Registrar of Societies. Of this total, the largest proportion (4,166) were religious bodies; 3,806 were categorized as 'social and recreation'; 3,500 were for sports; 2,687 were 'social welfare' groups; and 41 were political parties. Other categories included cultural associations, mutual benefit societies, trade and commerce groups, youth groups, and educational associations (Makmor 1998: 63). Only a small proportion of registered societies are advocacy-oriented NGOs, probably only about 100 groups (Tan and Bishan 1994: 7).[18] Given the difficulties of obtaining registration as a society – not just the paperwork and formal procedures, though these are substantial, but the fact that organisations perceived as politicised may be denied registration or left in limbo for years – many advocacy-oriented NGOs are actually registered as companies or businesses instead.[19]

Involuntary deregistration is rare, but it is threatened and does happen. For instance, in 1980, the sociopolitical reform group Aliran Kesedaran Negara (Aliran, National Consciousness Movement) was threatened with deregistration and ordered to 'show cause' why it should be allowed to persist. What sparked the investigation was a letter by Aliran president Chandra Muzaffar regarding new allowances and salary increases for public servants as well as an indictment of Aliran's adherence to the principles of the *Rukunegara* (Malaysia's national ideology). The Registrar charged that Aliran was 'likely to be used for purposes prejudicial to, or incompatible with, peace in the Federation' and that the group was pursuing objectives other than those for which it was registered (Aliran 1981: 322–3). In response, Aliran rebutted the specific charge and discussed the important place of a reform movement such as theirs in Malaysian society, and also appealed successfully to the public for support. The group was eventually allowed to remain in operation (Aliran 1981: 321–80). At around the same time, Angkatan Belia Islam Malaysia (ABIM, the Muslim Youth Movement of Malaysia), which was constantly critical of state policies and enjoyed widespread influence among tertiary students and the Malay middle class, was asked by the Registrar to sever all its contacts and affiliations with foreign organisations. The group was viewed as too much under the influence of 'radical' and militant Islamic movements abroad (Tan and Bishan 1994: 22–3).

More recently, the Islamic organisation Darul Arqam (Abode of Arqam) came under attack in 1994 for its allegedly deviationist teachings and practices. Darul Arqam, a religious study group established in Kuala Lumpur in 1968 by Ustaz Ashaari Muhammad, posed a political threat through its 'capacity to manage a self-sustaining and comprehensive socio-economic order, based on Islamic values and principles, whilst remaining within but virtually independent of Malaysia's liberal capitalist system' (Ahmad Fauzi 1999: 2). The government banned the group and arrested eight leaders under the Internal Security Act (ISA), citing religious reasons, though the motive for the crackdown may have been more political than theological, given Darul Arqam's challenge to the government's legitimacy (Ahmad Fauzi 1999). NGOs registered other than as societies are not immune, either. For instance, Institut Pengajaran Komuniti (IPK, Institute for Community Education), a

Sarawak-based NGO registered as a business and an active member of a coalition of NGOs opposed to the Bakun Dam project, was deregistered in early 1996 (Kua 1998: 3).

Additional constraints

Other laws similarly constrain NGOs and activists.[20] For instance, spontaneous protest is largely precluded by the Police Act 1967 (amended 1988), which requires that a police permit be obtained fourteen days in advance for any public meeting of more than five people. The police have frequently refused permits for assemblies organised by NGOs and opposition political parties. In response, NGOs tend to rely on seminars, symposia and their own publications as well as representations to government officials and the state-controlled mass media rather than mass rallies to reach both the public and the government. However, these initiatives, too, are limited by the Printing Presses and Publications Act 1984 (amended 1987), which requires a yearly permit from the Ministry of Home Affairs (with no redress to the courts) for all publications,[21] as well as stiff legislation on libel, contempt of court and official secrets. Indeed, one of the most widespread and mass-based (though largely unsuccessful) campaigns against a government policy in Malaysia so far was in response to proposed amendments to the Official Secrets Act (OSA, 1972) in 1986. The amendments strengthened a law that already denied public information to public interest societies, journalists and others, complicating discussion and debate. The law provides few safeguards against over-zealousness in declaring documents classified, including those regarding the operations and functions of the government – in fact, virtually any government information may be declared an official secret (see Gurmit 1987; Means 1991: 196–8).

In addition, aside from the restrictions on NGOs' membership and office-bearers enumerated in the Societies Act, all students are further constrained by the Universities and University Colleges Act 1971 (UUCA, amended 1975). While campuses are prime grounds for political mobilisation elsewhere, contemporary Malaysian tertiary students are forbidden from engaging in political activities and the laws on students' activism have been tightened after sporadic bursts of mobilisation. Malaysian students do have a tradition of activism, however, dating back to Chinese secondary school students' demonstrations against what they saw as the government's stifling of Chinese culture and education in the 1950s. Then in the 1960s and early 1970s, Malaysian student groups joined their counterparts elsewhere in protesting American aggression in Indochina and were active in welfare and community projects for the poor and underprivileged. The University of Malaya Students' Union (UMSU) went so far as to stage non-partisan public rallies around the country during the 1969 general elections to inform people about important issues and problems facing the country, also issuing a manifesto outlining its views and demands.

With student bodies and university political clubs increasingly vocal in critiquing government policies and actions, the government required in 1964 that all applicants for admission to universities and colleges obtain a 'suitability certificate' to weed out suspected communists, pro-communists and otherwise subversive or 'undesirable' elements. The UUCA was then introduced during the Emergency following the 1969 elections and subsequent racial riots, prohibiting all student and faculty organisations from affiliation with, support for, or opposition to any political party, trade union or unlawful group. University students were also prohibited from holding office in any trade union or political party, and student bodies could be dissolved for behaviour detrimental to the well-being of the university. Regardless, university and college students still protested against the demolition of squatter houses near Johor Bahru in September 1974, then demonstrated in support of a peasant movement in Baling, Kedah, that November. The authorities cracked down on these protests, detaining scores of students, lecturers, and youth and religious leaders under the ISA (which allows detention without trial) or other laws. The government claimed that the Malay-dominated UMSU was being used by an allegedly pro-communist Chinese Language Society member to spur campus unrest. All student publications in the universities were subsequently suspended or banned and the UUCA was amended in 1975 with new restrictions and tougher penalties. Supplementary regulations further restricted university lecturers and staff (Fan 1988: 238–55). Campus activism does still resurface, though, in times of mass political unrest. For instance, students of all races have been key players in the Reformasi movement launched in September 1998, with opposition to the UUCA a key factor in their agitation.[22]

Among NGOs, human rights groups typically face the greatest difficulties in organising, not only because of the dominant ideology and regulations that discourage debate or even critical thinking on 'sensitive' topics, but also because of public disinterest or fear. Furthermore, as Gordon Means (1991: 198–9) points out related to NGOs' campaigns on human rights and democracy, 'The fact that the DAP [opposition Democratic Action Party] usually played a highly visible role in the various seminars and conferences considering such issues only served to identify these interest groups with what the government considered to be implacable hard-line critics of the regime.'[23] The government also frowns especially severely upon challenges to economic development, for instance protests against large government projects such as the Bakun Dam in Sarawak.

Sharp remarks and constructive engagement

The government belittles its critics by portraying them as marginal and out of touch with the mass public. For instance, in late 1986 the government launched an attack against 'negative', too-critical interest groups, challenging them to register as political parties to prove they had public support, and naming five NGOs and two political parties 'thorns in the flesh'.[24] Mahathir lambasted these 'intellectual elites' as 'tools of foreign powers' and saboteurs of democracy, referring in particular to the campaign against the amendments to the OSA and NGOs' criticism and protests regarding banking scandals, corruption or impropriety in the awarding of government contracts, judicial independence, and resource development and environmental issues (Means 1991: 194). Moreover, after a 1987 Aliran-sponsored conference on the Malaysian Constitution, Mahathir 'depicted the participants as frustrated intellectuals attempting to seize power and presuming "to make policies for the government"'. Former critical activist Anwar Ibrahim, then Deputy Prime Minister, called the organisers 'arrogant intellectuals' who wanted to 'force their views down the government's throat' (Means 1991: 198–9).

More generally, Mahathir and other officials reiterate that Malaysian democracy is not like western liberal democracy but accepts some controls as necessary, particularly to check the demands of 'special interests' that could potentially impinge on the rights of the majority and endanger ethnic harmony and the political stability needed for development. These statements do influence the general public, especially since for many, such remarks are their primary exposure to NGOs. While critical and voluble, NGOs like Aliran reach primarily western-educated, middle-class, urban elites, while Mahathir's statements reach everyone. Moreover, the government's heavy-handed rhetoric has been reinforced by periodic crackdowns, including October 1987's Operation Lalang, when over 100 activists and politicians were detained for alleged Marxist tendencies.[25] Such arrests further deter the public from supporting NGOs or related oppositional activities, though simultaneously sparking some degree of indignant protest, such as the formation of the human rights group Suara Rakyat Malaysia (SUARAM) in the wake of Operation Lalang.

Malaysian NGOs: history, legal framework and characteristics 37

Relations between the state and NGOs deteriorated anew in late 1996, when the Second Asia Pacific Conference on East Timor in Kuala Lumpur was broken up by protesters, including members of UMNO Youth. More than 100 participants were arrested, including ten foreign human rights activists who were then deported. The government also decried a proposed NGO-organised public tribunal on the abuse of police powers: 'Mahathir claimed that some NGOs were deliberately challenging the government to take action against them and threatened that he would do so, if they had broken the law' (Milne and Mauzy 1999: 119). Then in 1997, the government investigated the ways in which NGOs were being managed, insinuating that their funds were being diverted from their original purpose for the benefit of individuals, or that they were co-operating too closely with foreign governments (Milne and Mauzy 1999: 119–20).

Despite this antagonism, NGOs do collaborate with the government in formulating and implementing policies on certain environmental, consumers', women's and other issues when their expertise is needed.[26] While NGOs – or, so that the state need not officially endorse the organisations, specific individual leaders of NGOs – may be invited to sit with representatives of the government and business community on legislation-forming committees, the NGOs have no veto power and the state retains the final say.[27] Moreover, the state is most likely to call upon 'professional' or 'moderate' NGOs whose contributions will complement rather than challenge its governance. Many NGOs accede to this arrangement since it at least allows their ideas to be heard. Still, greater state–NGO co-operation could generate more complementary efforts and less overlapping of functions and waste of scarce resources, as well as guarantee more participatory democracy (Lim 1995: 167–8; Tan and Bishan 1994: 16–23).

Regardless, however haltingly, public support for such issues as environmentalism and human rights has increased over the years, bolstered by a few high-profile cases. Environmentalism, for instance, was of concern to few Malaysians prior to the mid-1980s Asian Rare Earth case, when the improper dumping of radioactive waste products spurred the formation of activist support groups and a series of high-profile court cases and drew wide public sympathy (see CAP 1993). Then, in the late 1980s, increased attention to logging and development in Sarawak, including both environmental and native land rights issues, similarly heightened public awareness (Means 1991: 195–6). In terms of human rights, the September 1998 detention of Anwar Ibrahim under the ISA and his maltreatment while under police custody helped spark an enormous mass movement for justice, transparency and good governance, despite the government's threats and cajoling. Nonetheless, the ranks of committed NGO supporters remain thin, with only a small core of activists sustaining their movements between surges of wider public support.

Ideological and organisational attributes

Though relatively few in number, Malaysian advocacy-oriented NGOs are heterogeneous in structure, function and ideology. These NGOs may be classified by sector, as Lim Teck Ghee (1995: 166) does – the five he identifies are environmental, consumer, human rights, development and women's groups.[28] Alternatively, NGOs may be divided by constituency and framework, including community-based organisations, community service associations, worker–employer oriented organisations, women's organisations, youth organisations, professional organisations, and coalitions and campaign groups. However, as Tan and Bishan (1994: 3–4) point out, given the wide diversity of organisations in some of these categories, simply differentiating between 'community service and welfare NGOs' and 'development and issue-oriented NGOs' makes more sense.

Most Malaysian advocacy NGOs are small and urban-based, concentrated particularly in Kuala Lumpur and Penang.[29] Recruitment of members and especially leaders for advocacy NGOs is difficult because of fear of the ISA and other laws, lack of information about NGOs and their activities, plus the very low pay to be earned by working for an NGO and lack of time for volunteer work. Even NGOs with few formal members, though, may be able to rally widespread support for particular causes or campaigns.[30] Their small size and preponderance of professionals – lecturers, lawyers, teachers, engineers, journalists and the like – do prompt occasional accusations that NGOs are elitist or irrelevant.

While many NGOs are not really internally democratic or tightly linked with grassroots constituencies, others are more mass-based, such as consumers' associations. These are also the NGOs that are sustained less by highly educated middle-class activists (though such individuals still provide leadership) than by non-graduates or non-professionals. Many NGOs are highly personalistic in nature. Several key NGOs, such as CAP (S. M. Mohamed Idris), Environmental Protection Society Malaysia and Selangor Graduates Society (Gurmit Singh), Tenaganita (Irene Fernandez), the Malaysian AIDS Council (MAC, Marina Mahathir) and the International Movement for a Just World (JUST, Chandra Muzaffar, previously the central figure in Aliran) are over-

Malaysian NGOs: history, legal framework and characteristics 39

whelmingly associated with their leader regardless of how large the staff or how wide-ranging and decentralised the activities of the group may be.[31] On the other hand, though the Societies Act requires that all registered societies have office-bearers, for some NGOs assignation of these titles is just a formality, with work shared, decisions by consensus, and hierarchy minimised in practice.

Funding

Many Malaysian NGOs rely on foreign funds when they can get them, but such aid is limited and dwindling.[32] The bulk of foreign funding for development projects and technical assistance is still on a bilateral (government to government) basis and the bulk of multilateral aid goes to government-organised NGOs (GONGOs) and government agencies. Although all NGOs must report the sources of their foreign funding to the Registrar of Societies each year, the Registrar has never disclosed the extent of foreign funding for development NGOs. However, the United Nations Development Program (UNDP) found that funds from foreign NGOs, which usually go towards development NGOs, accounted for only 2.5 per cent of externally financed technical assistance grants to Malaysia in 1987. Of this sum, up to 90 per cent came from major institutions like the Asia Foundation and the International Planned Parenthood Federation, with the bulk going towards research, travel and projects of local universities, schools and research bodies. Foreign NGOs more concerned with grassroots development work by autonomous NGOs contributed a rather minuscule sum. The total foreign assistance provided by these foreign NGOs to Malaysian development NGOs in 1987 was only US$270,000, compared with US$108 million disbursed to state-sponsored NGOs and state agencies (cited in Tan and Bishan 1994: 10–11). The Malaysian government also provides funds to some NGOs for projects such as consumer protection or anti-domestic violence programs. However, such funds are limited and some NGOs prefer not to accept government support for fear of compromising their independence.[33]

Some NGOs prefer not to accept foreign aid as a matter of principle, if only because accepting it would leave them open to charges by the government that they are being manipulated by foreign elements.[34] Most deny any intrusion of foreign donors in decision-making processes, though acknowledging that the choice of projects may be influenced by what will be funded and that the contest for funds may contribute to infighting within the NGO community.[35] Even among those NGOs that do accept foreign aid, given that funds are scarce, they still strive to minimize costs and raise funds locally, as through sales of books and t-shirts, membership dues, donations, cultural events or fun fairs, jumble sales, and paid forums and dinners. Also, for specific campaigns, such as against the amendments to the OSA or to preserve Endau Rompin state park, NGO coalitions raise funds domestically through seminars and donations from individuals and groups. Private or corporate philanthropy remains minimal, though it is comparatively more forthcoming for campaigns or projects against issues such as domestic violence or HIV/AIDS, especially from multinational corporations, than for other sorts of issues. Overall, NGOs focusing on issues that conflict with the state's priorities – such as concerning labour, the environment or human rights – have a hard time raising local funds.

Networking

Networking is a definite strength among Malaysian NGOs, particularly at the domestic level. Major campaigns may involve over 100 NGOs, though most attract fewer than 50 participating groups, many with only minimal engagement in campaign projects.[36] Tan and Bishan suggest that the state has actually encouraged otherwise self-absorbed and independent NGOs towards solidarity and networking, since:

> the state's many reactive attempts to encapsulate and force the NGOs into the confines of its own corporatist politics provided the NGOs with the experience of working together, organising national campaigns and forming solidarity networks, as well as generating unwanted international publicity for the state. With each successive campaign, NGO links grew stronger. Moreover, the public increasingly accepted NGOs as mainstream political alternatives – if one were to judge from the letters to the editors supporting the NGOs and the campaigns.
> (Tan and Bishan 1994: 24)

International – particularly regional – networking also occurs, though it is heavily reliant upon international funding and inconsistently pursued, depending on the relative pressure of domestic concerns. Human rights groups' regional initiatives include joining in the drafting of an Asian Human Rights Charter and supporting the East Timorese and Acehnese independence movements, the movement for a democratic Burma, and political reform in Cambodia. Earlier initiatives include 1987's Human Rights Support Group, which agitated for the release of sixteen men and women detained in Singapore. Women's groups such as

Tenaganita participate in campaigns against trafficking in women, against the spread of HIV/AIDS and for a range of other issues affecting women. Islamic NGOs engage in a range of regional and international campaigns, too, such as in support of Muslims in Palestine or Kosovo, though these campaigns are generally less likely to be seen as politically aggressive by the Malaysian government.[37]

Racial and religious cleavages

The primary lines of cleavage among Malaysian NGOs are racial and religious, especially between secular and Islamic groups. Moreover, while advocacy NGOs are usually open in principle to members of all races, most are segregated in practice, both because communalism is so deeply engrained in Malaysian life and because language barriers complicate inter-racial communications.[38] In general, English-speaking, middle-class, urban non-Malays dominate advocacy groups. Politicised Islamic groups are, not surprisingly, dominated by Malays, with secular groups or those linked with other religions comprised of primarily Chinese and Indians. Secular women's groups pose an exception, as proportionately more Malays seem to join them than other groups.[39] Secular NGOs call for public accountability, reclamation of rights lost through the arbitrary use of state power, state intervention and regulation on matters of public interest, preservation of the physical environment, political detentions, abuse of executive privileges, and so on. Religious NGOs, especially the Islamic movement, on the other hand, have raised the spectre of the loss of religiosity and spiritual values among state actors (Nair 1999: 96–7).[40] Not surprisingly, though, subdivisions exist within these subgroups, given different schools of thought within Islam and the distinctions among secular, Christian, and other groups' motivations.

The tendency of more critical NGOs still to be predominantly non-Malay in composition may reflect 'the wider divisions and diversity in the non-Malay political spectrum compared to the closeted Malay sector' (Tan and Bishan 1994: 13). However, with the recent Reformasi movement,[41] a range of Malay-dominated or Islamic groups (among them, ABIM, Jamaah Islah Malaysia, and Persatuan Ulama Malaysia) have become just as critical and outspoken as predominantly non-Malay NGOs on issues relating to human rights, social justice and democracy. Regardless, even campaigns around apparently non-racial issues may be limited to a particular ethnic group. For example, over two dozen Chinese guilds and associations issued a 'Joint Declaration' in 1985 against racial polarisation, Malay-centric policies that failed satisfactorily to address poverty and the growing rich–poor gap, human rights violations and the transgression of freedom and democracy, discrimination and chauvinism, religious fanaticism, and the like (Chinese Guilds and Associations 1985). Though some of these demands are clearly more in the interests of non-Malays than Malays, the fact that so many of these issues have since been adopted by the Reformasi movement suggests that the 1985 campaign could conceivably have been more multiracial. Despite some non-Chinese support, though, the campaign around the Joint Declaration was – and was perceived as – primarily a Chinese initiative. Muhammad Ikmal Said explains that both Malay and non-Malay leftists tend to be communal, improvements in communication between groups notwithstanding, even when their programmes are fairly 'universal' and despite the fact that their distance from one another deflects mass support. He attributes this racialism to characteristics of colonialism, immigration and the contemporary state, in addition to the different market positions of Chinese and Malays, which have entrenched a communal culture (Muhammad Ikmal 1992).

In general, then, Malaysian NGOs operate within a constrained space, as the political process is officially reserved for political parties and there is limited scope for traditional lobbying activities. However, their supposedly non-political status empowers NGOs in specific ways, since 'when these groups speak critically on issues of public policy, they can claim that they do so not as party or politically-motivated agents exploiting an issue for electoral gain, but as non-partisan groups voicing the concerns of all citizens' (Nair 1999: 97–8). Regardless, many NGOs do maintain links with opposition political parties, especially the DAP, PAS, Parti Rakyat Malaysia (PRM) and Parti Keadilan Nasional. Relations with component parties of the governing Barisan Nasional coalition, on the other hand, are complicated by NGOs' often non-negotiable areas of concern and lack of bargaining power, as well as a tradition of mutual mistrust.

Conclusions

An unsympathetic regime, relatively low popular commitment to voluntarism and political activism, persistent racial and religious cleavages, and enduring stifling regulations have curtailed the development of a vibrant and effective civil society in Malaysia. All the same, what NGOs there are have played a key role in exploring and espousing political, social and economic reforms, in the process sustaining a nucleus of committed activists. Clearly, though, Malaysian NGOs do not fit the theoretical ideal of democratic, grassroots-oriented, politically transformative organisations for building social capital and keeping the government in line. Too few of them are truly independent, self-financing, and racially and linguistically inclusive.

Malaysian activists have developed strategies over the years for working around the government's regulations and for educating and mobilising a broader public. For instance, the formation of campaign networks not only spreads the work and costs among a larger base – a crucial benefit, given NGOs' scarce human and financial resources – but also reduces risk. A few lone activists make easy targets for the government to attack, but as Zaitun Kasim exclaims, 'What can they do to twenty groups?' (interview, 1 August 1997). Selective accommodation to the government is also an adaptive strategy as it grants NGOs a degree of recognition and legitimacy and ensures that their voices are not completely marginalised or ignored. Similarly, since NGOs know the government-controlled media will be of little benefit (aside from influential but rare features by concerned journalists on the environment, domestic violence or other social issues), NGOs have learned to take advantage of alternative media. The internet is transforming NGO communications in Malaysia as elsewhere, with most advocacy NGOs now supporting e-mail and often a website. Other channels include NGO-published journals and newsletters, such as the *Aliran Monthly*, CAP's *Utusan Konsumer* and SUARAM's *Hak*, plus opposition-party organs, including *Harakah* (PAS), *Roket* (DAP) and *Suara PRM* (PRM).

Where Malaysian NGOs are weakest is in critical self-evaluation, long-range planning and sustainability. The press of projects and general lack of resources mean that even the best-intentioned NGOs often fail to complete project-based or overall periodic evaluations, or fail really to incorporate the lessons from past evaluations into plans for subsequent programmes. In the same vein, the exigencies of immediate needs, the volatility of popular support and the unpredictability of government crackdowns make long-range planning seem an unattainable luxury. At best, NGO plans extend through a donor agency's three-year funding cycle. However, without strategic plans that extend beyond the short term, budgeting for long-term campaigns and formulating more systematic rather than reactive initiatives are not possible. Finally, the current extent of reliance on particular leaders and foreign funding sources cannot be maintained; the majority of advocacy NGOs need to be far more aggressive in making their organisations and enterprises sustainable.

Efforts by NGOs at reflection and reform must begin with full-scale, honest evaluations, and continue through the articulation of precise goals to the development and implementation of long-range plans. Internal democracy and large-scale consultation of constituents would make this process more legitimate and bring in fresh ideas and perspectives. Regardless, as advocates for democratic procedures and social justice in governance, NGOs must set an example by promoting regular transitions in leadership, racial and religious tolerance, and genuine links with the grassroots within their own sphere. Through such steps the Malaysian NGO community may renew and reinvigorate itself while also serving as an example for social activists in other countries facing comparable opportunities and obstacles.

2 The women's movement in peninsular Malaysia, 1900–99
A historical analysis

Lai Suat Yan

Introduction

Various women's voluntary organisations, popularly referred to as non-governmental organisations (NGOs), along with women's sections of other NGOs, trade unions and political parties have fought for the advancement of women's interests and rights since before Malaya (Malaysia) achieved independence in 1957. This chapter will discuss the struggles and the gains of the women's movement as well as evaluating the approaches used to improve the status of women in society. The article will also address other social forces and facets of the political environment upon which the success or failure of women's struggles is contingent. A definition of what the women's movement embodies will first be discussed, as this framework suggests the challenges faced in the struggle for a society that embodies justice for women.

Defining a women's movement

Defining a women's movement necessitates setting a boundary, as broad or as narrow as it may be. This is not an easy task due to the complex nature of the women's movement and its multiple subjects. A woman is defined not only by her sex but also by her ethnicity, religious/cultural background, educational background, class, age and ideology. The subject position that she takes depends on the sociocultural context of a particular time. Mouffe aptly describes subjectivity as 'always precarious and provisionally fixed' (cited in Vargas 1995: 98), whilst Butler (1993) uses the term 'contingent foundations' and Braidotti (1994), 'nomadic subjects'. Depending on the particular context, gender, ethnic or class identity may play the most crucial role. For instance, in a civil war among different ethnic groups, ethnicity comes to the fore as a person is killed for belonging to a particular ethnic group. Even then, the particular way in which women and men are treated is gendered. For women, war often takes the form of rape (for example, the rape of Bosnian Muslim women) whilst men are battered and killed.

The particular way in which one subject position intersects with another produces specific effects. In Malaysia, the intersection of gender with ethnicity may enforce gender subordination. This is because, as observed by Chhachhi, 'A call for a return to culture and tradition is almost always a call first directed at women' (1988: 262). As biological reproducers, Chinese and Malay women in Malaysia were urged to have more children to secure the future of their communal groups (Ng 1989).

Given the different subject positions occupied by women in Malaysia, the struggle to advance women's rights and interests has needed to take these traits into consideration, particularly factors relating to ethnicity, religion and culture, class and age. A good example of this is the campaign to enact a Domestic Violence Act that would protect all women, irrespective of their ethnicity or religion. Activists had to take into account the religious factor and potential opposition from certain quarters since domestic violence, as a matter pertaining to the family, is under the jurisdiction of *Syariah* laws for Muslims rather than under the civil laws as for non-Muslims. Hence, discussions were held with Islamic agencies to lobby for their support. Notwithstanding these distinctions, campaigns against violence against women in Malaysia tend to bridge differences along class and ethnic lines, as women are battered and raped irrespective of these subject positions. The dominant theme in these campaigns is that gender inequality is the main cause of violence against women.

A feminist struggle will have to take into consideration these intersections and link up with other related struggles, for instance the struggle against racism, workers' struggles and the struggle for democracy in general. Vargas summarised beautifully that it is not an either/or case, as besides 'the risk of hiding the specificity of women's struggles among all other subject positions and contradictions women confront', we must also be aware 'of subsuming all other contradictions to gender' (1995: 89). Nonetheless, the relationship is not a simple one, either between the women's movement and other social movements or within the women's movement itself. In the first example, sections of the women's movement are supportive of issues pertaining to social justice and related to human rights, and have linked up with other progressive movements on these issues. Still, there is no guarantee that these wider social movements will not subsume women's issues as being less important compared to class issues, rather than giving these equal weight, or will not agree with certain issues raised, such as women's sexual rights – a divisive issue even within the women's movement. On the other hand, while sections of other social movements have been supportive of women's issues, they are sometimes frustrated with the apolitical stance adopted by sections of the women's movement.

To be as inclusive as possible, I will adopt Wieringa's definition of a women's movement as:

> the whole spectrum of conscious or unconscious individuals or collective acts, activities, groups or organisations concerned with diminishing gender subordination, which is understood as intersecting with race and class oppression.
>
> (1995: 7)

As the aim of the women's movement is to diminish gender subordination, the focus of this chapter is on the mobilisation of women in Malaysia to achieve this aim, whether in the political, socioeconomic or cultural arena. However, in the Malaysian context, as in other postcolonial 'Third World' countries, the struggle for women's rights has historically been contained within the larger struggle for independence or subsumed under class struggle. Even in these contexts, though, there were moments of rupture, as when women stood up and asked the leadership to recognise their equal status or fought for their equal rights. The autonomous women's NGOs set up more recently are a departure from this trend, as women's rights and interests always remain their main priority. Here, though, the 'danger' is to ignore political or class dimensions.

As noted by Tarrow (cited in Foweraker 1995), supporters of the ideals and aspirations of a movement are spread across the society and not all are activists. In Malaysia, they can be found in the networks of women in neighbourhoods, workplaces, schools, mosques, churches, temples and other areas of everyday social life. Sometimes, support is expressed through daily discourses, sometimes in deliberate actions and sometimes by women's joining organisations. At the same time, these supporters may also endorse a number of other social movements. However, this chapter will focus only on organised groups as these lend themselves more easily to study. The women's movement, like other social movements, is observable when a proliferation of claims is made in public spaces and social grievances are made visible (Touraine cited in Foweraker 1995), although the movement's full breadth may remain submerged from view.

As women are constituted by multiple factors, the women's movement does not speak with a single voice but with multiple voices.

However, what becomes accepted, defined or portrayed as 'the women's voice' at a particular juncture is the consensus or the lowest common denominator of the majority of women. It may also be the dominant view among the most powerful or influential section of the movement. Then again, this position may be the result of contact or contestation between the women's movement and the state and society. For example, women's reproductive and sexual rights are usually raised within the context of rape or together with health issues, such as HIV/AIDS, to gain legitimacy in discussing them.

Two points merit clarification to help with understanding the women's movement better. Firstly, a common accusation periodically thrown at the women's movement is that feminism is a western import with no relevance for Malaysian society. Western feminists are portrayed as aggressive, confrontational, morally loose, and responsible for the decay in their societies, where the institution of the family is falling apart. In contrast, Malaysian women and their eastern values are projected unilaterally as soft, gentle and virtuous. The message is that their counterparts in the West are not to be followed by Malaysian women as the family institution is an important pillar in Malaysian society.

This accusation is not credible for several reasons. Western women are inaccurately portrayed, displaying a lack of sensitivity to the struggles they go through, and hence, are unfairly blamed for everything. This image also overlooks men's role, as well as that of capitalism, in bringing about the break-up of the family institution. Moreover, in the painting of a unified, docile picture of Malaysian women, we can discern an effort to erase the history of women in Malaysia. Many Malaysian women have fought valiantly for women's rights, to the extent of being expelled from positions of power in a political party (for example, the case of Khadijah Sidek in 1954) or even imprisoned (for instance, women activists such as Irene Xavier, Cecilia Ng, Chee Heng Leng and Lim Chin Chin were detained without trial during Operation Lalang in 1987). Furthermore, this discourse is hypocritical, as Malaysia is zealously following in the footsteps of the West in terms of economic development, not to mention in men's attire and mannerisms.

On the other hand, in the quest for women's votes in the general election held in November 1999 and as a response to Parti Islam SeMalaysia, PAS (Pan-Malaysian Islamic Party) and its patriarchal comments on women's roles and other issues in society, women's issues are being embraced by parties in the ruling National Front (Barisan Nasional, BN). For example, the government tabled the Guardianship of Infants (Amendment) Bill in July 1999 to grant equal guardianship rights to non-Muslim mothers and the BN Member of Parliament from

Kota Baru, Kelantan, Ilani Ishak, called for an Equality Act to be established to ensure the equality of the sexes in all spheres of their lives (*Sunday Star*, 25 July 1999).

Going even further, the newly elected chief of the Malaysian Chinese Association Women's Wing (Wanita MCA, the women's wing of a member of the BN), Dr Ng Yen Yen, is portrayed as a feminist with a westernised outlook as well as the first English-educated head of the movement. Dr Heng Pek Koon, who has written on the history of the MCA, contrasted Ng's persona as a dynamic woman with that of the Chinese-educated women who previously dominated the Wanita MCA and are perceived to be more tradition-bound (Heng 1999). She hailed Ng as the 'agent of change' who will advance the interests of women in the following areas:

> increased women's participation in decision-making roles in government bodies; more education and training opportunities, particularly in information technology and in the running of small businesses, that will make Chinese women more competitive in the workplace; improved child-care facilities so that more women can enter the work force; workplaces where women can be free from sexual harassment; and amendments in legislation dealing with divorce and child custody that currently discriminate against women and children.
>
> (Heng 1999: 12)

Heng takes a positive view of being a feminist, westernised champion of women's causes, as opposed to being a traditional, conservative woman.

Even in situations in which the struggle for women's emancipation in the West does have an influence, the agency involved in subscribing to this agenda and modifying it for the Malaysian context is not to be ignored. I concur with Jayawardena's (1986) view that feminism is not a foreign ideology being imposed on 'Third World' countries. Indeed, Wieringa (1995) relates an account of the constructed myth that feminists in the south are solely focused on issues of food and labour, whilst feminists in the North are into body politics and discourse analysis. In the Malaysian scenario, the advancement of women's interests and rights in party politics, the labour movement and women's NGOs in the twentieth century showed that the issues struggled for straddled both these domains. This perspective on the place of western feminism by no means denies the presence of Eurocentrism in some of feminists' struggles and writings, as highlighted by Mohanty (1991), Trinh (1989), Lazreg (1988), Spivak (1987) and Hooks (1984).

Finally, I purposely use the term 'women's movement' rather than 'feminist movement' in spite of my own preference. Since the term 'feminist' has negative connotations ascribed to it, it may be strategically unwise to use it. However, some women activists in Malaysia are proud to acknowledge themselves as feminists. Nonetheless, it is difficult to label neatly someone as feminist or not, as women are struggling within a set of concrete constraints (Kandiyoti 1997; Vargas 1995).

The struggle for women's interests and rights in party politics

The most successful mobilisation of women in Malaysian history has been in the anti-colonial and nationalist movements. Both the right and left wings of these movements were mainly organised along ethnic lines. Within the left-wing tradition were the Angkatan Wanita Sedar (AWAS, Conscious Women's Front) and the Women's Federation. AWAS, the women's section of the Malay Nationalist Party (MNP), was formed in late 1945 as the president of the MNP recognised that women had a role to play in the struggle for independence and were needed by the party.[1] On the other hand, the leader of the MNP's youth section argued that women were brought into the party so as to 'arouse in Malay women the consciousness of the equal rights they have with men, free them from the old bonds of tradition, and to socialise them' (Asiah 1960: 13). This claim is not supported by the first president of AWAS, who later became the fifth president of the Kaum Ibu, discussed below (Dancz 1987: 86).

The MNP demanded independence and aimed to form an Indonesian republic that included Malaya. Membership figures of AWAS were low, peaking at 2,000 (Asiah 1960: 15), compared to the highest membership figure for the MNP, 60,000 (*Malaya Tribune*, 3 April 1946). AWAS held discussions, provided a forum for Indonesian women visitors (Asiah 1960: 14) and played a prominent role in organising and taking part in a six-mile march to protest the British prohibition against the use of motorised vehicles in processions.[2]

The Federation of Women, comprising mainly Chinese women, was established in 1946 with the aim to 'educate women to take part in public life' (*Straits Times*, 23 October 1947). Together with eleven branches established throughout Malaya (also with predominantly Chinese women as members), it formed the All-Malaya Women's Federation (Manderson 1980) and numbered about 20,000 (*Malaya Tribune*, 12 February 1947). Activities and campaigns organised for women included teaching, dressmaking skills for destitute women, holding Mandarin evening classes and dissuading housewives from using the black market. Resolutions demanding suffrage for women in Malaya were also passed by the various branches. The Women's Federation joined with several other organisations to form the All-Malayan Council for Joint Action (AMCJA), which aimed to establish a United Malaya (including Singapore), self-government with a fully elected legislature and citizenship rights for everyone who regarded Malaya as their home. AMCJA joined forces with the MNP, with the additional goals of preserving the status of the Malays and using the Indonesian colours for a flag.

The struggles of these two women's sections/organisations were short-lived as all left-wing groups were banned when the British imposed Emergency Rule in 1948. The non-communal political parties that were subsequently established, including the Independence of Malaya Party, founded in 1951, and the Pan-Malayan Labour Party, established in 1952, did not flourish even though these parties promoted gender equality. This is because women's participation in politics is circumscribed by ethnic boundaries and communal considerations (Ng and Yong 1990).

The United Malays National Organisation (UMNO), representing the right-wing tradition, was formed in 1946 to protest against the formation of Malayan Union as proposed by the colonial government. Kaum Ibu (KI, Women's Association), its women's section, was formed a year later in 1947, when mostly women's associations that began as independent, nationalist organisations joined together. The KI played a prominent role in public demonstrations and rallies opposing the Malayan Union. In fact, KI's primary objective was to strengthen UMNO to oppose the Malayan Union and later to push for independence. Other goals of advancing Malay women's interests and rights, such as through marriage and divorce reform, higher education for girls and getting women to participate in politics remained secondary. Nonetheless, through Puteh Mariah and the support of the then-president of UMNO and several members, the KI ensured that women were granted the vote in the constitutional draft of the Federation of Malaya Agreement that was ratified by the British in 1947. In 1952, the KI, with the support of the then-president of UMNO, also successfully thwarted the Council of Ulamas' (Islamic Religious Teachers) banning of women from taking part in politics. The Council had argued that women's involvement in politics would lead to excessive mixing of the sexes, which would be contrary to Islam (*Utusan Melayu*, 18 September 1952). Ten years later, in April 1962, the KI initiated the celebration of Women's Day, to be observed for the first time that year on 25 August.

A meeting was called of all women's organisations to organise the celebration together. The significance of Women's Day for women's organisations was to mark the role women played in their nation's history, to unite women so as to improve their lot and to make women feel they had a major role to play in developing the country (Report of the NCWO First Biennial Conference, 25 August 1965).

In 1951, the KI (renamed Wanita UMNO in 1971) only commanded 10,000 members out of 100,000 UMNO members (*Suara of UMNO*, 15 May 1951). By 1982, that figure had reached 430,000, or 54 per cent of total party membership (*New Straits Times*, 22 March 1982). Despite the bargaining power afforded by the size of its membership, Wanita UMNO has continued to play a supportive role. Women's main roles in UMNO are as canvassers and voters during general elections rather than as leaders or electoral candidates. The under-representation of women in the party's top hierarchy and government still persists today. The KI/Wanita UMNO has dealt with the lack of opportunities given to women to govern by passing resolutions at their general assembly (for instance, in 1962), sending memoranda to the Prime Minister (as in 1976) and sending a Wanita delegation to see the Deputy Prime Minister in 1981 to request the allocation of more seats for positions of power in the government or as electoral candidates (Dancz 1987). While these demands have not been accommodated, Wanita UMNO has remained loyal to the party and still throws its support behind the party.

The exception to this approach was the response of Khadijah Sidek, the third KI president (1954–6), to women's being deliberately excluded from the Johor state election lists. Khadijah took the party general assembly to task by taking other delegates with her and walking out of the assembly in protest. She had also vocally fought for an autonomous status for the women's section and greater female representation in decision-making bodies in the party. She was finally sacked in 1956 for party indiscipline. Although many KI members threatened a mass protest against the expulsion, they finally followed the party directive not to do so. Khadijah's expulsion may have dissuaded other women leaders who might have contemplated following in her footsteps (Manderson 1980).

The KI/Wanita UMNO has generally used a passive approach in seeking changes for women. This approach includes passing resolutions, sending memoranda and personal lobbying by women leaders with the president of UMNO. These passive approaches were used, for example, in the reform of legislation for equal pay for equal work in the tertiary sector and of family law governing Muslims (Manderson 1980). The success of the reform depends on whether there is sustained lobbying or pressure from other NGOs or women's organisations. For instance, in the battle for equal pay, as discussed in more detail in the next section, it was the continuous effort of the union movement that led to equal pay for women in the public sector being granted in 1969 (Manderson 1980). The political environment also plays a role, as equal pay for women in the public sector was acceded to by the government partly to counter the election promises of opposition parties such as the Gerakan Rakyat Malaysia and the Democratic Action Party (Manderson 1980).

The potential strength of KI/Wanita UMNO, the most well organised and largest mass-based women's section of any Malaysian political party, lies in its numbers. However, this strength has not been exploited to the fullest because in general, women members accept their supportive role in the party, a reflection of their traditional roles in society (Manderson 1980). The official party line also hampers the KI/Wanita UMNO. For example, the leader of KI/Wanita UMNO spoke against equal pay when the opposition unsuccessfully brought a motion requesting enactment of such legislation (Manderson 1980).

The women's sections of other political parties in Malaysia have never either been so well organised as KI/Wanita UMNO or commanded such broad membership. However, these women's wings, for instance Wanita MCA and the Women's Section of the Democratic Action Party (DAP), have also taken up or raised issues in Parliament of concern to women, such as sexual harassment at the workplace and laws to recognise women as equal in different spheres (*Star*, 4 April 2000). Women leaders of these parties are also not autonomous and are subject to maintaining the party line.

In general, there has been a growth of conservatism for Muslim women in society. This shift can be gauged by the regression in *Syariah* laws. For example, polygamous marriages contracted without the permission of the court and divorces pronounced outside the court that were once illegal are now considered valid after a fine is paid (Zainah Anwar, quoted in *Star*, 29 March 2000). Also, the Guardianship Amendment Bill that was tabled in July 1999 only accords non-Muslim women equal parental rights (*Star*, 21 July 1999). The current political environment, with PAS in government in Kelantan and Terengganu, has further contracted women's rights, as with the PAS government's directive in Terengganu that all female Muslim workers must wear a *tudung* (headscarf) to cover their heads (*Star*, 29 March 2000). Likewise in Kelantan, the Chief Minister issued a directive to state government officers not to employ beautiful women during job interviews, based on the assumption that they could easily find rich husbands (*Star*, 21 July

1999). Still, PAS's retrogressive views on women have at least generated space for discussion on these issues and have been criticised by the UMNO leadership, women's organisations, newspaper readers and academics (*Star*, 21 and 22 July 1999; *Utusan Malaysia*, 27 September 1999).

In this context, even the PAS women's wing, Dewan Muslimat, has started to question the party leadership, including its not allowing female leaders to sit on the stage with male leaders of the party during the PAS general assembly. When debating the presidential address, Dr Lo'Lo' Mohd. Ghazali, a Dewan Muslimat committee member, had this to say: 'We see smartly dressed PAS leaders sitting on stage but what happened to us [women], why are we side-lined? . . . Is there women discrimination in PAS or is it not Islamic if women were on stage with men?' (*Star*, 5 June 2000). Even if largely obliged to follow the party line, then, women's wings of Malaysian political parties do at times articulate policy preferences or concerns that are specific to women and that would otherwise likely be ignored.

The struggle for women's interests and rights in the labour movement

Until 1950, women workers' struggles were mainly documented in the rubber estates. Women sometimes took a leading role, aggressively and bravely standing for what they wanted: good working conditions, fair pay and an end to sexual harassment. For example, in the Klang Estate workers' strike and the Panavan Karupiah Estate in Perak, one of the workers' main issues was ending sexual harassment (Ng and Yong 1990). The Labour Commission noted in 1937 that Chinese women took a leading part in the strikes for wages in Ulu Langat, Negeri Sembilan and Kuala Lumpur (Rohana 1988). Women also held meetings to discuss the non-provision of maternity leave by employers in the Batu Arang Estate and another estate near Kajang (Rohana 1988). With a strike that lasted 700 days, the longest in Malayan labour history, Chinese women in five rubber-packing firms succeeded in reversing the decision of the management to reduce their wages in 1949. This victory was the more remarkable because there was neither a union nor a prominent leader (Josey 1958). While Indian women became more active in labour struggles in the 1940s, their activism in the estates was mainly as supporters rather than leaders (Rohana 1997b). For Malay women, a significant event was establishing the Malay Women's Teachers' Union in 1929 with the aim of encouraging more Malay girls' entry into formal education and thereby improving their status in society.

In the 1950s and 1960s the dominant cry was 'equal pay for equal work'. Unequal pay had existed since the 1930s, with wage rates in estates varying by gender and ethnic group (Li 1982). A 1946 report by the Labour Department noted that children were paid the least, followed by women, with men being paid the most in estates. The Plantation Workers' Union, the forerunner of the National Union of Plantation Workers (NUPW), negotiated for equal pay for all workers in 1950. By 1953, most women rubber tappers received the same pay packet as men (Rohana 1997b).

In the public sector, the battle for equal pay as well as for provisions regarding maternity leave and the temporary work status of women gained momentum after 1957, when greater numbers of women joined the government service. Discriminatory pay rates were 'justified' by various salaries commissions on the grounds that it was more difficult to transfer women due to their family obligations, that women were less permanent in service due to marriage and that women were not considered the main breadwinners (Rohana 1997b).

The Federation of Malaya Women's Teachers Union (WTU) was formed in March 1960 specifically to pursue matters affecting the status of women teachers, including equal pay, discrimination against married women and paid maternity leave (*Straits Times*, 11 March 1960). The National Union of Teachers (NUT) initially resented the WTU, as the NUT was already representing women teachers in advancing their rights, such as by pressing for permanent status for married women (Manderson 1980: 180). However, the NUT later joined with the WTU to demand equal pay (*Straits Times*, 14 August 1960). Also, in a move to step up its efforts to advance the cause of eradicating unequal treatment towards women employees, the Congress of Unions of Employees in the Public and Civil Service (CUEPACS) established a women's section, the Women's Action Front, in January 1968 (Manderson 1980: 183). In addition to the various teachers' unions, the chief proponents of equal pay were nurses' unions and several women's organisations, including the National Council of Women's Organisations (NCWO) (Rohana 1997b: 60). These various unions and organisations agitated for equal pay by passing resolutions; sending petitions; submitting memoranda; and organising rallies, marches and demonstrations. The government finally acceded to their demands in 1969. While the union movement, particularly its women members, was the chief agent in initiating and sustaining the pressure on the government, the networking and combined efforts with the women's movement, including the NCWO and KI/Wanita UMNO, also contributed to the success of the equal pay campaign for women in the public sector. The pressures exerted in the broader political environment further ensured the success of this campaign.

The industrialisation of the Malaysian economy in the 1970s and 1980s saw the expansion of the manufacturing sector and the large-scale entry of Malay women into the labour market. These women were active in labour activism and took a leadership role in these struggles. Two significant cases involving the electronics industry were the Mostek strike in 1985 (Lochead 1987) and the struggle to establish an in-house union by the electronics workers at RCA in 1989 (Tan 1994–5; Loh 1992–3; Grace 1990). In the case of the Mostek Electronics factory in the Bayan Lepas Free Trade Zone in Penang, the workers, predominantly women, picketed, staged a sit-in outside the Chief Minister's office, presented the Prime Minister with a memorandum during a public rally, marched and waved banners demanding jobs. The struggle of these 700 retrenched workers during the recession of the mid-1980s for reinstatement or rightful compensation was supported by many other workers of all ethnic backgrounds in the Free Trade Zone.

The RCA Workers' Union (RCAWU) was registered in January 1989 but its efforts to represent workers' interests and rights were blocked by the American company. Several tactics, including changing the name of the company to Harris Solid State Malaysia (HSSM) on 8 August 1989, transferring workers to Harris Advanced Technology (HAT) on 10 January 1990 and isolating 24 employees, most of them union officials and active members, were employed to frustrate unionisation efforts. The workers, particularly women, were also harassed.[3] This case illustrates not only the harassment and intimidation confronting workers and the union-busting tactics of an American company, but also indirect state collusion to frustrate workers' rights in order to attract and ensure the steady inflow of foreign investment into Malaysia (Grace 1990). In this struggle, several NGOs, including women's groups, played a part by initiating a support group for the HSSM workers (Ng and Yong 1990).

From the 1980s onwards, the issue of sexual harassment at the workplace became prominent again due to the efforts of the Women's Section of the MTUC and women's organisations. As discussed in more detail below, in 1985 the Women's Section of the MTUC joined with other women's groups and individuals to form the Joint Action Group Against Violence Against Women (JAG-VAW) to raise awareness about violence against women, including sexual harassment. The issue of sexual harassment at the workplace has been of particular importance to the MTUC. The organisation conducted a survey in 1987 which showed that between 11 and 90 per cent of women faced sexual harassment at the workplace (*New Straits Times*, 4 April 1996). Concerned with the situation surrounding women workers who are sexually harassed, the women's section of the MTUC produced a Code of Conduct on Sexual Harassment and raised awareness on the issues surrounding sexual harassment at the workplace by organising group discussions, seminars and workshops. Counselling was also made available by the MTUC for victims of such harassment. As there are no specific laws to deal with sexual harassment, one of the most effective protections and redress for workers is through the unions: for instance, by inserting a clause against sexual harassment in collective agreements, as has been done in the case of the Penang Textile and Garment Workers' Union and the Pen-Group Companies. Besides that approach, the Academic Staff Union of the University of Malaya has had a committee since 1999 to lobby the management to adopt a policy to prevent and eradicate sexual harassment in the university.

Outside the unions, women's organisations have sometimes taken the lead in urging better protection for women against sexual harassment at the workplace, as will be discussed in the next section. In addition, there are women's NGOs that have been established solely to advance the interests and rights of women workers, including Sahabat Wanita (Friends of Women) and Tenaganita (Women's Force). These groups will also be discussed in the next section.

Since the beginning of the twentieth century, women workers have struggled as both supporters and leaders to advance their rights as workers. Sometimes, these struggles are based on women's subject position as workers in general, for instance for fair wages, safe working conditions, job security and freedom to organise. At other times, the struggles are specific to their subject position as women, as for equal pay, against sexual harassment at the workplace and for provision of crèches by employers. Although labour struggles in the 1940s were mainly a struggle against capital (Stenson 1970; Caldwell 1977), sexism and patriarchy were questioned to a certain extent even then. Male dominance still persists in unions even today, as evidenced by the subordinate status of the women's wings of the Malaysian Trade Union Congress (MTUC), which represents private sector workers, and CUEPACS, its public sector counterpart, and by the predominantly male leadership of most unions, including those with substantial numbers of women members, such as the NUPW and the National Union of the Teaching Profession (Rohana 1997b). However, this questioning and asserting of women workers' particular interests continues, as with the issue of sexual harassment at the workplace and the involvement of women's organisations in women workers' struggles.

The struggle to advance women workers' interests and rights reflects Vargas' emphasis on the contextualisation of women's struggles among other frames, problems and contradictions (1995: 89). Workers fighting for their rights may not deal with specific issues affecting women. On the other hand, issues affecting women may not pertain to their gender position alone, but may also be due to their class position as workers exploited by capitalists. In this respect, the issue of democratic leadership is another important dimension to consider. Leadership in the unions tends to remain unchanged for years, preventing not only women but also other men from assuming these posts (Rohana 1997b). At the broader level, the labour movement in Malaysia has had to confront an increasingly authoritarian state over the years, which has weakened the movement. From a radical labour movement at its height in 1947, when the General Labour Union commanded a membership of 263,598 (over 50 per cent of the total labour force) and had around 85 per cent of all unions under its wing (Morgan cited in Rohana 1997b), the labour movement became weakened and fragmented in the 1990s. In 1995, 706,253 workers, or less than 10 per cent of the labour force, were unionised (Jomo and Kanapathy 1996).[4]

The struggle for women's interests and rights in women's NGOs

Prior to independence, women's organisations were primarily concerned with issues related to girls' and women's education and welfare. One of the earliest demands intended to elevate the status of women in society was for access to formal schooling for women. The Malay Women Teachers' Union was established in 1929 for this purpose. Efforts to improve the education of Chinese women also coalesced by the 1940s. The first such instance was the founding of the Penang Women's Association in January 1946, which sought to organise night schooling for girls (*Straits Times*, 14 January 1946). Three months later, the Selangor Women's Relief Association was formed to make available free education for women and relief for unemployed Chinese women in Selangor (*Straits Times*, 24 January 1946). Another example of a women's organisation formed during that period and concerned with social welfare matters was the National Association of Women's Institute in West Malaysia (NAWIM) in 1952. NAWIM catered to rural Malay women, with the objectives of raising their standard of living, improving their knowledge in home economics and encouraging women to work together. The organisation's activities included organising nursery classes, setting up co-operatives, undertaking food catering, providing foster homes and keeping livestock (National Clearinghouse on Women in Development 1987).

After independence, the struggle for women's emancipation was represented by the National Council of Women's Organisations (NCWO). The NCWO was formed when two organisations merged in 1963. One was the Women's Council, an advisory and consultative body established in 1961 to 'act as a spearhead group initiating action for [the] betterment of women' (*Straits Times*, 5 June 1961, quoted in Dancz 1987: 139). The Council had representatives from eight women's organisations representing 35,000 women (*Straits Times*, 5 June 1961). The other organisation was the KI. The success of the celebration of the first Women's Day in 1962, a joint effort between KI and sixteen other women's organisations, prompted Fatimah binti Hashim, then the leader of KI, to propose to Rasamma Bhupalan, the leader of the pro-tem committee of the Women's Council, that the two organisations merge. Some of the NCWO's main objectives are:

1. To bring all women's organisations together,
2. To raise the standard of living of women and to work for the welfare and advancement of women and children, and
3. To serve as a consultative and advisory body to women's organisations in the country.

(Nik Safiah 1984: 220)

The NCWO was also to co-ordinate the activities of both political and non-political women's organisations.

As of its first conference on 25 August 1965, the NCWO had twelve affiliates, including the KI UMNO, the MCA Women's Section and the Malaysian Indian Congress Women's Section.[5] The Parti Sosialis Rakyat Malaysia (Malaysian Socialist People's Party) Women's Section and the Pan-Malayan Islamic Party Women's Council (Dewan Muslimat), though among the women's organisations involved in organising the first Women's Day, were no longer members. From twelve affiliates, NCWO had grown over the years to 52 affiliates as of the early 1990s (see Appendix A). Wanita UMNO and Wanita MCA are no longer members of the NCWO, having withdrawn their membership in 1983 (Nik Safiah 1984). Nonetheless, a close working relationship prevails, as the leadership in the NCWO and Wanita UMNO has sometimes overlapped. For example, Zaleha Ismail, the president of the NCWO, was also the Minister of National Unity and Community Development until the general election in 1999. Fatimah Hashim, the president of Kaum Ibu/Wanita UMNO from 1956 to 1972, was also the president of the NCWO from 1965 to 1989. In the early 1990s, the Democratic Action Party Women's Section joined the NCWO, but given its marginal position there, it has had no influence over the direction of NCWO.

The NCWO is comprised mainly of welfare, religious and service-oriented women's organisations, representing primarily educated, middle- and upper-class women. Given its history, the NCWO opts to work for reform for women from within the establishment. The undeniable advantages to this approach are access to government resources such as funding and access to information and influence within political structures. Conversely, this strategy may also work to limit the organisation's autonomy and activism.

From its inception, one of the major contributions of the NCWO has been the annual celebration of Women's Day. The NCWO has also jointly organised seminars and conferences concerning women's issues with the Women's Affairs Department (HAWA), established by the government in 1983.[6] Some of the NCWO's other notable achievements have been in the area of lobbying for laws that do not discriminate against women, such as job security and maternity leave for women in the public sector (1969), separate taxation for women (1972 and 1991),[7] outlawing polygamy for non-Muslims (1976), and raising the age of marriage to eighteen years and instituting civil family laws for all non-Muslims. At the height of the Islamisation process in 1983,[8] the NCWO engaged with Muslim family laws, requesting that the Muslim family laws codified in each state be made uniform. This standardisation would, for instance, prevent a Muslim man from circumventing the family law of a particular state by crossing the border to remarry in a state where he is allowed to do so without his first wife's permission.[9] The NCWO also managed to secure the appointment of women members as jurors and on national councils, including the National Council for Islamic Affairs, and state Islamic boards. Finally, the NCWO submitted the National Policy on Women, a watered-down version of which was approved in 1989. The policy's section on principles includes the statement, 'the special needs and feminine characteristics of women are not affected and that their maternal and familial responsibilities are not sacrificed' (Ng and Yong 1990: 10). This policy was included in the Sixth Malaysia Plan of 1991–5.

The 1980s brought a shift in orientation as Malaysian women, influenced by international feminist trends and concerned with the violence that women experience at home, on the street, at the workplace and in the media, decided to focus their energies on campaigning on the issue of violence against women. Initially, a group of over twenty women in their twenties and thirties, most of them previously student activists, met informally as a study group in the early 1980s. This group expanded to over 50 women and several men once they embarked on a two-day exhibition-cum-workshop focusing on violence against women.[10] The event, which was to celebrate International Women's Day in March 1985, highlighted violence against women in five areas: domestic violence, rape, sexual harassment in general and at the workplace in particular, prostitution and the portrayal of women in the media. As some of the women involved either held leadership positions or worked full-time in NGOs, these existing platforms were utilised.

The Joint Action Group Against Violence Against Women (JAG-VAW), which was formally launched on 1 October 1984, consisted of five NGOs together with individuals. These NGOs were the Women's Aid Organisation (WAO), the Association of Women Lawyers (AWL), the University Women's Association (UWA), the MTUC Women's Section and the Selangor and Federal Territory Consumers' Association (SFTCA).[11] With the exception of the SFTCA, all of these groups were affiliates of the NCWO. Nonetheless, the groups within the JAG 'functioned autonomously of NCWO and were not linked to the government or any political party'.[12] Still, this independence did not preclude the JAG from working together with the NCWO or on similar issues. The JAG and NCWO served as co-organisers of a national workshop on laws that discriminate against women a few months after the March event. Subsequently, they presented a memorandum seeking reform of these laws to the government. The NCWO had also organised a series of seminars on rape crisis services in the mid-1980s on its own. The NCWO even became part of the JAG when meetings were held to discuss lobbying for a Domestic Violence Act in Malaysia in the 1990s.

The JAG is fluid and its membership changes depending on the specific campaign mounted. What stood out about the JAG was its principle of working as a collective rather than a hierarchy, as reflected in one of its main workshop objectives: 'the actual process of working together as a group, as a collective, where the values of cooperation, sharing and group decision-making were experienced' (JAG-VAW 1986: 1). Meetings were informal, held at women activists' offices or in the living rooms of their houses.

The March 1985 event raised awareness of issues of violence against women. Around 1,200 women and men of all races, income groups and ages participated in the workshops (JAG-VAW 1986). Moreover, publicity in newspapers and the holding of similar events in Sarawak, Penang, Ipoh and Sabah throughout 1985 and 1986 spread the message further. Also of significance were the formation of new women's NGOs by women who had either organised or participated in these workshops. Among these NGOs were the All Women's Action Society (AWAM), the Women's Crisis Centre (WCC), the Sabah Women's Organisation (SAWO) and the Sarawak Women for Women Society (SWWS). These women's NGOs continue to work on the issue of violence against women.

Initially, the focus of the JAG-VAW campaign was on rape, following five cases of brutal child rape-murders in the span of five months in early 1987. A coalition of women's, environmental and children's NGOs and individuals known as Citizens Against Rape (CAR) was established. CAR reached out to the masses by holding a public demonstration and street dramas, and initiating a signature campaign to reform the gender-insensitive rape laws. At the same time, the Malaysian police, with the co-operation of the Canadian Mounted Police and input from women's NGOs, were conducting a series of training sessions on how to work with rape survivors in a gender-sensitive manner. In the hospitals, the Health Ministry set up a task force to study the management of rape cases. The task force proposed that rape crisis units be established in hospitals, including counselling, and that a rape kit to collect evidence for trial be developed. Also, the women's wing of the BN tabled a resolution in early 1987 to lobby the government to implement legal reforms.

The CAR campaign was short-lived. Amidst a political crisis in the country, mass detentions without trial of social activists were carried out in late 1987 under the Internal Security Act (ISA). Among those detained were four women activists, arrested under the charges of mobilising workers and women to overthrow the state. Three of them were members of the Women's Development Collective (WDC) and the other was from Sahabat Wanita.[13]

Nonetheless, the laws pertaining to rape were amended in 1989, thanks to media coverage and the efforts of women's NGOs. In lobbying for the amendments, various meetings and discussions were held involving the Bar, the Attorney-General, the Ministry of Justice and HAWA. The amendments to the rape laws provide for a minimum sentence of five years' jail for convicted rapists, the prohibition of cross-examination of a victim's sexual history except under certain circumstances, and allowing abortions to be performed on rape survivors whose pregnancies threaten their mental and physical health (previously, they were only allowed when the life of the mother was threatened). While these amendments signified to a certain degree the achievements of the women's movement, they also reflected co-optation by the state, as the definition of rape is still limited to penile penetration. This patriarchal view does not consider as rape the penetration of the vagina or anus by other objects or parts of the body, oral penetration or forced cunnilingus. Instead, as mandated by the dominant cultural/religious interpretation, the insertion of the penis into the anus or mouth, irrespective of whether the act is consensual, is a crime, defined in the statute books as carnal intercourse against the order of nature. The experience of lobbying for rape law reform also reflected the more secure base of the state in comparison to that of the women's movement, which enabled the state to subvert the proposed definition of rape.

Despite the gender-sensitisation training for police, the setting-up of one-stop crisis centres and amendments to the laws pertaining to rape, recent research conducted by women's NGOs – namely, the WCC, with the co-operation of the Women and Human Resource Studies Unit, AWAM and Suara Rakyat Malaysia (SUARAM), a human rights NGO – from the mid-1990s onwards shows that there is still much to be done for rape survivors (Lai et al. 2002; Rohana 1997a; Suaram Komunikasi 1998). While Penang's WCC took up the issue of sexual abuse of children, AWAM is currently working on further reforms to the law and to procedures governing rape trials.

Following the amendments to the laws pertaining to rape, the focus of women's activism changed to working for the enactment of a Domestic Violence Act (DVA). Some of the members of the JAG working towards this aim were AWAM, the WAO, AWL, the Women's Section of the Selangor Chinese Assembly Hall (SCAH) and the NCWO. In May 1989, AWAM, AWL and the WAO organised a public seminar entitled 'Mother's Day: Confronting Domestic Violence'. The aim of the seminar was to bring attention back to the memorandum submitted in June 1985, which amongst other demands called for the enactment of a DVA. A signature campaign by the WAO in support of the proposed DVA collected 14,000 signatures. Later the same year, in August, the AWL initiated a discussion between the Malaysian Royal Police and women's NGOs on the issue of domestic violence. A Joint Committee, comprising AWAM, AWL, the WAO, the NCWO, HAWA, the Bar Council, the Social Welfare Department, the Health Department, the Islamic Centre and the Royal Malaysian Police, was established to examine the DVA (*Waves*, 1993). The Committee revised the 1985 DVA proposal and submitted it to the Minister of National Unity and Social Development in March 1992.

Various activities were organised by women's NGOs to raise awareness of and garner public support on this issue. For instance, AWAM, the SCAH Women's Section and *Sin Chew Jit Poh* (a Chinese newspaper) organised a workshop-cum-exhibition for the Chinese community; AWAM and *The Star* (an English newspaper) conducted a survey on domestic violence; the WCC in Penang launched an outreach programme on this issue; and the SWWS conducted a public forum on 'Domestic Violence and the Proposed Domestic Violence Bill'. Learning from the previous experience of working for amendments to the rape laws, when many of the Members of Parliament (MPs) treated the issue 'with much levity and inane laughter' (Fernandez 1992: 116) during the debate, lobbying for MPs' support also became part of the strategy (*Waves*, 1993). Activists lobbied MPs from both the ruling and opposition parties.

After continuous persistent efforts, the DVA was finally enacted in 1994. As with the amendments to the laws pertaining to rape, the enacted DVA falls short of the demands of the JAG-VAW and is still very much steeped in a patriarchal worldview. One of the DVA's shortcomings is the non-recognition of marital rape, as women are deemed to have signed away their rights over their body upon marriage. Another shortcoming is the lack of a feminist perspective on the dynamics of abuse, denying battered women immediate protection. Once again, the state had the upper hand over the final version of the DVA. This balance of forces indicates the need for the women's movement to grow and develop a wider base so that the state will have no choice but to concede to the movement's demands. On another level, the compromise version reflected differences within the women's movement (Ng 1999). When the Women's Affairs Division took over the final drafting of the Act in 1993, some women's NGOs pointed out its shortcomings and issued a press statement criticising it. However, this statement was not supported or signed by the NCWO. The NCWO's position is understandable, given its relationship with the women's wing of the ruling coalition. Regardless, the DVA was only implemented two years later, after women activists took to the street following the handing over of a memorandum to the Minister in Charge of Women's Affairs on 8 March 1996.

While the women's movement has not achieved all that those involved set out to do with regard to domestic violence, its various activities have provided a feminist analysis of this issue as a social problem and not a private one. The resounding message broadcast through the media is that, regardless of the circumstances, men have no right to beat women. Abused women also have nothing to be ashamed of and are instead encouraged to come forward and lodge police reports or seek help to end the violence. Amidst this atmosphere, the years following the enactment and implementation of the DVA saw a sharp increase in the number of cases reported to the police, from 532 cases in 1994 to 1,413 in 1996 and 5,799 in 1997 (Lai 2000). At the very least, increasing numbers of women are breaking the silence on domestic violence.

Although ethnicity can be a divisive factor in communal Malaysia, the experience of lobbying for the DVA demonstrated that their gendered subject position can unify women. In this instance, the women's movement sought for the DVA to cover all women, irrespective of their religious background, to ensure uniformity in handling these cases. Hence, it was necessary to initiate discussions with various Islamic agencies, since the argument against this universal application was that Muslim women are protected from their abusive husbands under *Syariah* laws. Ultimately, uniform coverage was not completely achieved, as although a Muslim woman can seek protection under the DVA, matters pertaining to maintenance and the welfare of children are still governed by *Syariah* laws.

As mentioned earlier, women's NGOs have worked together with unions on issues pertaining to women workers, such as sexual harassment at the workplace. When the situation demanded it, women's NGOs even took the lead. For instance, the WCC initiated a petition in mid-2000 in response to the sacking of four women workers at an international hotel in Penang who complained of sexual harassment by the general manager. Working with other NGOs such as AWAM and the WAO, the WCC collected 12,000 signatures in six weeks demanding a proper and transparent investigation of these harassment cases and an enactment of effective laws against sexual harassment. Initially, the four women were accused by their employer of making false allegations and suspended. They were later dismissed after a domestic inquiry was convened. Another two women workers who complained of sexual harassment decided to resign. The petition was also in response to the pitiful number of companies in Malaysia – only 50 as of March 2000 – which have adopted the Code of Practice on the Prevention and Eradication of Sexual Harassment launched in 1999 by the Ministry of Human Resources.

Sexual harassment at the workplace has been one of the main concerns of AWAM since the late 1990s. The NGO has run numerous training sessions for companies, given talks to various audiences and been interviewed by the media on the issues. AWAM and the WDC are currently conducting research on sexual harassment at the workplace, assessing knowledge and awareness of the Code as well as its effectiveness in the pioneer companies that have adopted it. AWAM and the NCWO were part of a committee comprised of representatives of the government, private agencies, NGOs and institutions of higher learning formed by the government in July 1998 to study the definition of sexual harassment, conduct research and carry out an action plan to address the problem (*Star*, 14 and 16 July 1998).

Women's NGOs have also been established solely to work on women workers' issues, most notably Sahabat Wanita and Tenaganita. Sahabat Wanita originated from the coming together of a group of women to discuss the situation of women workers in the Sungai Way Free Trade Zone in the late 1970s. Registered in 1985, Sahabat Wanita currently runs two main programmes for women, the Women Workers' Programme and the Children and Young Women's Programme. The Women Workers' Programme covers education and training on a range of issues, including employment laws, family laws, sexual harassment, land issues and women and politics. Community organisation work is another feature of the programme, providing women with support to handle community problems such as the forced eviction of urban settler communities. In handling these issues, Sahabat Wanita also networks with other organisations. The Children and Young Women's Programme comprises kindergartens and day-care centres as well as regular meetings with young women for them to learn about and share knowledge on issues affecting them, such as education, discrimination against girls, the environment and work.

Established in 1990, Tenaganita currently carries out projects in four areas, with a designated desk for each: plantation women workers, industrial women workers, migrant workers, and women and health. Both Tenaganita and Sahabat Wanita are not only concerned with specific issues affecting women but also committed to issues of democracy, justice and equality in Malaysia, and have participated in joint actions, campaigns and forums. For example the Director of Tenaganita, Irene Fernandez, has been charged under Section 8A(1) of the Printing Presses and Publications Act for exercising her freedom of speech and standing up for the rights of migrant workers by 'maliciously' publishing a memorandum on the abuse, torture and dehumanised treatment of migrant labour at detention camps.

Women's NGOs that have been part of the JAG or work on issues of violence against women, such as AWAM and SAWO, have also networked around and supported other women's issues, among them women's rights to land and housing, as well as broader issues of justice and democracy. Seeing the need to work together, AWAM initiated a meeting to discuss issues faced by autonomous and relatively radical women's NGOs and women's sections of more progressive NGOs in the early 1990s. Subsequently, the National Women's Coalition (NWC) was established with representation from seventeen NGOs.[14] The NWC was delineated into four commissions: land, labour, culture and religion, and violence against women. However, the NWC failed in its bid for registration as it was not sufficiently organised across the country. The coalition ceased activity in 1995, apparently lacking the human resources and financial support to keep going.[15] Nonetheless, some former members have continued to work together on issues. The NWC could either be seen as a challenge to the established NCWO or as a complement to the NCWO's efforts to diminish gender subordination. Working on the issue of violence against women has brought diverse women's organisations together, as this issue cuts across class and ethnic lines and is considered as 'non-political' or 'humanitarian'. For example, member organisations of both the NWC and the NCWO came together to work on the campaign against violence against women.

The strength of the JAG that has been working on the issue of violence against women lies in its commitment to a feminist perspective. The activists involved espouse the perspective that violence against women is a consequence of the imbalance in power or unequal relationship between men and women, reinforced by sexist structures in society. The organisations in the JAG have challenged the dominant view that blames women for being battered or raped, and have introduced the notion of offering gender-sensitive services to meet the needs of abused women, such as one-stop crisis centres. These NGOs have also demanded gender-sensitive laws, such as laws pertaining to rape that will not take into consideration the sexual history of the rape survivor/victim in determining whether rape has been committed. The services set up by women's NGOs themselves, such as crisis phone lines, face-to-face counselling and shelter, are rendered as a form of empowerment and not as charity for women (Fernandez 1992). These organisations are usually autonomous and function as collectives. Hierarchy, nevertheless, does persist, although in informal or less rigid ways.

These groups are mainly led by and comprised of middle-class and non-Malay women (Fernandez 1992) and are urban based. The chief exceptions are the WCC and Sisters in Islam (SIS).[16] Muslim women from these two organisations (and other organisations) played an important role in challenging the view that a Muslim man has a right to beat his wife. Their contribution was necessary as the proposed DVA was to cover all women, irrespective of ethnicity. Domestic violence falls within the parameters of the family, so any law enacted has to take into account the separate jurisdiction in family laws for Muslims – these fall under *Syariah* law for Muslims and under civil law for non-Muslims. Furthermore, it is difficult for non-Muslims to speak on these issues on behalf of Muslims. Being from a different religious background, they may be viewed as lacking legitimacy.

In Malaysia, women's NGOs engage with specific women's issues: not only violence against women, but also such issues as single motherhood or the status of women in culture and religion. Some women's NGOs have gone beyond these concrete concerns and engaged with what are traditionally perceived as 'bigger' issues, including democracy, justice and uneven development. For example, the Women's Manifesto, prepared by the Women's Manifesto Coordinating Committee for the 1990 general election, included concerns such as democracy and human rights, corruption and people-centred development besides traditional women's issues such as violence against women, women and work, and women and law. However, in line with women's NGOs' generally non-political stance, the response from women's NGOs was poor, with only ten groups – not all of them even women's groups *per se* – endorsing the document.[17] There are two possible explanations for this reluctance. First, some women's NGOs are welfare-oriented groups and will not comment on any issues considered political, let alone endorse such a manifesto. Second, even if a women's NGO is concerned with political issues, it may have decided not to engage at that level so as not to jeopardise its relationship with the government, which is the provider of funds and services, and which the NGO may hope to influence in policy or legal matters concerning women. However, women may still campaign for these broader issues through other NGOs, such as SUARAM, a human rights NGO that campaigned for the release of those detained without trial under the ISA during Operation Lalang in 1987.

The tenth general elections in November 1999 saw sections of the women's movement taking on a new challenge by entering into formal politics. This move was to gain visibility for women's issues and to provide the space and encouragement to increase women's participation in politics and, ultimately, decision making.

Making history: the Women's Candidacy Initiative in Malaysia

The tenth general election was a momentous one. For the first time, beginning in late 1998, a group of women came together to work collectively towards fielding a woman candidate at the national level based on a platform of women's issues. This campaign was known as the Women's Candidacy Initiative (WCI). The WCI predominantly involved middle-class, urban (from Petaling Jaya and Kuala Lumpur), younger (in their twenties and thirties) women of all races. While the WCI gave women's issues top priority, it was also concerned with issues pertaining to justice and democratic governance. This initiative signalled a further development in the advancement of women's interests and rights in the realm of formal politics, as it encouraged women to be involved in politics without the hindrances posed by party structures or party lines.

The WCI candidate was initially intended to be one of a group of independents running based on issues, along with candidates for justice, the environment, labour and consumers. The aim of the proposal was to expand the conception of politics beyond being organised just along racial or party lines. However, except in the case of the women's candidate, the plan did not take off for various reasons, including that a few of the possible candidates for the issues in question joined opposition parties instead. As it was not viable to run as an independent, the WCI candidate, Zaitun Kasim, finally ran under the DAP ticket, though without being bound by the DAP party line as she was not even a DAP member. She ran as part of the Alternative Front in the attempt to deny the ruling coalition, the BN, a two-thirds majority. Although Zaitun did not win, she did well, garnering 26,144 (42.8 per cent) of the votes in the constituency.[18]

The number of votes the WCI candidate managed to garner is reflective of the support for political change following the sacking of Anwar Ibrahim, the former Deputy Prime Minister, and support for the Alternative Front. Nonetheless, the fact that WCI positioned itself as not only concerned with women's issues but as representing both men's and women's interests helped. This stance was achieved by placing women's issues within the larger framework of justice and uneven development, whereby wealth is increasingly concentrated in the hands of a few, increasing the gap between the rich and the poor. Such a broadly appealing position allayed doubts regarding the candidate's possibly narrow areas of concern, in the process endearing her to supporters of change, particularly more conservative women or men not receptive to women's issues.

As there is a chapter in this volume solely on the WCI and the 'Women's Agenda for Change' (WAC),[19] suffice it to say here that the WCI was particularly significant for two reasons. First, the WCI pushed women's issues to the forefront of the political agenda alongside other issues of concern. This prioritisation is important to ensure that women's issues are not left out or just assumed to be taken into consideration by champions of change and justice – history has shown that this will not happen. Psychologically, running a woman candidate on the platform of women's issues in particular and other social issues in general serves as a reminder of the importance of those issues. The effort also underlined the need to have not just any woman candidate, but a woman candidate who will advance women's rights.[20]

Just as important, as this was the first effort in the history of the Malaysian women's movement to run a candidate on the platform of women's issues, it provided an invaluable exercise in allowing women to familiarise themselves with the mechanics of contesting an election. Inexperienced women learned from other women who had assisted with political parties' campaigns in the past. The experiences gained in deciding in which constituency to run, strategising for the election campaign, and mobilising the human and financial resources needed for the campaign have at the very least prepared the WCI for future engagement with electoral politics. Moreover, though few in number, some men also volunteered to help with the WCI before and during the election. Men were also involved through the machinery of the opposition parties, which worked together with the WCI during the electoral process.

The lobbying document, 'Women's Agenda for Change' (WAC) represents another significant achievement for women activists. The WAC is the result of a national workshop involving a total of 34 women's organisations and other NGOs in early 1999. The initial idea was to develop a platform for a woman candidate by updating the Women's Manifesto, but as a result of the zest and committed energy put into it, the document expanded beyond just an electoral platform. However, the WCI's platform is based on the WAC. The WAC was launched in May 1999 with the endorsement of 76 NGOs (WAC 1999). The WAC targets the government and related institutions regarding policy measures and actions that advance women's rights; politicians who can incorporate women's issues into their election manifestos and, if victorious, their constituency programmes; and lastly, the general public, to raise their awareness of issues affecting women.

The document outlines eleven major issues of concern to women. The issues covered are much wider than those included in the manifesto produced by sections of the women's movement in preparation for the 1990 general election. Besides specific issues affecting women, issues pertaining to just and sustainable development, democratisation, transparency, accountability and human rights – key concerns of social movements in general – are also included. Moreover, the title of the document highlights the term 'change', drawing a parallel with the present sentiment demanding change towards more democratic and just governance.

Of significance is the inclusion of the issues of sexuality and health. Sexuality is an issue seldom discussed in Malaysia even by the women's movement,[21] given the lack of consensus over the issue and the risks of being discredited as encouraging promiscuity and loose morals. A case in point was the publication of the comic strip 'Lina's Dilemma', which depicted single young women discussing sexuality and advocating the use of condoms (Ng and Chee 1996: 203). There was an uproar over the comic strip in a Malay newspaper and even a consumers' association that has generally been supportive of women's rights criticised the publication. In defence, concerned women's NGOs argued for the importance of such discussions to prevent the spread of HIV/AIDS.

As a consequence of the cultural and religious atmosphere,[22] the women's movement's public discourse on sexuality is narrow. Initially, sexuality was discussed in relation to the issue of sexual violence against women and later in the context of HIV/AIDS. I have argued elsewhere with reference to sexual violence that this approach in the discussion of sexuality hinders the emancipatory potential of the conception of women's human rights to include bodily integrity (Suat Yan 1998: 118). This limitation is because the justification for bringing up sexuality is anchored in adverse effects on women's reproductive and sexual rights, thus limiting the discussion to those contexts. If reproductive and sexual rights are seen as women's rights, then it should be possible to discuss sexuality on its own terms, with adverse health effects as a consequence rather than a justification. On the other hand, given the lack of consensus among women's NGOs on this issue and the possible repercussions of discussing sexuality, these circuitous approaches may be the best way of finding space to discuss this issue. Still, in the WAC, the combination in one section of the issues of sexuality and health is deceptive. The focus of the section is mainly on sexuality – the regulation of women's behaviour and sexuality – and the thrust of the section is to advance a human rights perspective towards women's sexuality. This effort is a move forward in the discussion of sexuality. Another step forward would be to popularise this discourse among the general public.

The sections of the women's movement involved with the WCI and the WAC face many challenges ahead. Now that the elections are over, the primary challenge for the WCI is to sustain itself. Most of the women who volunteered their time to the initiative have full-time jobs and the level of energy put into the WCI for a few months prior to and during the election is difficult to maintain in the long term. As with past projects, another hurdle confronting the WCI is the lack of resources, including finances, machinery and media exposure. This challenge is shared especially by women's candidates from opposition parties (Rashila 1998: 157). Such a lack of resources can have a deleterious effect on a candidate's performance, particularly on her ability to reach out to those who are still undecided. The problem is compounded by the lack of democratic space, as demonstrated by the laws against public assembly. The WCI will need to surmount this challenge as well in its efforts to run candidates in the future. As for the WAC, it currently has two full-time staff and the finances to support these human resources and to run its programmes until September 2001.[23] Beyond this, its future is uncertain, although it is likely that those who gave life to the WAC will continue to prioritise this project in their respective agendas, given the current political situation.

Conclusions

Currently, women's issues are receiving a boost from the government as it attempts to woo back its dwindling support, diminished since the sacking of Anwar Ibrahim in September 1998. The government is appealing in particular to women who may feel alienated by PAS's retrogressive views on women and the increasing infringement on women's rights in states in which PAS is now in power. In this context, Wanita UMNO and Wanita MCA are emerging as champions of women's issues.

At the same time, women's NGO activists, long disaffected by a patriarchal system that accedes only to piecemeal reforms, have now had the experience of engaging directly with formal politics by running a woman's candidate with a platform of women's issues. This entry into formal politics reflects the increasingly political orientation of some sections of the women's movement and efforts to empower women to participate more actively in the political arena. Aligned with the opposition, these women's activists are standing up not only for women's rights but also for just and democratic governance in Malaysia. Concern for these broader issues is not new for Malaysian women's NGOs. Since the mid-1980s, some women's NGOs, among them AWAM, WDC and Sahabat Wanita, have collaborated with other NGOs in these struggles. The recent form of this alliance, however, is distinctive. Nonetheless, this linkage among issues and activists remains uneasy, given PAS's conservative stance on women's issues and the different objectives of the opposition parties that have come together, whether PAS's quest for an Islamic state or the DAP's plan for a Malaysian Malaysia. Nonetheless, women's opposition politics, as represented by the WCI, have entered a new realm, uniting formal politics with NGO activism. At the same time, welfare-oriented or politically disinclined women's NGOs will likely persist in their eschewal of politics.

At the same time, although women workers have demonstrated their ability to fight for their rights in different eras, in general their level of activism has diminished. The main reasons for this decline are repression by the government, which has weakened unions, and women's secondary position within those unions. In some instances, this void has been filled by women's NGOs that have taken the lead to agitate for women workers' welfare, as with the recent attention given to sexual harassment, or by women's NGOs established specifically to cater to organised women workers.

Hence, the nature of the women's movement has shifted over time. The women's wings of political parties have remained active, but still relatively marginal to their respective parties. Trade unions have lost much of their clout and dynamism, but some of their tasks have been assumed by NGOs, instead. Women's NGOs, for their part, have evolved from more commonly narrow, welfare-focused organisations to include actively political, broad-based organisations and pioneering initiatives. These changes aside, however, by whatever means, the Malaysian women's movement has continued and will continue to strive for a society that gives women their fair due.

Appendix A

Affiliates of the National Council of Women's Organisations (NCWO)

1. Young Women's Christian Association
2. National Association of Women's Institute Peninsular Malaysia
3. Women's Section, Malaysian Indian Congress
4. Selangor Chinese Women Li Chee Association
5. University Women's Association
6. Muslim Women's Action Society
7. Girl Guides Association Malaysia
8. Women's Section, Malaysian Trade Union Congress
9. Secretaries Society Malaysia
10. Women Journalists' Association Malaysia
11. Kuala Lumpur Speakers' Club
12. Women International Club
13. National Women's Council, Malaysian Ceylonese Congress
14. The Malaysian Ministry of Foreign Affairs Women's Association
15. Women's Service Christian Society
16. Women's Section, Malaysian Association of Youth Clubs
17. National Electricity Board Women's Association
18. Women's Section, 4B Youth Movement Malaysia

19. National Union of Cooperatives Malaysia
20. Buddhist Missionary Society, Women's Section
21. Congress of Unions of Employees in the Public and Civil Service
22. Malaysian Armed Forces Public Employees Union
23. Women's Graduates Society Malaysia
24. Malaysia Hindu Sangam
25. Women's Association, Medical Faculty
26. Association of Welfare and Sports, Malaysian Citizens Volunteers Corps
27. Women's Aid Organisation
28. Bahai Women's Committee
29. Women's Wing, Hindu Youth Organisation
30. Women's Section, Malaysian People's Movement Party
31. Malayan Railway Women's Group, Federal Territory and Kuala Lumpur
32. National University of Malaysia Women's Association
33. Association of Bumiputra Women Entrepreneurs Malaysia
34. Association of Women Lawyers
35. Association of Sabah Women's Organisations
36. Women's Section, Association for the Advancement of Indians in Malaysia
37. Good Shepherd Sisters
38. Sarawak Women for Women Society
39. Women's Section, National Union of Petroleum and Chemical Industry Workers
40. Women's Section, Selangor Chinese Assembly Hall
41. Women's Crisis Centre, Penang
42. Women's Welfare Council, Penang
43. Inner Wheel Club of Kuala Lumpur
44. FELDA, Women's Association
45. Federation of Family Planning Associations Malaysia
46. Association of Bumiputra Women in Business and Professions, Selangor and Federal Territory
47. National Union of the Teaching Profession, Peninsular Malaysia
48. Telecom Athletic and Welfare Association
49. Soroptimist International Club of Kuala Lumpur
50. Women for Women Association Malaysia
51. Association of Nurse Tutors, Peninsular Malaysia
52. Women's Wing, Democratic Action Party

3 Complex configurations
The Women's Agenda for Change and the Women's Candidacy Initiative

Patricia A. Martinez

Introduction

This chapter is about two definitive developments for women in Malaysia: the Women's Agenda for Change (WAC), launched in May 1999, and the Women's Candidacy Initiative (WCI), launched in September 1999.[1] I offer a critical analysis of the WAC and WCI as a participant in their evolution, explore their relevance in the context of the tenth general elections and their aftermath in Malaysia, and reflect on how women's activism is shaped by their relationship with an authoritarian state.

The WAC is a comprehensive document detailing changes demanded in eleven areas that constitute public life in Malaysia. It is the most comprehensive document ever to articulate women's issues in Malaysia, covering major areas of importance to the nation beyond the more women-oriented concerns that women's NGOs have traditionally covered. The ambit of the WAC is beyond even the scope of the Memorandum on the National Policy on Women submitted by the National Council of Women's Organisations in Malaysia (NCWO) in 1989, the Malaysian government's subsequent National Policy on Women in 1995, and the Action Plan for Women in Development in 1997. The WCI developed in response to the same grievances as spawned the WAC, representing the move from non-governmental activism to political empowerment – an idea that had been considered over the years by women activists but did not crystallise until 1999. The WCI comprised a few of those involved in formulating and endorsing the WAC together with other individuals. In the general elections of 29 November 1999, the WCI fielded a female candidate whose platform included issues outlined in the WAC.

Both the WAC and the WCI are the result of the efforts of non-governmental organisations (NGOs) that work on women's issues and of individuals who are committed to realising social justice for women. These entities, together with the state, are the main sources of the discourse in Malaysia regarding women's rights, problems and needs. The women's sections of political parties, whether in the ruling coalition of the Barisan Nasional or in opposition political parties such as the Democratic Action Party (DAP), have historically mainly reacted to issues raised by NGOs and the state. Moreover, these women's sections are not necessarily responsive to or supportive of all initiatives by women.

There are over 10,000 NGOs in Malaysia. More than 250 are defined as working on women's issues, of which approximately 150 can be described as active (Rohana 1999). Among the more prominent women's NGOs are the Women's Aid Organisation (WAO, established 1982), the Women's Crisis Centre (WCC, 1982), the Sarawak Women for Women Society (SWWS, 1985), the All Women's Action Society (AWAM, 1985), the Sabah Women's Action Resource Group (SAWO, 1987), the Women's Development Collective (WDC, 1989) and Sisters in Islam (SIS, 1992). There are other NGOs that are very active and articulate on women's issues, too, among them Tenaganita, which addresses the issues of factory workers and other working-class women, and Sahabat Wanita, which focuses on women workers in rubber plantations. Both NGOs have worked together with WAO, AWAM, SIS and WDC on major issues. Also, at various times but especially recently, the women's sections of the Malaysian Trade Union Congress, the Selangor Chinese Assembly Hall, and Pertubuhan Jamaah Islah Malaysia (JIM) have worked collaboratively with women's NGOs. The organising committee of the WAC is a good example of groups' coalescing for a particular project.

There are three coalitions of women's groups in existence. In 1963, the National Council of Women's Organisations (NCWO) was formed as a coalition of women's organisations that were at that time oriented largely towards issues of welfare, religion and service. The NCWO functions presently as an umbrella organisation for over 80 women's groups. Its chair until recently was the Minister of National Unity and Social Development, in whose ministry the Women's Affairs Division (HAWA) was located until January 2000. HAWA then became the responsibility of a deputy minister, Sharizat Abdul Jalil, in the Prime Minister's Department, which was the original 'home' of HAWA. As such, the NCWO is perceived as enabling in negotiations with an authoritarian state and yet not always so, since women's NGOs and the state conceive of and address issues from different premises and agendas. In February 2001, a new ministry for Women and Family Development was established, headed by Sharizat, now a minister, and with HAWA under its ambit.

The two other coalitions of women's groups are less formal. In 1985, a Joint Action Group on Violence Against Women (popularly referred to as JAG) was formed. Its efforts culminated in the enactment of the Domestic Violence Act of 1994 and its gazetting two years later. JAG comprises most of the groups described above. It was reconvened in 2000 for a campaign for legislation against sexual harassment. There is also in existence a less prominent, currently fallow National Women's Coalition, established in the mid-1990s. This group comprises approximately twenty organisations representing women's autonomous groups and women's sections at the grassroots level.

It is important to note that the terms of reference, 'working on women's issues' or 'women's NGOs', should not be read to imply seamless cohesion among the groups involved. These terms indicate some degree of solidarity and ability to coalesce quickly and effectively over an issue or project. However, they gloss over dissimilarities, including ideological ones, among women's groups. Different women's NGOs privilege different issues, and/or have different constituencies, objectives and organisational structures.[2]

The Women's Agenda for Change (WAC)

The WAC could be described as the culmination of the efforts of women's NGOs, catalysed by a larger movement for social justice which has been growing over the last few years, especially among groups that work on related issues. While the WAC was launched in the midst of the political upheaval and push for alternative governance that began with the dismissal of former Deputy Prime Minister Anwar Ibrahim in September 1998, preparatory work for both it and the WCI began months before. The context at that time was the impending third millennium and the need to evaluate progress made on women's issues and to plan for future work.

Participants in the working committee that wrote the draft position papers of the WAC included representatives from the Women's Development Collective (WDC, which also co-ordinated the WAC), the All Women's Action Society (AWAM), Sisters in Islam, and individuals: Ivy Josiah, Carol Yong, Saira Shameen, Sri Husnaini and the author of this chapter. Representatives of 34 NGOs joined representatives from opposition political parties and church groups as well as individuals for a national consultation. Convened in January 1999, this meeting enabled others who work on women's rights and women's issues from across Malaysia to deliberate on the draft WAC. An interim WAC organising committee evolved from this assembly and continues to coordinate future projects resourced from the initiative. It is important to point out that the WAC is a collective effort, for there was considerable input by those present at the national consultation, even if not all their names appear on the document. In addition, I want to invoke especially the many women over very many years who have had the courage to seek redress for or speak up about their experiences of discrimination and oppression, motivating those of us who work on women's issues.

The document that in some ways was a precursor to the WAC is the booklet entitled 'As Malaysians and As Women: Questions for Our Politicians and a Manifesto for the '90s' (hereafter referred to as the Women's Manifesto). An examination of this document puts the trajectory taken by the WAC in context. Published before the 1990 general elections, the Women's Manifesto was drawn up by some of the same groups involved in the WAC. Its preamble acknowledges progress in developing the immense natural wealth of the nation and lauds the (then) recently approved National Policy on Women. The Women's Manifesto states that it deplores and regrets that race and religion continue to be divisive, that amendments to the Constitution erode fundamental civil rights, that women are still discriminated against, and that the fruits of development have been inequitably distributed, widening the gap between the rich and the poor. It covers six areas: women and work, violence against women, development, health, corruption, and democracy and human rights. The issues highlighted are dealt with briefly, presented as questions asked of politicians seeking election, such as whether his or her party would commit to people-centred development or support the participation of women in the formulation of a national health policy. The Women's Manifesto reflects the pressing issues of that time, many of which continue to be relevant. For example, questions such as 'What steps will your party take to restore the independence of the judiciary?' and 'Does your party have a vigorous human rights programme?' are as pertinent now as a decade ago (see Women's Manifesto 1990).

The WAC is a far more comprehensive and lengthy document. It has eleven sections covering women and development, participatory democracy, culture and religion, violence, land, health services, the law, work, AIDS, the environment, and health and sexuality. Each of the eleven papers of the WAC first sets out the context then highlights aspects of relevant issues that have an impact on women. A section on actions concludes each paper, providing a prescriptive list of what is required especially from the government, but also from the private sector and the rest of society. Only the last paper was not one of the original drafts presented to the national consultation convened in January 1999. Rather, it was an outcome of the consultation, since there was consensus on the need for a paper on 'Women, Health and Sexuality' even if it might be construed as controversial. Significantly, the proposal for such a paper was first raised by one of the oldest participants present, who represented a group of Christian women – not, as is commonly assumed, the initiative of younger, western-educated feminists. Moreover, despite a few initial expressions of misgivings, there were Muslim women's groups that endorsed the WAC with this section.

The introduction of the WAC states that the issues which constitute the document are not exhaustive and invites the reader to add her or his concerns. This invitation is relevant because it is a shortcoming of the WAC that the document does not reflect the issues of all women. Among those whose specific concerns are not covered are the disabled, the elderly and sex workers. Some of these groups, such as the disabled, were invited to the consultation but did not attend. The introduction frames the WAC with references to the Women's Manifesto of 1990, the Fourth World Conference on Women and the NGO forum in Beijing in 1995, the National Policy on Women of 1989, the Action Plan for Women in Development of 1997, the Sixth and Seventh Malaysia Plans and the Malaysian government's ratification of the United Nation's Convention to Eliminate All Forms of Discrimination Against Women (CEFDAW or CEDAW) in 1995. The introduction provides the major premises of the document: that key issues raised throughout the 1990s have not been addressed; that women are affected adversely by their subordinate status in society, especially in the context of economic development and globalisation; and that the manipulation of ethnicity and religion as well as the use of fear and oppressive force to divide Malaysians is deplorable.

In the exigencies of space, I will not summarise the various sections of the WAC.[3] Rather, I will present just a series of reflections on the initiative and offer some comments.

The WAC is the first detailed blueprint or envisioning by women of an ideal Malaysian nation. The document is over 30 pages long and packed with considerable detail on the context of the issues invoked and the kinds of redress sought.

Although the WAC was developed by women and written in terms of women and their issues, it is framed within larger concepts of democracy, development, land, religion, and so on.

The document represents a watershed in the way women's issues have been conceptualised and presented. Prior to the WAC (and in a more limited sense, the Women's Manifesto), women's NGOs were primarily reactive. They most often raised issues with a gender particularity (for example, rape, domestic violence or sexual harassment) or in relation to specific events first publicised by the media. The WAC is instead a proactive project and a deliberate attempt to bring together outstanding issues, problems and needs; it was not in reaction to any event, policy or programme. It also embodies a vision of a more egalitarian society, one that embraces all Malaysians regardless of gender. Some of the WAC's prescriptions and demands are not limited to women; they have relevance for society and nation inclusive of all Malaysians. Some examples of this broad relevance are found in the demands for transparency and accountability in governance and elections; for an alternative vision on development that ensures an equitable balance between economic development, social well-being and political participation; for public education programmes on sex and HIV/AIDS; and for environmental protection.

The fact that the WAC was first publicised at the consultation in January 1999 and was launched a few months later, in May – well before any of the opposition political parties unveiled their manifestos – gave rise to conjecture that women had raced to be the first to offer an alternative vision for Malaysia in anticipation of the upcoming general elections. However, the timing was merely coincidence. As stated earlier, the WAC was the product of many months of meetings, deliberations and drafts beginning in 1998. Nevertheless, the launch of the WAC – which received considerable coverage in the media – and the fact that it was endorsed by over 70 organisations, many of them not women's groups, catapulted women into prominence as the elections approached. There is speculation that it was because of the timing and impact of the WAC that the ensuing electoral rhetoric of both the ruling coalition and most of the main opposition political parties focused so considerably on the importance of obtaining women's votes.

Over the years, criticism by the government or those with political power has included carping about the 'western' orientation of women's NGOs and their issues.

It can be argued that the issues as well as the language of the WAC, or the way women and their issues are framed, are resonant with liberal and universalist discourses on human rights and democracy. However, it can also be argued that the issues which have emerged as relevant are those at the forefront of public rhetoric and media coverage in Malaysia, regardless of whether or not they are contiguous with human rights and liberal discourses.

It should be acknowledged that the WAC is resonant with the focus, language and education of the women who form the core of activists in NGOs in Malaysia, many of whom are middle class, some western educated, and many professionals. In addition, the perception of correlation with 'western' paradigms and concepts arises from women's collaboration and links with the United Nations and other global agencies as well as from events that are the source of policies, programmes and paradigms for women the world over, such as the Beijing Conference in 1995. Following the rhetoric and agendas of United Nations agencies and these formative events is a dynamic common to many women's groups in Third World countries. However, it must be pointed out that the correlation with universalist discourses on human rights is also self-conscious in the WAC. For example, the document deliberately distances itself from and repudiates the 'Asian Values' cultural relativist discourse that has been appropriated by those wielding authoritarian power in Malaysia. The WAC asserts, 'The record so far has shown that the Asian Values debate has been used to alienate Malaysians who do not conform to what has been dictated as the norm for this country' (WAC 1999: 7).[4]

It can be argued that this language and conceptual premises encoded within the WAC document do not resonate with the larger constituency of women in Malaysia. Assumptions are in operation that others reading it or using it for their own projects will understand what is inferred, for example, by the term 'transparency'. For a good number of even literate Malaysians, this term does not immediately evoke accountability or demystification of government administrative procedures and processes. Such words are found mostly on websites with links to or sympathies for the political opposition in Malaysia and in the rhetoric of politicians (especially from the opposition) and the work of academics. Therefore it can be argued that the audience and thus effectiveness of the WAC is somewhat curtailed when language such as this is deployed, as the groups mentioned above constitute a relatively small and elite percentage of the population whom the document seeks to address. This shortcoming is not unique to the WAC. Opposition political party campaigns and rhetoric for the last general elections were rife with such words, often with little attendant explanation of their powerful ramifications for critiques of the state.

The fact that the language and concepts in the WAC document do not correlate with those of the larger constituency of women in Malaysia is also perhaps indicative of the homogeneity presumed about 'women' by those who speak or work on behalf of women. While activists are clearly conscious of the diversity of their constituency (Ng and Chee 1996; Rohana 1999), they continue to make and operate from assumptions about women in Malaysia. Maznah Mohamed alludes to this tendency in an account of a gathering of women activists around the theme, 'Rethinking the Women's Movement'. She writes, 'One of the most enlightening aspects of the workshop was that women activists were finally attempting to look at *themselves* rather than at other women whom they've always assumed to represent' (Maznah 2000: 16, emphasis in original. Similarly, a group discussion at the women's NGO AWAM raised the questions, '[H]ow are we to gauge our achievements? How do we know we are succeeding . . . [since] the increasing number of calls to the Telenita counseling line is not necessarily indicative . . . [W]e have yet to come up with a method of measuring our success' (Beng Hui 2000: n.p.). These statements are indicative of a self-consciousness, if not discomfort, about the presumed constituency of women whom activists define and speak for.

Perhaps what is necessary – but not within the abilities of NGOs with their limited financial and human resources – is a database on women in Malaysia. There is a dearth of data on women in official statistical production and analysis, and if statistics are compiled, the priority is on economic indices. Perhaps one of the most urgent projects of the Ministry for Women and Family Development should be to establish such a database on women to provide a profile of what the majority of Malaysian women think, want and need.

> *The WAC describes and addresses specific problematic laws, policies and institutions. Thus, the document's criticisms are directed largely at the state because it has authority for most of the institutions, and certainly the official policies and laws, which have an adverse impact on women. The sections entitled 'Actions' often address the state directly in demanding change or intervention. Therefore, the WAC is addressed both explicitly and implicitly to the state.*

In large measure, this focus on the state has to be the paradigm of those with little power who spar from the margins with a powerful and pervasive authoritarian regime. Women strategise within a set of concrete constraints that reveal and define the blueprint of a patriarchal bargain, especially with the state, within any given society (Kandiyoti 1997). In the context of an authoritarian state, negotiation rather than outright confrontation is often the weapon of the weak (Scott 1985). NGOs in Malaysia have achieved substantial gains for women by working realistically within these limitations.

However, from another perspective it can be argued that the maintenance of this paradigm in the WAC reifies or at least consolidates women's situation at the margins, in supplication to power. One wonders if the assumption of this position and the consciousness it engenders has perhaps stymied the way women perceive their ability to negotiate with and beyond the state. One perspective on activism for women's rights in Malaysia suggests that it is not only contained but also scripted by the state. Activism is contained because there are laws that limit the ability to protest, critique or investigate.[5] It can be described as scripted because the state is overwhelmingly dominant and powerful, so the paradigm and rhetoric of women's activism combines protest with supplication to the state.

NGOs in Malaysia have achieved substantial gains for women by working with the possibilities that surface from approaching the state not as a single entity, but as a conglomeration of bureaucracies, institutions and individuals. With such an understanding, it is possible to locate and negotiate with those institutions or individuals who are more open to social justice for women. The point remains, though, that even this strategy represents negotiation from a position of a lack of power. A cursory look at any of the memoranda submitted by women's groups testifies to this structure, as the issues or problems to be addressed by the state are justified by their relevance to the nation's development plans and programmes.

Activist and academic Rohana Ariffin describes this stance as the way women's groups in Malaysia have resorted to achieving their objectives by going through official channels. She explains that in their interactions with relevant authorities, women 'cushioned their words so that they could not be construed as extremist or militant'. She adds, 'in their initial statement of introduction, [they] will ensure that they respect the sanctity of the state, religion and family. Their claims are made, therefore, within these parameters' (Rohana 1999: 421). The parameters of state, religion and family bound the paradigm of those in authority, as is obvious from the renaming of the newly established Ministry for Women's Affairs as the Ministry for Women and Family Development. The Minister herself was quoted as stating that this was to ensure that the nation's 'wider agendas and ambit' are included (*Star*, 18 February 2001: 5) The assumption of this position and the consciousness it engenders have also shaped the way women perceive their ability to negotiate with and beyond the state. It should be noted that this dynamic is common to other non-governmental institutions and individuals also when they are forced to deal with the various manifestations of the state.

Among the long-term effects of such a relationship is that it infantilises the entire population, not just women. The print media each day carry extensive examples: articles, letters and news items premised on exhorting, demanding or begging the government to note, recognise or take appropriate action with regard to a particular problem. A state's paternalism reduces its citizens to being obedient, wheedling or recalcitrant children. One outcome of such infantilising is that citizens become less inclined to assume responsibility for the well-being of the nation or for being self-motivated. The logic engendered is that, since the state controls everything, everything is the responsibility of the state.

Privileging the state to the extent of being unable to see beyond it is a common characteristic of the post-colonial Third World, in which public discourse is imbued with the rhetoric of national priorities. The imperatives of a newly independent nation were often the focus of nation building by all sectors of society, including women, who themselves accepted this priority. Perhaps now, more than 40 years later, it is time to put this post-colonial mindset in perspective. The powerfully persuasive rhetoric of national priorities has been appropriated by politically motivated nationalist agendas. Women's concerns, issues and problems no longer need to be subservient to the pressing needs of a fledgling nation (if that was justified in the first place). Women should be inherent and integral to any conception, analyses, planning and programmes of the nation.

The dynamic of women's negotiating from a perceived position of powerlessness with a pervasive and powerful state has significant ramifications. As Fatimah Hamid Don describes in her critique of the National Policy on Women, the main objectives of this policy did not carry strong statements of gender equality or the need to eliminate gender discrimination because these were relegated to lesser importance by women themselves as a strategy of negotiation with the state.[6] She explains that the reason for subverting gender was the priority given instead to inserting the National Policy on Women into the larger policies and programmes of the nation. She elaborates that this strategy was used in order to expedite approval of the paper submitted by women on the policy (Fatimah 1995). (It is perhaps significant to mention that this critique, found in the paper 'The National Policy on Women in Development: A Critique' distributed at the 1995 conference entitled Approaching the 21st Century: Challenges Facing Malaysian Women, is missing from the version of the paper published in the conference proceedings, a volume entitled *Malaysian Women in the Wake of Change*.) Fatimah states that activists' adoption of such a strategy enabled the promulgation of a National Policy on Women which addresses aspects of problems that women encounter, but without one of the founding premises of these problems: gender discrimination and the need for gender equity. Many years after the enactment of this policy, every section of the WAC resonates with the problem of gender equality. This, then, is an example of a curious formula whereby women achieve power by disempowering themselves consciously in competing realities.

The WAC section on women, health and sexuality represents the first time the issue of sexual orientation has been addressed in a general document on women and social justice in Malaysia.

Although the section on sexual orientation or identity is only a short paragraph in the two and a half pages on 'Women, Health and Sexuality', it is quite specific. The paragraph condemns the regulation of women's sexual behaviour, including 'their sexual orientation and lifestyle preference', and states that a person's sexual orientation and sexual practice should not be grounds for discrimination so long as they do not involve harm to anyone. The paragraph concludes, 'The widely held notion that a woman's primary role is to be a wife and mother, means that women who do not fulfill this expectation, such as single women, lesbians, celibate women, or childless married women, face a great deal of hostility and discrimination' (WAC 1999: 29). While the paragraph has been critiqued – legitimately – as being inadequate or unclear, it is important to recognise that this is the first articulation of a more inclusive understanding of sexuality in a general manifesto or policy document in Malaysia. In addition, it is noteworthy that despite this section, the WAC was endorsed by groups such as JIM, which define themselves as religion-oriented and more conservative. It is significant that there were more reservations voiced in private communications among those who were asked to endorse the WAC regarding the critique of the government and systems of authoritarianism than there were objections to this section on sexuality.

Concluding reflections on the WAC

In September 1999, Members of Parliament as well as opposition political parties were asked to endorse the WAC and raise its issues as part of their election platforms. They were sent a form letter with an attachment that required them to list five actions to which they would commit. Only seven out of 192 Members of Parliament responded to the exercise. Three of the responses were from opposition Members of Parliament, specifically from the Democratic Action Party (DAP). Out of fifteen female Members of Parliament, none committed to the WAC. Parti Rakyat Malaysia (PRM) and Parti Keadilan Nasional (Keadilan) did not have representatives in Parliament then, but they committed to the reintroduction of elected local governments and to reviewing existing civil and *Syariah* (Islamic) law. The women's wing of Parti Islam SeMalaysia (PAS) indicated that it was studying the WAC. In October 1999, the Manifesto of the Barisan Alternatif (BA, the loose opposition coalition comprised of PAS, Keadilan, PRM and the DAP) included the statement that the WAC would be studied and implemented.

The official response has been more ambiguous. The women's wings of the political parties of the ruling coalition, especially the most prominent among them, Wanita UMNO, were unresponsive. It is perhaps significant that one of the most influential women in Wanita UMNO at that time was the minister responsible for HAWA, the Women's Affairs Division in the government. Just before the elections, the WAC was endorsed by Abdullah Badawi, the newly appointed Deputy Prime Minister, and Sharizat Jalil, who was then Deputy Minister for Youth and Sport. Still, many women activists say that these two endorsements by leading government politicians have resulted in little of substance in terms of policies and laws, although the creation of a new ministry for women has left some feeling hopeful. Many women were upset that in the budget announced for 2001, special allocations were provided for some segments of society, such as the disabled, but not for women. There is an allocation for women in development in the latest of the nation's blueprints, the Eighth Malaysia Plan (spanning 2001–4), but social justice issues for women continue to be relegated chiefly to NGOs and their limited resources.

The WAC has evolved beyond being just a document. It is now an entity that signs on to other appeals, demands and protests related to the needs of civil society. Examples of this are the WAC's endorsement of various representations to the Malaysian Human Rights Commission (SUHAKAM), the 1 May 2001 declaration of Workers' Rights, and an official protest against the arrests of ten opposition party politicians in April 2001 under the Internal Security Act, a draconian law that allows for detention without trial. This dynamic ensures that the WAC intervenes to further the aims it describes and that it does not remain a document, but rather, serves as an active and tangible configuration of women's agendas.

The Women's Candidacy Initiative (WCI)

The Women's Candidacy Initiative was described by some as the next logical step in working for women or as an outcome of the frustrations of trying to effect change for women. Although it cannot be denied that advances have been made in getting redress for women's problems and that policies and laws have been amended, these improvements are only a portion of what is needed. This is obvious from the demands of the WAC. Besides, women's NGOs have had to make concessions and compromises in the process of negotiating these demands. For example, in working with HAWA as well as the police and religious authorities, women's organisations had to accept a Domestic Violence Act (DVA) that, in its final form, represents a compromised version of what they anticipated (Ng and Chee 1996: 201). In addition, it not only took many years before the Domestic Violence Act was finally enacted in 1994, but then took two more years and considerable lobbying and confrontation by women activists before the legislation was implemented (WAC 1999: 11–12).

The WCI grew out of the recognition that the political participation of women at every level of decision making is vital to advance and maintain the rights of women and to represent their concerns. In Malaysia, women from the women's wings of their respective parties who are selected to stand as parliamentary candidates essentially perceive themselves as playing supporting roles in furthering the agendas of their parties (Dancz 1987). The notion of having a woman in Parliament who would articulate women's issues had been expressed informally since at least 1997. This idea and resolve consolidated in August 1998 at approximately the same time that the WAC crystallised.

Representation in Parliament is the main objective of those working in the WCI. The initiative represents a transition from activism at the margins to political empowerment at the center of governance and public life in Malaysia. If there is a woman in Parliament whose mandate is a platform that includes women's needs and concerns, then the work of drawing attention to issues and events that have an impact on women is enhanced. This arrangement would be a vast improvement on the existing situation wherein women's NGOs have to work through the vagaries of the media and various sympathetic (or otherwise) officials in the government just to get an issue or event recognised as problematic, let alone rectified.

In reaction to the experiences in more structured NGOs of some of its members, the WCI was deliberately defined as an informal group. Participants do not need to complete a membership form or pay fees, as for some other NGOs. There is no formalised hierarchy, although obviously some assume leadership roles. Various women take on responsibilities depending on who volunteers and what tasks need to be done. The WCI is supported by a core of approximately twenty women and men, but the number fluctuates considerably, reaching its largest size during the elections. Also definitive of the WCI is a sense in the core group that women who have only limited experience as activists are just as capable of defining and leading a women's movement as their more experienced colleagues. Activists' seeking election to Parliament is a relatively new phenomenon and hence is a leap in the dark even for those with more experience in women's issues. There were times when some in the WCI acknowledged the enormity of an undertaking that seemed almost foolhardy for its daring, but there was considerable encouragement from both within and outside the group. The woman who stepped up to become a candidate at the launch of the WCI in September 1999 was Zaitun Kasim, an Australian-educated, Muslim activist with many years of experience in human rights and women's issues.

Aside from Persatuan Sahabat Wanita, which offered its offices for the WCI secretariat, no other NGOs were formal components of the WCI. The precise reasons for this remain difficult to ascertain, but could be attributed to a few main factors. Unlike the WAC, the WCI was convened less formally, so individuals rather than groups made the decision to participate. Also, some women activists were apolitical or were already members of a political party. Others supported the candidacy but could not participate actively because they were already fully committed to other projects. Finally and most importantly, time and human resources were so limited that within the short period between the WCI's becoming a functioning unit and the elections of November 1999 (a total of five months), the need to network and include other NGOs, although listed as imperative, became less of a priority. In retrospect, these lapses, even if exigent or inadvertent, may be described as shortsighted. Their ramifications may have a far-ranging impact on the WCI's relationship with other NGOs and on women's NGOs' sense of political empowerment.

From its inception, the WCI was conceived of as being separate and different from the existing array of political parties. Indeed, up until the announcement of the date of the elections, there was considerable debate within the group about whether the WCI was an NGO or a political party; the former conception prevailed.

Therefore the base of support for the WCI was small and the limitations of the project were considerable, not only because it was the first time that women were seeking political empowerment on their own or because of a lack of an established relationship with political parties. The limited support for the WCI was also because there were activists who were ambivalent about the transition from activism to political empowerment.

This ambivalence is relevant. It was a dilemma shared initially even by some of those within the WCI. The perceived premise of activism in a civil society is that individuals and groups are not contained by political allegiances – that one is free to critique the government and institutions at will. The perceived premise of politicisation is that one is constrained by alliances and political correctness. These premises hold. However, in dealing with a dominant and powerful state, activists have made political choices and moves in the past, especially in negotiating with the government, whose agendas are often openly synonymous with those of the political parties of the ruling coalition. Thus the definition of what constitutes 'political involvement' and its ramifications is debatable in terms of an ambivalence about seeking political empowerment. In this context but some years earlier, Noeleen Heyzer, then the director of the United Nations Development Fund for Women (Malaysia), wrote about the difficulty of enacting radical change in the functions of NGOs from welfare and service delivery to advocacy, lobbying and 'even political action' (1995: 6). She states:

> This change of roles is not an easy task. It requires NGOs to rethink their position, strategies and relationship with the government. It requires them to learn new skills of analysis, negotiation and alliance building nationally and transnationally. Whether Asian NGOs significantly seize the challenge and opportunities or not depends largely on whether they can step back and reflect on their conventional roles and work.
>
> (1995: 6)

In addition, the meeting described as 'Beijing Plus 5', convened in 1995 to evaluate the implementation of the Declaration of the Fourth World Conference on Women in Beijing, maintains the validity of women's achieving power in decision making, one of twelve areas defined as critical. Perhaps achieving political empowerment is one area that more Malaysian NGOs need to consider, although the ramifications of doing so in the context of their role in a civil society or with an authoritarian state also need to be weighed carefully.

The manifesto of the WCI encapsulates succinctly what the project was about and what it hoped to achieve:

- To promote an awareness in all Malaysians, but especially women, of their rights and power in a democratic process of elections and parliamentary representation.
- To promote a minimum of 30 percent participation of women at all levels of political and policy-making processes.
- To promote all causes of justice and democracy and to incorporate the views, aspirations and participation of women in this process.
- To work towards the abolition of the use of physical force or any form of violence by state institutions against all Malaysians but especially the most vulnerable – women and children – in any and all situations.
- To work towards repealing all oppressive laws that curtail the democratic rights of Malaysians, as well as revising all policies and laws which discriminate against or impact unfairly against women, including those of the *syariah* court system.
- To work towards provisions that would ensure people are never forcefully evicted from their land or homes under any circumstances and that alternative, quality housing is provided to those who are deliberately relocated from their homes as a result of development for public interest.
- To ensure that all development programmes are consultative and people-centered, with 'people' meaning all Malaysians citizens who are directly affected by these development programmes.
- To ensure that all decision-making and all business conducted by the government and its institutions are processes open to public scrutiny. To ensure also that the government and its institutions accept responsibility and are accountable for these decisions and their results. To ensure that local council elections are reinstated.
- To ensure the just and equitable distribution of the wealth of the nation so that it is not concentrated in the hands of a few but instead enjoyed by all Malaysians, and to ensure also that women are involved in the process of decision-making and in the distribution of national wealth and resources.
- To ensure a safe, comfortable and quality standard of living for all, prioritising the most vulnerable groups, especially single mothers, the elderly, children and the disabled. To ensure that the basic social service needs of all are met. (WCI 1999: n.p.)

Like that of the WAC, the manifesto of the WCI is broad-based. Its objectives include women's issues but these are conceptualised in wider terms. This positioning was not only to make the platform relevant to a constituency beyond women, but also because of the premise that women and their issues are not exclusive, but are framed within the larger context of Malaysian society.

A document dated 11 August 1999 and circulated to all decision-makers in the Barisan Alternatif (BA) argued that an independent candidate from the WCI would enhance the BA's base among the electorate. This was especially relevant because the incumbent Barisan Nasional (BN) had launched a vigorous campaign to woo women's votes and had stated repeatedly that this was its major strategy. The document proposed that endorsing the women's candidate would be a 'dramatic and explicit statement that the Alternative Coalition respects and cares about women; that the Alternative Coalition supports women's struggles for advancement and higher status in society'. On 1 September 1999, at a seminar convened to discuss women and the distribution of wealth in the nation, women representatives from PRM, DAP and Keadilan declared publicly that their parties would not stand against the independent woman candidate.

Over the next two months, the component parties of the BA and BN issued a number of statements expressing concern for women and support for their issues. For example, Datuk Napsiah Omar of the BN was quoted as saying that 'women can determine what type of government they want for their children's future' (*Star*, 4 October 1999: 7). As women's votes were crucial, she urged all Wanita UMNO leaders to reach out to women at the grassroots level and to teach them the 'proper' way to vote. Such statements and sentiments seemed to indicate the potential power of a candidate perceived as empathetic with women.

The toughest negotiations for the WCI were over which constituency and under which Barisan Alternatif (BA) party's logo its candidate would stand for election. Despite a preference to be independent because of its NGO orientation, the WCI had no alternative but to be a part of the BA. The WCI lacked the funds, human resources and sufficient time to consolidate a strong base or voter recognition for a logo of its own. Besides, it could not take on the BA as well as the BN in vying for a seat. Therefore it was decided that the WCI had to become a part of the coalition of opposition parties. Still, some in the core group had considerable misgivings about individual parties in the BA, especially PAS, with its track record on women (for example, PAS would not allow members of its women's wing, Dewan Muslimat, to stand for election, and its policies and rulings as well as statements reported in the BN-partisan media suggest that PAS discriminates against women). Members of the BA had strong misgivings, as well, including whether the WCI candidacy was so new and so small as to be facetious, whether women were being opportunistic and selfish in wanting to fight for women's rights, and most importantly, whether the WCI candidate would lose the opposition coalition one more seat.

Ultimately, the DAP offered the parliamentary seat of Selayang in the state of Selangor to the WCI and announced the candidate as part of the DAP selection, even though Zaitun Kasim did not actually join the party. This arrangement is significant and testifies to the determination of the WCI to maintain its alternative features despite its participation in politics. The incumbent in the Selayang constituency was Dato Chan Kong Choy, a vice-president of the Malaysian Chinese Association (MCA), a component party of the ruling coalition. He had won his seat in 1995 by a 70 per cent margin. The WCI worked closely with the Muslim opposition party PAS in Selayang to try to win the significant Malay segment of the vote. The working relationship with PAS was relatively easy and smooth despite the fact that Zaitun does not wear a *hijab* and that many members of the WCI are not Malay or Muslim.

While Zaitun lost to Dato Chan, analyses show that there was a considerable swing of votes towards her, although not enough to ensure a win. Of the valid votes cast, 52 per cent were for Dato Chan and 43 per cent for Zaitun. Postal votes, mostly from the armed forces and police, were close, as well: Dato Chan garnered 846 votes and Zaitun, 751. On her first try, the WCI candidate significantly reduced the margin of one of the most popular and powerful candidates in the MCA, which was cause for some celebration. However, it is also pertinent that the WCI candidate ran on the DAP logo and track record. Because of the DAP's history and because it was a member of the BA coalition, some of the support from voters was more for the DAP or opposition per se than for the individual candidate.

> *Women's lack of political power – the result of their lack of political participation – remains an area that women need to address and yet are reluctant to tackle.*

One reason proffered even by political parties is that the nation is Islamic and women are discouraged from leadership roles in Islam. Yet women have grown increasingly visible and assertive in public life in Malaysia. Indeed, there is general consensus that Muslim women in Malaysia are less constrained than some of their sisters in other Muslim nations. They have easy access to the same opportunities as men in education, health services and the franchise. Women constitute more than 50 per cent of the enrolment in three out of four public universities. At present, Muslim women serve as governor of the central bank and Minister for International Trade and Industry, one of the most senior appointments in the Cabinet. The university at which I work has three female deans. They head the law, engineering and economics faculties, all of which are still deemed male preserves in quite a few nations around the world. Still, although these are powerful appointments, women have documented and protested the pervasive resistance to women's advancement or lack of opportunities in white-collar, supervisory or managerial positions.

Similarly, women encounter resistance in being nominated or chosen as candidates in elections or as appointees to political office even though they are politically active. Women form approximately half the membership of most of the main political parties in Malaysia. However, their role has been largely as supporters, albeit vital ones.[7] It is women who go from door to door in their *kampung* (villages) to convince those who are eligible to vote to support their party. It is women also who do the administrative work necessary to ensure that the party machinery runs smoothly, as well as raising funds for the party. These roles were especially significant early in Malaysia's political history. Finally, women themselves turn out in large numbers to vote.

In the November 1999 general elections, Malaysia's tenth, only 53 out of over 300 candidates who stood for election were women. The common terminology 'stood for election' is misleading, for candidates are appointed by those in power within their political parties. Of the 53 women candidates, 36 were from the ruling coalition. This figure needs to be understood in context, however. For example, the MCA fielded just six women despite having over 600,000 members, almost half of them women. This ratio is indicative of the extent to which women are excluded from political office.[8]

In an interview with *Aliran Monthly* before her candidacy, in response to the question, 'How can women participate more actively in politics in this country?' Zaitun Kasim replied,

> Asking *how* can women participate assumes that it is easy enough for women to participate. Maybe we don't ask often enough '*Why do they not participate?*' What is it about the structures of political parties that make it so difficult and at times, frightening, to participate in the management and running of the party? Do party processes fully accommodate the needs of women and the multiple

roles they are expected to play, which male political members may not be expected to? Political parties should reach out, foster and encourage a more supportive environment if they are truly committed to not only representing 'the people', but also the women in their parties.

(quoted in Maznah 1999: 37, emphasis in original)

Zaitun's words seemed almost prescient more than a year later, when UMNO sought to develop new sectors of support by establishing Puteri UMNO, a movement for younger women, who are almost invisible in Wanita UMNO. On 10 July 2000, Prime Minister Mahathir Mohamad (who is also president of UMNO) announced the decision to create the new division. Over the next few months, it was primarily women in the party, especially the leader of Wanita UMNO, who made statements that intimated their discomfort with having Puteri UMNO as a fully fledged component of the party. There were even suggestions to reduce it to the status of a club. Some younger women were outraged, drawing a parallel with the male equivalent in the party – the members of UMNO Youth have voting rights and representation up to the Supreme Council of the party, its highest level. It is interesting that even within a party that is eager to increase its support in the aftermath of its poor showing in the last general elections and that has identified women as vital to this endeavour, younger women find enormous obstacles to their full political participation. This difficulty is indicative of both political culture in Malaysia, which exemplifies the feudalism inherent in virtually all the cultures of its population, and the larger context of authoritarian paternalism which women learn, conform with to achieve their objectives, and then replicate. If a significant section of women within a political party that openly woos them have major problems, then the move from activism on the margins to political power at the centre for other women seems doomed to failure. Yet, as the WCI's foray into politics showed, this imperative is within reach.

Although women constituted 55 per cent of registered voters in November 1999, and despite the considerable courting of 'the women's vote' which continues even now, women won only twenty seats in the tenth general elections.

These twenty seats represent women's best showing yet. In the aftermath of the elections, perhaps in the context of the emergence of Islam as definitive in the way Malaysians voted, only three women were initially appointed to the Cabinet, two as ministers and one as a deputy minister, although an additional deputy minister was appointed later. This was a decrease from the four previously appointed throughout at least the past five years, despite all the rhetoric about the importance of women and their vote and the presence of the largest number of women ever in Parliament. The Prime Minister commented that he had difficulty finding appropriate women candidates who fulfilled all the relevent party, state, ministry and other considerations (*New Straits Times*, 10 December 1999). Disappointed, Dr Ng Yen Yen, head of the women's wing of the MCA, asked that the criteria for the selection of cabinet members be made known so that women within the BN could 'better equip themselves' (ibid.). No women from the other BN parties protested this decline in representation or issued any statement. Less than two weeks later, at a forum entitled 'Women, Politics and the Media Today', academician Nik Safiah Karim expressed her shock that women's groups did not protest the reduction of women in the Cabinet (*New Straits Times*, 23 December 1999).

These developments beg the question of whether the messages directed at women in the last elections, whether by the BN or the BA (and largely from the top down, in either case), largely missed their mark in terms of developing women's political consciousness. If we do not wish to continue to perpetuate the assumptions that limit women politically, how do we reach this constituency? Would conscientisation be an effective method, alerting women to policies, laws and programmes that have an adverse impact on them (instead of focusing on issues such as rape, domestic violence and sexual harassment), thus awakening a gendered political consciousness? Or would the reverse work more effectively?

There is a need to explore the findings of a survey (which because of serious flaws is described as best serving a 'confirm or deny' purpose in evaluating conventional wisdom on popular attitudes) conducted through the Political Science Department of Universiti Kebangsaan Malaysia. Only 47 per cent of the mostly Malay respondents aged 39 and younger disagreed with the statement, 'Political and social matters are more appropriately managed by males.' Still, a full 70 per cent agreed that 'Women's active involvement in a political movement is important' (Weiss 2000). In other words, the attitudes expressed towards women's political involvement are ambivalent. Patriarchy is pervasive in Malaysian cultures and religions. It does not enhance the potential of women in public office that the leading opposition political party, PAS, does not field female candidates and that its women's wing faces considerable restrictions in terms of public space and access during its party conventions (*muktamar*). On a wider scale, public perceptions of women are largely sexist. Patriarchy and sexism are not conducive to recognising women's capabilities in dispensing the responsibilities of public office.

An incident during the elections and the furore in Parliament in February 2000 over sexist remarks suggest the way in which women are rendered negligible, if not ultimately irrelevant, in public office. In his campaign against DAP candidate Theresa Kok, the MCA candidate for the seat of Seputeh, Dr Sua Chong Keh, declared at a dinner organised by the women's wing of his party that he 'does his business' standing up while a woman does hers squatting down, and that as such he is a better candidate. Then in February 2000, two BN Members of Parliament caused an uproar by their use of sexist language. Thong Fah Chong and Bung Moktar on separate occasions said *boleh masuk sedikit* instead of *minta penjelasan*, the usual phrase for interrupting a parliamentary debate to seek clarification. The phrase *boleh masuk sedikit* has sexual overtones of penetration. Neither MP has been censored, although the Hansard shows that both men used the phrase to interrupt women Members of Parliament. I have collected a few examples of the Prime Minister himself trivialising women[9] and attended an academic conference in Malaysia in which some men found the session on feminist issues hilarious. While these examples are the exception rather than the norm, the fact that such attitudes are articulated by men in high public office is testament to the sexism that continues to pervade Malaysian society.

Malaysian political scientist Johan Saravanamuttu writes, 'I would argue that sexism and hierarchy form the underpinnings of contemporary male social discourse in Malaysian society cutting across ethnicity and class' (1994: 212). Given this reality, one might conjecture that gender equality is imperative. Yet, as Fatimah Hamid Don pointed out in her analysis of women's strategies to enable passage of the National Policy on Women, and as their chequered progress towards full political empowerment suggests, women have de-prioritised privileging this imperative. Obviously, in addressing specific issues such as the latest campaign against sexual harassment that was launched by JAG in March 2001, gender equality is implicit or at least foundational. However, it is the absence of the reiteration of gender equality in and of itself as a stated imperative which is perhaps at the root of the sexism or lack of gender sensitivity that grounds many of the problems that women encounter.

Nevertheless, the development and trajectories of the WAC and the WCI give cause to hope that women are renegotiating their conceptions of power and polity in their complex configurations.

4 Islamic non-governmental organisations
Saliha Hassan

Introduction

In its general management of democracy in the country, the Malaysian government remains wary of non-governmental organisations (NGOs) that involve themselves with political issues or specifically advocate reviews of policy decisions and legal restrictions within the realm of civil and democratic rights. The regime's trepidation extends to Islamic and/or Islamic-oriented NGOs (IONGOs), which appear to enjoy substantial grassroots goodwill among the Malay Muslim community that makes up about 45 per cent of Malaysia's population. This attitude may be a legacy of the colonial days, when indigenous anti-colonial movements in the late nineteenth century that were led by religious figures usually had greater grassroots support than others led by displaced traditional elites. Examples of these earlier leaders are Haji Abdul Rahman Limbong, Lebai Hassan, Haji Zakaria and Tok Janggut in Terengganu and Kelantan. Religious leaders were often closer to the people than other feudal or administrative leaders, thus making them more effective in influencing the grassroots towards political actions, despite existing feudal political structures and values. In fact, the strength of their religious fervour made individuals bold and greatly committed to their cause.

During this early period, Islamic movements often began as associations focused on non-partisan religious activities such as general communal welfare and specific social issues such as religious education. These associations would later turn political as independence and the notion of self-government began to take root. A few actually came to act as fronts for nationalist movements. This development was followed in the 1920s by the *Islah* or Islamic reform movement, which empowered ordinary Malays with greater confidence in themselves and defined for them an indigenous perspective for a nationalist movement. By the

1950s, Malay nationalism was characterised by some of its leaders, such as Dr Burhanuddin alHelmy, as inseparable from the religion of the Malays, Islam, both in the context of the Islamic interpretation that there is no concept of 'separation between church and state' and in terms of culturally synonymous identification of Malay and Muslim in Malaysia.[1]

For the Malay community, the contest between the United Malays National Organisation (UMNO) and the Parti Islam Se Malaysia (PAS), known at that time as the Parti Islam Se Malaya,[2] dominated politics in the immediate post-independence period of the 1960s (Funston 1985). UMNO's leadership was leading the nation towards interracial co-operation among the three major races, the Malays, Chinese and Indians, with the objective of securing a conducive political climate for socioeconomic development. Its stance was more secular than PAS's and it commanded greater grassroots support among the Malay- and English-educated Malays. In contrast, PAS maintained a more rural constituency, particularly among Arabic- and religious-educated Malays. PAS's discourse at the time revolved around the issue of *merdeka kosong* or 'empty independence', since the young nation's foreign policy, defence system, judicial and administrative structure, social programmes and much of its economy remained in the hands of its former colonial master. Beyond politics, PAS adopted a discourse of morality not only in matters touching on the marginalised position of Islamic laws in the Federation of Malaya but also related to the lack of understanding and observance of Islamic ethics and morals, especially among the political leadership. The party thus challenged the moral legitimacy of the UMNO leadership. In what can be seen as a response to this challenge, the government – UMNO in particular – took the initiative of forming special agencies dealing with Islamic issues and independent Islamic organisations that could promote its commitment to Malay interests, among which Islam remains a dominant concern. These bodies are discussed in detail below (see also Saliha and Che Hamdan 2000).

Perhaps recognising the embeddedness of Islamic concerns in the Malay community, the government continues to perceive Islamic organisations and movements as reliable indicators of the feelings, aspirations and concerns of its Malay Muslim-majority electorate. Hence, continuing to be wary of a possible political challenge from them, the government is mindful of Islamic organisations' evaluation of its policies. This attention gives Islamic non-governmental organisations a measure of public space and a political role in Malaysia's largely state-defined civil society. This aspect of civil society development in

Malaysia became more visible amidst the general increase of NGO activities on various issues in the 1970s. The government itself sponsored a number of Islamic NGOs, both to counter independent grassroots Islamic NGOs and to touch base directly with its Malay Muslim electorate. An example of these is the Malaysian Dakwah Foundation, Yayasan Dakwah Islamiah Malaysia (YADIM). Established in 1974 as a trust foundation, YADIM's objectives include the streamlining of all *dakwah* activities (the act of calling others towards an appreciation of Islam, enjoined upon every Muslim) and containing as well as overcoming deviant teachings amongst *dakwah* organisations.

Government-sponsored Islamisation

Internationally, Malaysia is anxious to be understood and accepted as a modern, non-belligerent Muslim state and to present a 'friendly face of Islam'. Domestically, by way of recognising the political legitimacy of the Malays as the identifying indigenous entity, Article 3 of the Malaysian Constitution firmly establishes that the official religion of the nation is the religion of the Malays, namely Islam. The *Yang di Pertuan Agong*, who is the Malaysian sovereign head of state (per Article 32 of the Constitution) elected every five years from among the nine Malaysian sultans, is also the head of religion.[3] Furthermore, the prime minister, who is the head of government, is also the leader of UMNO, the dominant political force in Malaysia ever since the party's inception in 1946. UMNO first took shape in resistance to the British Malayan Union proposal, which, if implemented, was seen to entail the obliteration of Malays' political dominance on their own soil. It follows quite naturally then that UMNO, founded on the principles of protection of Malay rights and sovereignty, would be the main influence in charting the nation's course and identity. Although mindful of the impacts of its policies on ethnic harmony and the general good of multi-ethnic, multicultural, multi-ideological and multi-religious Malaysia, UMNO's efforts towards developing a united *bangsa Malaysia* (Malaysian nation) have remained focused on the role and position of Malays as Malaysia's dominant indigenous group.

In this sense, in pushing for a Malay agenda within the wider Malaysian agenda, the national Malay leadership walks a sensitive divide of value systems and political tightropes strung among ethnic interests and sensitivities. Nonetheless, the UMNO leadership has continued to call upon the Malays to maintain their traditional and legitimate political leadership. Prime Minister Mahathir Mohamad, for example, has tirelessly urged the Malays to do so and to maintain the strength of character and identity to face up to contemporary global challenges, backed by twenty-first-century know-how (Mahathir 1986, 1997). He also exhorts them to transform their culture and society towards greater conformity with Islamic teachings, emphasising particularly those progressive aspects that encourage more assertive economic and intellectual participation.

These aspirations have been translated into pertinent government policies and programmes, many of them introduced after the 13 May 1969 racial riots in Kuala Lumpur and, on a lesser scale, in some other parts of the country. Among these initiatives are the much-debated New Economic Policy (1970–90), which proposed to restructure the Malaysian economy so that economic sectors no longer conform to racial divides; the National Culture Policy (1971), which is based on Malay culture; and a revamp of the 1961 National Education Policy based on the newly formulated national philosophy of *Rukun Negara* (1970). The five pillars of this philosophy are: belief in God, loyalty to king and country, sanctity of the constitution, sovereignty of the laws and civic virtues.

Another such government programme is the 1982 official policy of assimilation of Islamic values in the civil service, *Dasar Penerapan Nilai-nilai Islam*. The first stage of this policy's implementation was the identification of several universal values, such as sincerity, honesty, dedication, accountability, reliability and sense of responsibility, to be upheld by government administrative personnel. The policy further stresses the universal values of good character, fair and accountable leadership, and enlightened attitudes as hallmarks of Islam. The policy was said to be intended as a government initiative towards securing balanced material and spiritual development for Malays as well as for the nation at large. Later, in the mid-1980s, other Islamic-oriented institutions followed. These were implemented mainly in the banking and financial sectors. Concurrently, Islamic and universal values that were identified for assimilation in the government sector also permeated other areas of social life such as education, media policies and welfare. In short, Islamic values were introduced into all areas of state-sponsored activity.

The former Deputy Prime Minister, Anwar Ibrahim, was a major figure in articulating this policy and vision.[4] Anwar's ideal political framework was an ethical political system that would provide for a responsible civil society and an accountable state. He termed this order a *masyarakat madani*, or society in which societal and political discourses and practices thrive within an Islamic and ethical framework. In such a civil society, issues of democracy, pluralism and participation, social justice, accountability, democratic fairness and good governance are debated and acted upon responsibly. Such underlying principles obviously promise the government's accountability and a greater scope for fundamental liberties, and thus a greater role for citizen participation.

This idea seems to be in line with Mahathir's agenda for Malay intellectual and economic development via progressive Islamic values. In his book, *The Challenge* (1986), and his speech at UMNO's fortieth general assembly, 'Menebus Maruah Bangsa' ('To Reaffirm Malay Dignity', 1997), Mahathir outlines clearly his political philosophy that Malays can only progress if they embody the true Islamic spirit of resilience, high achievements, self-confidence and humbleness before God. This message has been echoed and amplified by other government and UMNO leaders at all levels. Relatively speaking, however, Anwar was more concerned with ideological and ethical paradigms than Mahathir. Mahathir is more focused on the pragmatic implications of Islamisation both as a government policy and object of sponsorship in multi-religious Malaysia and as a political strategy to buttress UMNO vis-à-vis its Islamic 'fundamentalist' challengers.

Government-sponsored Islamic NGOs

In what appears to be a strategy against the development of independent and autonomous Islamic organisations, the government has formed and supported its own Islamic NGOs. An example of an early government-established Islamic NGO that has enjoyed its significant support is the Malaysian Islamic Welfare Organisation or the Persatuan Kebajikan Islam Malaysia (PERKIM). Tunku Abdul Rahman Putra Alhaj, the first prime minister of Malaysia, set up PERKIM in 1960 and led the organisation until his death in 1990. PERKIM's objective is non-partisan *dakwah*. Its main concerns include the welfare of new Muslim converts. The Tunku's domestic and international stature lent PERKIM credibility and earned it recognition from the international Islamic world. PERKIM remains functional today.

There are also government-supported Islamic NGOs that address the rights, positions and roles of Muslim women in the private and public spheres. An example is the Lembaga Kebajikan Perempuan Islam (LKPI), or Council for the Welfare of Muslim Women (Wan Rahimi 1986). LKPI was formed in 1960 at the initiative of the then-Queen, Raja Permaisuri Agong Tunku Khurshiah, to help Muslim women who were victims of domestic strife. LKPI has continued to focus on protecting Islamic women's rights, especially within the context of variations in Malaysian states' Islamic laws. The majority of its active members as well as officers are Malay women from the upper echelon of Malay society – wives of dignitaries, representatives from ministries, Muslim women community leaders at all levels, and politicians from UMNO women's wing. LKPI therefore enjoys the government's patronage.

In 1981, LKPI launched its own version of the Girl Guide movement, the Pergerakan Puteri Islam (PPI). PPI is a uniformed group for young women whose purpose is 'to make young girls good Muslim women who are educated, progressive and accepted by society' (Wan Rahimi 1986). Although its original target groups included young female workers in factories and the government sector, PPI is currently confined to secondary school girls. Other youth groups formed by Malay Muslim youths that enjoy similar benign support from the government are the Gabungan Pelajar Melayu Semenanjung (GPMS), which is a Malay students' organisation mainly based in peninsular Malaysia, and Belia 4B, a youth organisation comprising a larger rural Malay youth constituency.

Islamic NGOs sponsored by the government or formed independently but dependent on the government's patronage tend to enjoy greater access to policy-making bodies, financial assistance and other facilities from the government than those that are not. While this supportive form of government–NGO relationship promotes Islamic NGOs' objectives, it also constrains them within the framework of what is politically correct for the government, or more specifically for the dominant component of the ruling political party, UMNO. These Islamic NGOs therefore seldom if ever publicly express critical or evaluative opinions on government policies touching upon Islam and the Muslim community. What is played out on the ground becomes less about the democratic activities of a component of civil society than about maintaining an Islamic image for Malaysia and the notion of UMNO as the guardian of the nation's official religion, Islam. The latter priority in particular is directly related to UMNO's competition for the hearts and minds of the Malay electorate vis-à-vis its major political rival, PAS.[5]

The *dakwah* movement

In the 1970s and 1980s, Malaysia experienced what was known as 'Islamic assertiveness', 'Islamic resurgence' or 'Islamic revivalism'.[6] This phenomenon permeated every stratum of Malay society. Among the general Malay public, Islamic revivalism was outwardly manifested in ways such as significantly bigger congregations at Friday prayers, well-attended religious activities and the donning of Islamic dress by Malay women, which basically means wearing headscarves. At the government level, it was seen in the conscientious observance of explicit Islamic rituals and requirements during official government functions. For example, the recital of Islamic *doa* (prayers) became a regular feature at all official functions organised by government bodies or any Malay-dominated organisations, together with the non-serving of alcoholic drinks and strict observance of *halal* (religiously permitted) foods. Friday lunch hours were lengthened for all government agencies in order to allow government employees, the majority of whom are Malays, to attend Friday prayers, which is obligatory for all Muslims. These changes were in turn backed by substantive official Islamisation policies, including the revamping of the Islamic religious teachings in the National Education Policy, culminating in the establishment of the Islamic International University, and the setting up of various Islamic structures, such as Islamic banking practices, in the economic sector.

A number of independent contemporary *dakwah* organisations took root during this period. These ranged from the Angkatan Belia Islam Malaysia (ABIM), or Malaysian Islamic Youth Movement, which maintained a modern and progressive Islamic outlook, to the more 'fundamentalist' Jamaat Tabligh (Tabligh) and Darul Arqam (Al Arqam). These groups' activities heightened Malays' consciousness of Islamic traditions and enthusiasm to live life according to Islamic tenets. Some of these groups, especially ABIM and Al Arqam, enjoyed widespread grassroots support in the Malay community, especially in the 1970s and 1980s, and hence defined themselves as movements rather than NGOs.[7] Through both their activities and their principles, ABIM and Al Arqam became the dominant influences during the period of Islamic resurgence. Their agendas began as moral ones in the sense that they started by addressing moral issues in daily life. In the process, explicitly in the case of ABIM and by way of their choosing to practice an alternative lifestyle in the case of Al Arqam, they began a critique of the Malay political leadership for what they perceived as its un-Islamic policies and practices. *Dakwah* groups took on a political mantle and started to lead public discussions and grassroots programmes relating to democratic participation, civil rights and societal development delineated by Islamic principles (Zainah 1987; Chandra 1987). These precepts informed what ABIM's Anwar Ibrahim termed *masyarakat madani* when he later became deputy prime minister.

Key politically engaged IONGOs

In general, Malaysian IONGOs prefer to maintain a non-political identity and a non-ethnic basis. Most seem to be content to function as service and welfare organisations. The majority of IONGO activists are urban professionals with exposure to western education and liberal democracy; this shared ideological-structural framework is no doubt significant. Among more politically engaged IONGOs, their advocacy and conscientisation efforts cover broad fields of legal and human rights, including labour issues, the rights and status of women, and monitoring government policies and political processes. These groups aim at providing checks and balances to the powers of the authorities, while at the same time enhancing public understanding of the nature of participatory democracy.

Among the main politically engaged IONGOs are ABIM, Al Arqam and Sisters in Islam (SIS). These three organisations represent widely divergent types of IONGO. ABIM remains mainstream, widely accepted and respected, especially among the younger generation of Malays. Al Arqam, whose main trademark was living in what they purported to be an Islamic commune, was banned for deviant teachings in 1994, although recently there has been some talk about its regrouping on the outskirts of Kuala Lumpur. SIS is a controversial Islamic IONGO as far as the mainstream Malay community is concerned due to some of its radical and feminist reinterpretations of Islamic texts with regard to women's positions and rights. However, with the economic and political crises of the late 1990s, like many of their non-Islamic counterparts, a number of other IONGOs that normally focus on apolitical concerns became more evidently politicised. These groups include the Jamaah Islah Malaysia (JIM), a society of Muslims oriented towards addressing current social and religious issues, especially those within the Malay community; the Pertubuhan Kebangsaan Pelajar Islam Malaysia (PKPIM), a national Muslim student association; and Muslim professional organisations, such as the Persatuan Peguam Islam Malaysia, which is a society for Muslim lawyers, and the Persatuan Ulama Malaysia, which is the association of Malaysian Islamic religious scholars.

Angkatan Belia Islam Malaysia (ABIM)

ABIM was established on 6 August 1971. It was an outgrowth of the National Muslim Students' Association or Pertubuhan Kebangsaan Pelajar Islam Malaysia (PKPIM). ABIM was proposed in order to provide a platform (a *harakah*, or movement) for graduating students from universities and colleges who had been active in *dakwah* activities to continue their Islamic activities and to generate an Islamic movement as the path to Islamic revival in Malaysia (Funston 1985: 171–9). The group enjoyed wide popularity among educated Malay youths and professionals. ABIM stresses the fact that it stands on the principle of moderation (*kesederhanaan* or *wasatiyyah*).

During the 1970s and early 1980s, under the charismatic leadership of Anwar Ibrahim, ABIM was vociferous in denouncing the government's Islamisation efforts as 'insufficient', 'superficial' and 'measured in material terms'. ABIM criticised the state's efforts as being opposed to the development of the true Islamic personality (*sahsiyah Islamiyyah*) and genuine *penghayatan Islam*, or the sincere Islamic practices based on Islam as a way of life for which ABIM aimed. ABIM's Islamic revivalist discourse addressed almost all aspects of private and public life in the social, economic, political and religious spheres. Among IONGOs, ABIM's discourse was the loudest and best informed. The group debated, explained and challenged the state on key issues such as the character of an Islamic state and Islamic leadership, Islamic education and the Islamic way of life, and Malaysia's involvement in international politics as part of the global Muslim brotherhood. It criticised evident un-Islamic values and practices of the state and Malay society, and called for radical reforms. Indeed, it has been reputed that when PAS joined the Barisan Nasional (ruling National Front coalition) for a short stint from 1974 to 1977, thousands of PAS members joined ABIM in search of a purer Islamic organisation.

Despite its initially confrontational stance, ABIM later fell more in line with the government's development agenda and Islamic orientation, namely progressive, moderate and friendly Islam (Muhammad Nur 1996). Funston explains this shift, noting that 'the ready employment opportunities available to Malay graduates served to still much religious fervour' and 'groups such as ABIM are certainly not opposed to economic development per se' (Funston 1985: 171–9). Indeed, many older members of ABIM are now affluent corporate figures and in influential UMNO positions.

The movement of ABIM members into UMNO really began when its leader since 1972, Anwar Ibrahim, resigned to join the party under Mahathir's leadership in 1982 (Jesudasan 1995: 345). By the time of Anwar's removal from office and UMNO in September 1998 on charges of corruption and sexual misconduct, ABIM veterans had established an influential network in the political structure with significant impact on state policies. More importantly, these individuals were key to the power bases of a number of UMNO political leaders under the prevailing patron–client framework. Partly due to the influx of Anwar and his fellow ABIM members, UMNO soon changed its image from that of a 'secular Malay-nationalist political party' to that of a progressive, modern, Islamic Malay national movement. UMNO more or less embraced the agenda of the 1970s and early 1980s *dakwah* movement, though stopping short of establishing an Islamic state. The state's international propagation of moderate Islam is in line with ABIM's agenda, as well, particularly as reflected in the state and ABIM's mutual support for policies towards Muslim international communities, such as related to Bosnia and Chechnya, and investment abroad.

Nonetheless, ABIM has continued to warn of a spreading corporate subculture that is so unashamedly materialistic, profit-driven, hedonistic and ridden with un-Islamic practices (Siddiq Fadil 1982, 1983). While ABIM continues to voice concerns and make suggestions on solutions to various current social ills and negative aspects of development, it does so in a much more muted manner than it did in the 1970s. For example, ABIM criticised a proposed 30 billion ringgit coastline reclamation project in the Malay Muslim-majority northern state of Kedah, alleging that it would only benefit the rich while ruining the livelihood of fishermen. Kedah chief minister Sanusi Junid promptly replied that the state's plan may actually be one of the best ways to reduce acquisition of land for development purposes, suggesting the government was addressing one of ABIM's common concerns (*Sun*, 7 April 1996: 4 5 September 1996: 5).

Throughout its history, ABIM has gone beyond Islamic discourses and *dakwah* activities within the Malay-Islamic context. It has consistently also been active in pressing for civil rights, including freedom of expression, freedom of association and the independence of the judiciary. Together with other NGOs active during the 1980s, such as Aliran Kesedaran Negara (Aliran, the National Consciousness Movement) and the Selangor Graduates Society (SGS), ABIM agitated for the repeal of the Internal Security Act (ISA) 1960, which allows detention without trial, and the 1981 amendments to the Societies Act, which would have severely limited the activities of non-political organisations while greatly enhancing the powers of the Registrar of Societies.

ABIM offered an Islamic justification for condemning these policies. For instance, ABIM pointed out that the ISA threatened the security of personal freedom, right to a fair and public trial and protection from arbitrary imprisonment guaranteed in Islam. Meanwhile, ABIM charged that the Societies Act prevented *dakwah* organisations from fulfilling their Islamic responsibilities to enjoin fellow Muslims to do good and reject evil (*amar ma'aruf nahi munkar*). ABIM alleged that this restriction could even be construed as challenging the laws of Allah *s.w.t.*, since *dakwah* is the responsibility of every Muslim and co-operating in group activities for good is encouraged by Islam. Since this period also coincided with the government's Look East Policy, which focused on Japan and South Korea as successful economic models, ABIM leaders regularly included in their speeches the call to government leaders, especially Malay government leaders from UMNO, to 'just look back to the Qur'ān and Hadith'. ABIM also criticised the executive for making the Malaysian judiciary 'impotent', thus contradicting the Islamic precept relating to the independence of the judiciary. The acting president of ABIM at that time quoted the Pakistani Muslim religious figure, Abul 'Ala Al Mawdudi, to illustrate the Islamic tradition that 'if the caliph had any complaint against any citizen, he did not use his administrative powers and authority to set the matter right but had to refer the case to the court of law for proper jurisdiction' (Siddiq Fadil 1982, 1983). In short, ABIM had broken ground by discussing issues of democracy and civil society within an Islamic framework in Malaysia. Such discussions gained new prominence after the Anwar's removal from the government in 1998. The difference is that, in recent years, Anwar has drawn increasingly on an ethical framework based also on the other great traditions that have followers in Malaysia.

Darul Arqam (Al Arqam)

The contrast between Al Arqam and ABIM illustrates the fact that Malaysian Islam and *dakwah* have diverse faces. Twelve Muslims under the leadership of Ashaari Muhammad founded Al Arqam in 1968. Following the Prophet Muhammad's *s.a.w.* tradition of *Hijrah* (pilgrimage), Ashaari led his followers to Sungai Pencala, Selangor, a region on the outskirts of Kuala Lumpur, where they cleared eight acres of land and set up homes, a mosque and a school. According to Al Arqam, in order to establish an Islamic state, a true Islamic community must first be established. Al Arqam criticised PAS's and ABIM's approach as rhetorical and lacking in a committed practical agenda. Al Arqam denounced the Muslim-led Malaysian government as secular and influenced by Jewish and Christian practices. It sought to offer a sample of a true Islamic alternative that should replace the existing western-based political and economic systems (Jomo and Ahmad Shabery 1992: 80). However, by the late 1970s, Al Arqam had appeared to withdraw from public involvement, focusing itself on internal matters.

By 1986, charges of heresy had emerged over Ashaari's teachings and Al Arqam's cultic practices. In 1988, its publication, *Aurat Muhammadiah*, was banned by state religious departments as promoting deviant teachings. In the end, Al Arqam was banned in 1994 after the Malaysian National Fatwa Council declared that it had deviated from the true teachings of Islam. Furthermore, in order 'to erase the movement's identity' as well as 'to integrate them with surrounding villages', its various settlements, including not only its original settlement in Sungai Pencala but also others in Kelantan, Terengganu, Pulau Pinang, Pahang and elsewhere, were disbanded and remodelled under a staggered programme supervised by the Islamic Affairs Department, part of the Prime Minister's Department. Also, Al Arqam's members were directed to undergo Islamic rehabilitation programmes, *Kursus Pemurnian Akidah*, which were organised and co-ordinated by the same agency (*Sun*, 3 January 1997: 5).

Al Arqam was politically significant since it questioned the political system, the Malay national leadership and Malaysian socioeconomic practices from an Islamic perspective, thus challenging the state's secularist philosophy and policies at both the discursive and practical levels (Sharifah Zaleha 1995). Its potential lay in its organisational discipline, economic independence and direct interaction with the grassroots through its daily economic and social dealings. For these reasons, the government considered Al Arqam a political threat that could disrupt Malaysia's fragile interethnic and religious balance. Besides, Al Arqam's discourses also encouraged Malay Muslims to scrutinise the secularist Malay leadership, especially in UMNO, in an Islamic light.

Sisters in Islam (SIS)

SIS presents a distinct contrast with both ABIM and Al Arqam. SIS was formed in 1985 by a group of Malay Muslim women professionals, each with her own circle of influence in the legal, journalistic and academic fields. SIS has caught its share of domestic and international attention primarily by articulating and highlighting pertinent current debates on issues relating to Muslim women's rights and roles. The group has also addressed wider issues affecting Malaysian and Muslim society as a whole, such as the nature and implications of *Hudud* (Islamic criminal code) laws and notions of an Islamic state. For example, SIS's discourse and publications on topics such as the contextual relevance of PAS's proposed *Hudud* law and the right of a Muslim husband to beat his wife generated much public and media discussion. SIS also works together at both the domestic and international levels with other NGOs addressing women's issues in Malaysia, either in separate groupings or under the umbrella of the National Council of Women's Organisations (NCWO).

Most importantly, the measure of prominence that SIS has achieved has provoked a lively informed discussion on what Said Ramadan has identified as one of the major problems confronting the world of Islam, namely 'the plight of womenfolk in Muslim society', with regard to which he contends, 'we are in a state of complete chaos, a hotch-potch of competing forces: the remaining Islamic influence, our inherited traditions and extraneous influences which have crept into our life as a result of the enveloping wave of blind imitation of the west' (Said Ramadan 1985: 332–5). On the whole, the government has remained benevolent towards SIS. This tolerance may be because SIS is not about to turn into a radical feminist mass movement, but will likely remain exclusive and intellectual, and because it realises that the group in fact enhances Malaysia's international image as a progressive, modernist and moderate Muslim country.

IONGOs as part of Malaysian civil society

The legal constraints on democracy in Malaysia are well documented and clearly evident. Complaints about Malaysia's lack of democratic space and freedom of action for politically engaged NGOs have made international headlines. IONGOs and their members have not been immune. The most serious crackdowns on criticism have been October 1987's Operasi Lalang, when about a hundred social activists and critics, including some Muslim activists, were detained without trial under the Internal Security Act (ISA), and the banning of the allegedly deviationist Al Arqam movement in 1994.

The issues that IONGOs tackle are closely related to ongoing debates on civil society in Malaysia. The key question for IONGOs is to what extent they themselves address theoretical and philosophical questions regarding their functions in a Malaysian civil society that includes a substantial ratio of non-Muslim citizens. An important function of NGOs in a state is to empower individuals with the ability to influence political positions and the capability to pursue personal choices within the limits of common civic virtues. Nonetheless, most IONGOs seem content to remain service and welfare organisations. Hence, there seems much scope for discussion and new forms of action among IONGOs. This is especially true given the political role of Malays, and therefore Islam, in Malaysia.

IONGOs are actively engaged with discourses on the notion of democracy vis-à-vis the role of Islam as a defining factor in the political life of the nation. These NGOs clearly base their aims and agendas on Islamic principles. Nevertheless, although they actively participate in the mainstream political NGO discourse on issues relating to Malaysian democratic practices and processes from an Islamic perspective, they do not appear to have explicitly articulated how they perceive their specific role in Malaysian civil society. Meanwhile, other NGOs, as well as non-Muslim Malaysians, have generally avoided engaging in public discussion about the political role of Islam in Malaysian democracy. Instead, non-Islamic NGOs have collaborated with IONGOs whenever their positions on issues have found congruence, but remain detached on other issues directly involving the Muslim community.

On the other hand, the government, particularly the Prime Minister, has clearly indicated that Islam is the underpinning of the moral life of the nation. IONGOs have hence been operating in an environment increasingly conducive to their perspectives and aims. Mahathir calls upon religious leaders, the *ulama*, to practise *ijtihad* (reasoning) in reconstructing societal doctrines to enable Malaysian Muslims to participate fully in Malaysian developments in years to come without the trauma of losing their values and identity. Moreover, Mahathir advocates the rejection of *taqlid buta*, or blind acceptance of traditional ulamas' teachings, that might inhibit economic development, while also urging Muslim unity. Mahathir's exhortation to adopt progressive Islamic values – directed not only towards UMNO members, but to all Malaysian Muslims – is translated into pertinent government policies. However, in political terms, the regime's intention seems to be to maintain a basically secular polity.

The state's response to IONGOs

Although the Malaysian government does not liberally accommodate political opposition or politically inclined NGOs, nor does it marginalise or eliminate them completely. It monitors their discourses and activities and does not always take repressive actions against them. In fact it tolerates and sometimes facilitates NGO activities that benefit its policies or give it political mileage domestically or internationally. This policy of forbearance is extended also towards IONGOs, even those often aligned with government critics, such as ABIM.

The state has long tried to keep the management of Islamic affairs in its own hands. As early as October 1968, the Majlis Raja-Raja Melayu (Council of Malay Rulers) established the National Council for Islamic Affairs or Majlis Kebangsaan Bagi Hal Ehwal Agama Islam (MKI).

The MKI was officially launched in July 1969 and had its first secretariat in the Jabatan Perdana Menteri (Prime Minister's Department, JPM). In 1974, the MKI was upgraded to a department in the JPM. By 1985, it had moved to its own building next to the National Mosque in Kuala Lumpur. The department is now better known as Pusat Islam Malaysia (Malaysian Islamic Centre). Its objective is to co-ordinate and centralise Islamic activities, including Islamic education and teaching, at the federal level. Furthermore, in 1971, the government set up an Islamic Dakwah and Training Institute or Institut Dakwah dan Latihan Islam (INDAH), and an Islamic Research Centre or Pusat Penyelidikan Islam (PPI). The government has successfully used these Islamic research facilities, as well as others such as the Institut Kefahaman Islam Malaysia (IKIM) or Malaysian Institute of Islamic Understanding, established in 1992, to formulate Islamic policies and explain the government's development projects in terms of Islamic precepts. The MKI later formed the National Fatwa Council or Jawatankuasa Fatwa Kebangsaan to give *fatwa*, or definitive Islamic rulings, on matters indicated by the Council of Malay Rulers. Meanwhile, the Islamic Missionary Foundation or Yayasan Dakwah Islamiah (YADIM) was registered in 1974. YADIM was to be directly responsible to the Prime Minister, with powers to spread Islam and its teachings as well as to promote the general welfare of Malaysian Muslims. By 1981, there was also an Islamic consultancy body called Badan Perunding Islam to act in an advisory capacity to the federal government (Arkib Negara Malaysia File: AU/20/F).

The Mahathir era that followed (1981 to the present) brought UMNO in line with contemporary Malays' general Islamic aspirations. Mahathir is backed especially by a privileged middle class that is anxious to keep its distinct identity rather than adopting a typical urban and westernised image. This balance is to be maintained through a pragmatic, moderate and incremental Islamisation of values and culture. The government has consistently made it clear that Malaysia abhors all forms of extremist fundamentalism. Mahathir's main concern is social and political stability in order to pursue economic developmentalism. Towards that end, the government decided in 1986 to implement an amendment proposed previously to the Federal Constitution to establish the *Sunnah wal Jamaah* sect – defined as the sect that follows the teachings of the Prophet Muhammad *s.a.w.*, the Qur'ān and Sunnah – as the official sect of Muslims in Malaysia. The government explained that doing so would avoid divisions among the Malaysian *ummah* (Islamic community) and prevent the spread of Shi'ite teachings in the country (*Sun*, 8 April 1996: 3). Apart from distancing Malaysia from an image of revolutionary Islam, mandating a single official sect also ensures greater domestic conformity to the state's orientation on Islam.

In general, the state does not ignore views and criticisms voiced by NGOs, including IONGOs. In fact, the government has quite effectively utilised its Islamic agencies to counter or act upon criticisms and issues brought up by IONGOs. The most important of these agencies today is the Unit Hal Ehwal Agama Islam or Islamic Affairs Unit, headed by a deputy minister in the Prime Minister's Department. In short, the state has taken care to ensure that it is seen to be seriously committed to its Islamisation policy. Doing so effectively neutralises the criticisms from IONGOs that the state is developing too materialistic a culture, bringing social ills. Indeed, IONGOs may be considered to have been successful in their aims in as much as the state has responded to many of the issues they have highlighted.

The Malaysian state's response to IONGOs can also be seen as being more tolerant in most cases than its response to some other sorts of NGO. After all, IONGOs are reliable additional indicators for UMNO of the Malay voters' pulse. Also, the fact that they play the role of society's Islamic conscience gives them wider space and influence, given UMNO's special concern for Islam. However, this space is very much bounded by the state's secular structure and basic orientation. The state as spearheaded by UMNO emphasises multi-ethnic power sharing, the special position of the Malays and other *bumiputra* (indigenous groups), multi-religious co-existence and economic development. As long as IONGOs, or any other NGOs, do not radically challenge or oppose the state's position, the state remains accommodative and may even be responsive to their aims and interests. In the case of IONGOs, the state's sensitivity to them is determined by their likely impact in relation to UMNO's political interests, especially vis-à-vis PAS.

By responding to some of the IONGOs' demands, the state can also neutralise possible challenges to its political power. Recently, in fact, Malaysian government leaders have been inviting and encouraging NGOs to come forward and participate in some aspects of policy implementation, particularly those relating to development. NGOs are invited to be 'partners in development' by helping to tackle social ills in Malaysian communities, such as prisoners' rehabilitation, drug addiction, alcoholism and the promotion of healthy living styles, as well as the organisation of youth activities to promote good moral and Malaysian (especially Malay Muslim) civic virtues. In fact it has been observed that some IONGOs, being so often welfare-oriented even if also politicised, can be absorbed quite nicely into these sorts of role.

This involvement of NGOs on the government's terms further ensures conformity with the state's preferences in public matters.

Aside from these efforts at neutralisation, the state's response to IONGOs has also employed other stratagems. One of these approaches is the dissemination of a negative portrayal of IONGOs as 'dangerous' to political stability and inter-ethnic as well as inter-religious harmony, since they tend to deviate from or challenge government policies and interpretations of issues. A second tactic is to co-opt Islamic religious leaders at all levels. This strategy has the added effect of contributing to the greater Islamic stature of the state and providing it with a religious endorsement. A third is to resort to harsher measures, such as the use of the ISA to detain critics without trial and the Societies Act to monitor and discipline NGOs whenever necessary. A fourth response is to encourage and patronise groups that are moderate and supportive of state policies and ideology, especially with regard to economic development and pragmatic multi-ethnic co-existence. Finally, the state has often set up its own parallel organisations under its various ministries. These organisations enjoy state patronage and thus tend to prosper better than their non-governmental counterparts.

Conclusion

Since independence in 1957, UMNO and its coalition partners have maintained a secular, capitalistic form of governance that is friendly to Islam. In recent years, UMNO has gradually developed a more Muslim character, particularly in response to more aggressive pressure from PAS as well as from increasingly empowered Islamic organisations that enjoy wide acceptance at the Malay grassroots. The latter have been ascendant due to the enhanced general enthusiasm among the Malay community for Islamic living that began in the wake of the 1979 Iranian revolution and global Islamic resurgence. Compared with earlier moments of Islamic resurgence in the country's history, such as the Islah or reform movement in the 1920s and the surge of support for PAS in the late 1950s, this more recent Islamic reawakening has prompted activism extending beyond the conventional circle of rural based religious *ulama* and teachers or graduates of Islamic religious studies. Instead the current activists and leaders are from the new crop of urban-based, Malay, middle-class professionals. Their advocacy extends also beyond the traditional aims of encouraging a more upright Islamic community from a moral and social perspective. Instead these activists have promoted political Islam. They may not have all joined partisan politics but their *dakwah* has now emphasised the Islamic obligation to enjoin good and deny evil within the political life of the nation.

Islamic activists have been particularly moved in recent times by the Anwar Ibrahim saga – his diatribes on the Mahathir-led government, the manner of his sacking, his trial and the abuse he suffered while in detention prior to his trial. Spurred by the Anwar case, a number of IONGOs joined partisan politics and many Islamic activists embraced a political platform and stood as candidates in the 1999 Malaysian general election. As a result, the efforts of these groups continue to influence the secular BN government to address Islamic concerns within the context of its politics and governance and in its pursuit of the majority Malay electorate. The effect of IONGOs in further strengthening the Islamic opposition affirms the significant influence of civil society on Malaysian politics.

5 The environmental movement in Malaysia
Sundari Ramakrishna

Introduction

The non-governmental sector plays an active, increasingly important role in environmental dialogue. During the Rio Earth Summit process, the non-governmental sector was a full partner in setting the environmental agenda for the coming decade. As part of a significant new pattern of interaction, non-governmental organisations (NGOs) have begun to work with local governments and business to promote environmentally sound development. Nowadays, the NGO sector often provides a grassroots complement to local government. Various activities in which the environmental non-governmental sector participates include:

- assisting with implementation of existing enterprises leading to forested wetlands and marine life conservation;
- collaborating in preparing economically and environmentally sound community-based plans for policy-makers, planners and practitioners;
- assisting local governments to draw up new or additional environmental legislation;
- implementing conferences and seminars on conservation;
- setting up and co-ordinating campaigns to support worthy environmental causes or against development projects that impact on local communities; and
- providing technical and scientific assistance in management of different ecosystems.

The Malaysian government and environmental NGOs

The Malaysian government is comprised of three levels: the federal government, state governments and various local governments which comprise municipal councils. The federal and state governments have different areas of competence in relation to the environment. In essence, all matters relating to environmental quality, such as pollution matters, are within the ambit of the federal government. Those matters related to natural resources management are largely in the domain of the states. The municipal councils or local authorities, on the other hand, deal with aspects such as spatial planning (structure and local plans), the granting of licences for businesses and the maintenance of public services. This division of powers and roles among the various layers of government in relation to environmental protection and management makes the implementation of integrated planning a real challenge. Often, this institutional weakness is cited as a hindrance to adopting an integrated approach to environmental management and enforcement of laws related to the environment.

General history and status of environmental NGOs

Even prior to the passing of Malaysia's Environmental Quality Act 1974 and the subsequent establishment of the Division of Environment (now the Department of Environment) in 1975, non-governmental organisations working on environmental issues (MENGOs, or Malaysian environmental NGOs) were in existence. Among the early pioneers were the Malayan Nature Society, the Consumers' Association of Penang (CAP), the Environmental Protection Society of Malaysia and the Worldwide Fund for Nature. These were later joined by organisations such as Sahabat Alam Malaysia, which came into being in the latter part of the 1970s, and others established in the 1980s and 1990s.

Beginning before the watershed Stockholm Conference on Environment in 1972, Malaysian NGOs such as CAP had held seminars and workshops on issues concerning the environment. These organisations were already lobbying the government to introduce environmental laws and policies in the country. These civil society organisations were pioneers of the environmental movement in Malaysia. Indeed, they can even be acknowledged as pioneers of the movement in the developing world, active since long before the word 'environment' became fashionable. The contribution of the MENGO community was even acknowledged by the first Minister of Environment, Tan Sri Ong Kee Hui, who credited MENGOs' activities with influencing Malaysia's environmental movement and management.

Some MENGOs were (and are still) working with communities impacted by environmental degradation and destruction. Over the years, they have organised communities who suffered from adverse impacts from development. Among these are:

- fishing villages whose livelihoods were affected by environmental pollution from the toxic wastes of industries;
- farmers and plantation workers who were exposed to pesticide poisonings;
- communities exposed to toxic radioactive waste dumping (most prominent among them Bukit Merah, Perak);
- indigenous peoples whose forests and resources were affected by logging and dam projects; and
- communities whose quality of life was affected by environmental pollution.

In mobilising these communities, MENGOS have sent frequent letters of complaint to the Department of Environment and other government agencies. These agencies' responsibilities have also been highlighted in the media, sparking the development of environmental journalism in the country.

Besides public awareness work, environmental NGOs have organised major conferences, bringing together international speakers, local researchers, government officials and members of civil society to address key subjects. Many of these conferences have challenged mainstream concepts of development and emphasised the need for development that is ecologically sound and socially just. All this activity began even before the Rio Summit, which led to the concept of sustainable development.

Roles played by Malaysian environmental NGOs

Today there are about seventeen non-governmental organisations in Malaysia involved in environmental issues. A fair number are based in peninsular Malaysia and the rest in Sabah and Sarawak. Issues addressed by MENGOs cover a wide range of special areas, including environmental professionalism, ethical practices, advocacy, improving environmental quality, capacity building in environmental protection, community participation, environmental education and awareness, information dissemination, nature appreciation, conservation of special ecosystems, sustainable agricultural practices, policy analysis and wildlife trade monitoring. A few of these NGOs started way back in the 1940s. For example, the Malaysian Nature Society was initially involved in promotion of nature appreciation but is now active in environmental protection campaigns. Most contemporary MENGOs are very much involved in generating consciousness and raising awareness among Malaysians about appreciating the earth and being more committed to environmental protection.

MENGOs play important roles in the country's path towards sustainable development and pushing the environmental agenda forward. These roles include:

- where appropriate, collaborating with and providing services to the government, thereby complementing and supplementing the initiatives of the government;
- providing education and raising awareness on environmental concerns;
- facilitating community mobilisation and participation around environmental issues;
- empowering ordinary citizens, including those from the grassroots, to defend their environmental rights;
- contributing fresh insights to environmental debates and advocating for improvements in environmental policy and legislation;
- acting as watchdogs in ensuring that the country genuinely embarks on a development model which is environmentally sound and socially just; and
- promoting the implementation of Agenda 21 and other appropriate international environmental agreements and conventions.

The objectives and aims of NGOs in the peninsula may differ from those of East Malaysian groups. Peninsular MENGOs are concerned largely with resource conservation and quality of life issues. By comparison, MENGOs in Sabah and Sarawak are more community-focused. In Sabah and Sarawak, MENGOs' efforts are geared towards the preservation of the environment and the natural forests. The needs of indigenous people and the preservation of their cultures and ways of life seem to be among the top priorities of the local NGOs.

Interviews suggest that although MENGOs are sometimes driven by different objectives, they share a number of common goals which at times draw them to co-operate with one another. Most of the organisations aim:

- to increase environmental awareness in Malaysian society;
- to promote activities that help preserve the environment;
- to prevent the further degradation of the environment;
- to enjoy the environment through non-destructive activities; and

- to encourage and develop policies to support sustainable development.

Towards these ends, MENGOs undertake a variety of activities, ranging from awareness raising to policy analysis, field research, community development, capacity building, fund raising, advocacy, demonstration projects, education, training, campaigning and more. They cover a broad spectrum of issues and initiatives, including the environment, consumers, community, gender, poverty, health, rights of the disabled, governance, ecotourism, promoting sustainable livelihoods, and so on. The more well-established MENGOs in Malaysia focus their attention essentially on 'green' (protection and/or promotion of nature and natural resources, including species, ecosystems, habitats and processes), 'brown' (pollution, environmental degradation) or 'blue' (marine) issues and initiatives.

A number of issue-oriented environmental NGO networks or coalitions have emerged over the years in response to specific environmental concerns and considerations. Among these are the Pesticide Action Network, Sustainable Development Network, Climate Action Network, Biodiversity Action Network, Dams Action Network, Malaysian Climate Change Group, and Hills Network. Some MENGOs undertake regional and international activities as well, especially in relation to international environmental conventions. There have been calls by the Economic Planning Unit in the past for the establishment of an umbrella organisation or focal point for different MENGOs.

Main types of environmental NGO

Malaysian environmental non-governmental organisations share key features. Structurally, they are identifiable as organised civil society representatives of those citizens concerned with environmental protection, conservation and sustainable development. They are non-governmental, meaning separate from national, state and local governments, in organisation. Some, but not all, MENGOs are community-based organisations (CBOs). MENGOs are non-profit organisations in the sense that income generation is not their primary objective. Their mission – formal or informal – embraces the promotion of activities in the field of environmental protection and conservation. It may also embrace advocacy for protection of the rights of indigenous peoples and local communities regarding the sustainable use and management of their natural resources.

The many types of environmental NGO in Malaysia fall into three main categories. First are 'grassroots' NGOs or CBOs. These organisations are primarily based on volunteer work involving local communities and usually employ a limited number of paid staff. They are normally very target specific, i.e. cater to the needs of their target group. The second category is 'membership' NGOs. These organisations, which work on a professional basis, engage paid staff for their offices (most of the office staff is paid) and projects, and only depend on a few volunteers for their basic work. They are usually membership based, with members receiving regular newsletters and having to pay subscriptions. Besides addressing a broad range of environmental issues, some of these organisations also hire external consultants as experts for specific projects. Third, 'consultant' NGOs are staffed by professionals who offer their services as consultants to the government or other sectors in environment-related fields. They do not usually embark on advocacy activities and are perceived as experts in certain technical areas.

How Malaysian NGOs operate

Legal framework

MENGOs have to operate within a prescribed legal framework. They may be established in Malaysia as societies, trust funds, companies, organised local communities, or any other legally constituted not-for-profit organisations. Organisations that are established as societies under the Societies Act are registered with the Registrar of Societies, which comes under the Home Ministry. These organisations are usually membership based. They are required to hold annual general meetings and submit annual reports to the Registrar of Societies. MENGOs set up as trusts are run by a Board of Trustees, which must ensure the organisations are run according to a trust deed. Those organised as companies (not having shares but limited by guarantee) are incorporated under the Companies Act. They have to submit annual returns to the Registrar of Companies. If MENGOs intend to publish newsletters/magazines to circulate to the wider public, they must get approval from the Ministry of Home Affairs. Holding a meeting for the general public usually requires a permit from the police. It is illegal to hold demonstrations without police permits. In short, whilst Malaysians are free to set up organisations, these NGOs are subject to legal controls.

Power of information

The majority of MENGOs firmly believe in the power of information, as recognition of problems and sharing of information are the first steps towards progress. MENGOs' main aim is to challenge and change perceptions, promoting awareness of current environmental problems and new development strategies, amongst the general public. This aim is pursued through the distribution of leaflets, newsletters and other news updates, talks, workshops and the mass media (television, radio and newspapers). Over the past fifteen years or so, the computer has increasingly been seen as an important tool to promote awareness. Websites, web-based fact sheets and web links inspire both young and old to take action where and when possible on environmental issues. Many NGO networks and partnerships have been created via the internet. More recently, mailing lists have become popular as an information exchange service where facts and opinions can be shared and discussions carried out electronically. This method can be a very quick and productive way to highlight environmental problems and seek quick solutions from mailing list subscribers who have encountered similar problems or have the scientific and technical expertise to assist.

If sharing of information is the first step towards solving problems, the second is to educate the young. MENGOs believe that environmental education should start in preschools, where malleable younger generations can be made to think, understand and appreciate the richness of Mother Earth and what has to be done to prevent environmental degradation. Environmental education has become an integral part of all environmental projects carried out by the NGOs. This component is carried out in two main ways. Both the Malaysian Nature Society (MNS) and the World Wide Fund for Nature Malaysia (WWFM) have been actively involved with setting up Nature Education Centres in strategic locations to educate people from all walks of life. The MNS has also helped establish Nature Clubs in schools to help promote the appreciation of local ecosystems and Malaysia's unique biological diversity. MENGOs have also prepared and produced educational kits on the environment. WWFM has produced the 'Marine Kit' in conjunction with the Ministry of Education, and Wetlands International – Malaysia Program (WIMP) has developed the 'Wetland Education Kit on the Tasek Bera Wetlands'. These kits contain information and a wide variety of activities that can be done in a classroom atmosphere, including cassettes, videotapes, story books, posters, board games, teachers' guides and exercises to be completed by individual students.

Some MENGOs also share skills and scientific expertise among themselves. However, a majority of them are more involved in transfer of technical knowledge to local communities, government agencies and graduate students interested in environmental management or conservation biology. Many environmental conservation projects involve special, intricate ecosystems like montane forests, peat swamps, mangroves and coral reefs. In implementing projects, skills and scientific knowledge are transferred to stakeholders at project sites. Unfortunately, there is a lack of experts to manage some of these fragile ecosystems, which are rich in biological diversity and require expertise across various sectors. For instance, management of wetlands requires a multidisciplinary approach and co-operation among the Drainage and Irrigation Unit and departments of Fisheries, Forestry, Wildlife, Environment (monitoring and enforcement units), Agriculture and Indigenous Peoples.

Achievements

Compared with environmental NGOs from other countries, it is fair to state that most Malaysian environmental NGOs are skilled and possess a strong background of knowledge, motivation and commitment. The local NGOs that are most active and dominate the environmental sector are the Malaysian Nature Society (MNS), World Wide Fund for Nature Malaysia (WWFM) and Wetlands International – Malaysia Programme (WIMP). Some of these groups' achievements are described below.

International environmental conventions

WWFM was instrumental in getting Malaysia to ratify the Convention on Biological Diversity on 24 June 1994. This Convention is a legally binding agreement for conservation and the sustainable use of biological diversity. In the same year, WIMP was the driving force behind the Malaysian government's ratification of the Convention on Wetlands of International Importance (the Ramsar Convention). This convention is an intergovernmental treaty adopted to ensure the conservation and wise use of wetlands. As part of Malaysia's obligation as a contracting party to these international agreements, a biodiversity policy was formulated. The MNS and WWFM helped, serving as the only NGO members of the steering/drafting committee. The Minister of Science, Technology and the Environment launched the Malaysian National Policy on Biological Diversity in April 1998.

In a similar light, with financial assistance from Switzerland's

The environmental movement in Malaysia 123

Ramsar Bureau, WIMP worked together with the Ministry of Science, Technology and the Environment to develop a Malaysian National Wetland Policy Framework in 1996. This document was completed in 1999. Thereafter, a Wetland Action Plan was to be developed for the whole country.

Institutional reports on the environment

MENGOs have produced a number of significant documents on conservation and the environment. Early on, the MNS produced the first Blueprint for Conservation in the early 1980s. The information contained there was utilised by the government in formulating the socioeconomic developmental plan known as the Malaysia Plan (Leong 1996). These blueprints contain detailed information on ecologically sensitive areas such as rainforests, mangroves and marine environments, which aids in planning and management by key government agencies.

More recently, in 1993, WWFM developed the four-volume Malaysian National Conservation Strategy (NCS) for the Regional Economics Division of the Economic Planning Unit in the Prime Minister's Department. The NCS aims to integrate fully the many existing efforts towards natural resource management for conservation and development.

Then, in 1996, the Assessment of Biological Diversity in Malaysia was produced by a task force comprising key NGO personnel from the MNS and WWFM, together with academicians from universities and research organisations. This document outlines all the different ecosystems in Malaysia, provides relevant statistics and identifies threats (both potential and current) to these natural resources (MOSTE 1997). That same year, the National Ecotourism Plan was developed by a team of WWFM staff and external consultants. This document consists of six volumes, prepared for the Malaysian Ministry of Culture, Arts and Tourism. Its main objective is to assist the state and federal governments in developing Malaysia's ecotourism potential as an effective tool for conservation of the natural and cultural heritage of the country.

Fighting for a good cause

The approach of environmental NGOs is most often one of consultation instead of confrontation when it comes to speaking out and advising the nation on matters of conservation. The views that these NGOs put forward are based solidly on scientific facts, uninfluenced by hearsay and emotional groundswell. Over the years, MENGOs have raised a number of significant issues in relation to major projects that were environmentally destructive. These projects were subsequently shelved because of the strong concerns raised. They included:

- The saving of Taman Negara from the Tembeling Dam. This issue galvanised several NGOs to work together in the early 1980s. A dam was proposed in Taman Negara that would have destroyed Malaysia's premier national park. NGO advocacy led to the project's being halted.
- The saving of Penang Hill. Again, several NGOs, including the MNS, got together to fight what became one of Malaysia's best-known environmental cases. Penang Hill was saved from a project that would have turned it into a Disney-like theme park and caused much environmental destruction on the island. Following a major public campaign, Penang Hill was spared, as the state government decided to stop the project. NGOs were also involved in the official review of the Environmental Impact Assessment for the project together with the Department of Environment.
- The salvaging of Endau-Rompin. Thanks to the efforts of the MNS, Endau-Rompin is now a well-run state park. However, while the MNS fought hard for Pulau Redang – a beautiful island surrounded with coral reefs and rich in marine life – it lost (Leong 1996).

Not all campaigns have been successful. For example, all MENGOs have always maintained that Environmental Impact Assessments (EIAs) must be scrupulously adhered to in any massive development project. The most recent legal developments regarding the building of the Bakun Dam in Sarawak have proven these NGOs correct in their approach, although the NGOs have not won on the Bakun Dam issue. However, reasons, risks and doubts abound regarding why the dam should not and need not be built, and the government has not objectively shown or justified why it should be built.

In many of these fights, NGOs work closely with each other. Co-operation between NGOs was crucial to ensure success in the fights, for example, against the Bakun Dam and for Penang Hill. The Malaysian Hills Network, an alliance of NGOs interested in conserving the Main Range of peninsular Malaysia, was formed to crusade against one of the most environmentally disastrous projects of all, the proposed Hill Road linking three hill stations, Cameron Highlands, Frasers Hill and Genting Highlands (CAP 1997). The Main Range is a vital life-support system and backbone for the peninsula and provides many basic necessities of human life. At least for now the Hill Road project has been shelved.

The Selangor Dam project is probably the most talked-about and controversial project in Malaysia after the Bakun Dam. Environmental NGOs got together to protest the building of a dam in the pristine Selangor River, the only river in the state of Selangor which is clean and free from pollution. The NGOs demanded and urged the Department of Environment (DOE) to extend the period for public review of the Environmental Impact Assessment beyond the usual one month. They also urged the DOE to ensure public participation in the review panels for the EIA reports. The DOE eventually met both these demands. Also, the major issue in tropical dam construction is the analysis of adverse social impacts and resettlement problems, especially involving indigenous peoples. After a hard battle by environmental NGOs, the social impact study was done for the Selangor Dam with greater detail and provision for resettlement and re-establishment of the culture and lifestyles of indigenous groups.

From the above, it can be easily observed that when there is a particular proposed project that will ultimately degrade the environment or bring about environmental problems and the disruption of local communities' livelihood, both environmental and non-environmental NGOs (human rights, community-based, women's rights and consumer groups) work together to oppose such mega projects. NGOs in Malaysia work more efficiently together when there is a common issue about which they all feel strongly. Otherwise, each NGO, be it focused on environmental concerns or human rights or gender, tends to work independently with its own resources and according to its own mandate.

In most cases, environmental activism in Malaysia has relied upon patient, co-operative presentation of information, but in some instances that sort of approach has been complemented by more confrontational and emotional tactics. For instance, the Bakun Dam issue attracted worldwide attention. Greenpeace, Green Korea United and other environmental NGOs from at least twenty countries arrived in Sarawak, Malaysia between 1994 and 1996 to oppose the building of the dam, which would have resulted in the loss to many indigenous tribes of their native land and the disruption of their livelihood. Street protests and campaigns were held in Sarawak to protest this mega project. In a written statement in 1996, 120 NGOs worldwide urged the Swedish–Swiss engineering corporation to withdraw from the controversial Bakun Hydroelectric Power Project. This sort of confrontation did help in putting off the building of Bakun Dam temporarily and made the authorities rethink and scale down the project to minimise its social and environmental impacts. Similarly, anti-logging protests were carried out in Sarawak in the 1980s. Timber concessions had been given out to large timber tycoons who deforested valuable land, displacing some local communities and infringing upon their rights to harvest forest products.

Such tactics were not confined to Sarawak. In 1985, a factory called Asian Rare Earth (ARE), partly owned by Mitsubishi of Japan, was producing and storing radioactive wastes near a village in Bukit Merah, Perak. Exposure to these wastes threatened residents' lives; there were already some reported dead as a result of the exposure. Amidst lobbying, discussions and demonstrations involving NGOs, political parties and the public, the Bukit Merah residents took their battle to court, setting the first of many precedents and winning a civil case which ruled that ARE be shut down. In this case, environmental and consumer groups worked hand in hand to help the Bukit Merah residents win what was to become Malaysia's most famous environmental battle.

However, even with these interventions from local NGOs, we still have a long way to go yet to ensure that EIAs for mega projects with environmental consequences are properly done and comprehensive in nature, and that a transparent review process is put in place.

Regional co-operation among NGOs

The Association of South East Asian Nations (ASEAN) may be a vehicle for sustainable development. Notably, the ASEAN Senior Official on Environment (ASOEN) has been urged to take the initiative in linking with international clearing houses on environmentally sound technologies. Also, the ASEAN Action Plan on Transboundary Pollution was adopted by the ministerial meeting, a significant move for the region.

The ASEAN Plan is very encouraging in many respects and reflects many of the concerns and action proposals that Sahabat Alam Malaysia (Friends of the Earth Malaysia or SAM), CAP and the MNS have been urging the Malaysian government to undertake. In 1997, a dialogue was held between the ASOEN and members of the ASEAN Secretariat and NGOs from the region to discuss co-operation on regional environmental and development issues. In particular, since the occasion was the meeting of the parties to the Biodiversity Convention, NGOs called for regional cooperation to establish strong bio-safety laws, regulate access by transnational corporations to the region's biological and genetic resources and protect the rights of local communities and indigenous people (Chee 1996). Moreover, ASEAN officials supported a proposal by the Malaysian Secretary-General of the Ministry of Science, Technology and the Environment that NGOs be present at meetings of the ASOEN and ministers to continue the dialogue on regional issues.

Thus, the ASOEN and the ASEAN Secretariat agreed that there should be stronger NGO co-operation with the Secretariat and more public awareness of and involvement in ASEAN's activities. The role of NGOs in alerting ASEAN governments to the dumping of banned or restricted chemicals and toxic wastes in the region, the passage of nuclear-powered submarines in the Malacca Straits, the hazards of genetic engineering and so on has been significant. This influence is augmented by effective North–South NGO networks, which allow crucial information required by southern governments to be obtained and help southern NGOs put public pressure on northern governments. The strong co-operation between NGOs and ASEAN governments and the Secretariat has gone far and will continue to do so in implementing the ASEAN environment plan for action (Chee 1996).

Outside the ASEAN framework, Third World Network (TWN), an NGO based in Penang which represents southern interests and perspectives at international forums and United Nations conferences, played an important role in preventing harmonisation of intellectual property rights (IPR) laws and policies in accordance with the GATT (General Agreement on Tariffs and Trade). TWN stressed that potential conflict with biodiversity conservation and rights of local communities and indigenous peoples under the Biodiversity Convention should be resolved before harmonisation took place.

Critical assessment of environmental NGOs in Malaysia

The government's approach to environmental NGOs

The relationship between MENGOs and the state is ambiguous. During a January 2001 DANCED[1] workshop on the role of environmental NGOs in policy dialogue, a questionnaire on the government's approach to MENGOs was circulated to various participants. On a question as to whether the government recognises and appreciates the roles of MENGOs, there was no clear consensus. Many qualified their responses to indicate that the government's approach to a given MENGO depends on the type of activities it pursues. The government's response is usually positive in relation to environmental education and awareness-raising activities. However, it was widely felt that in relation to advocacy activities and in policy formulation efforts, the MENGO role is less appreciated. On the issue of access to official government information regarding environmental protection, the majority view was that it is not easy to access such information. The responses were further qualified by comments that, while it is relatively easy to obtain some information from reports like those provided by the Department of Environment, there is much useful information which is classified as 'official secrets' and therefore not available for public consumption. In some instances, even when the law allows for information to be provided, as in the case of Environmental Impact Assessment reports, the cost of obtaining such reports is sometimes prohibitive and out of reach.

MENGOs find that they have several opportunities and mechanisms to participate in policy dialogues on environmental protection. However, it is widely felt that the government response has not been very encouraging and leaves much to be desired as to the extent to which MENGOs' views are taken into account. Government consultations with MENGOs are sometimes perceived as mere formalities, token gestures and public relations exercises. One often-heard response from the government to this perceived lack of NGO consultation is that NGOs are not professional enough or that NGO performance is poor when opportunities are provided. Whilst some MENGOs may lack sufficient capacity to provide meaningful inputs due to certain constraints, the solution must lie in building up such capacity where it is needed. In cases in which the activities and approaches of MENGOs, while legal, are not in line with the government's views, there is a general perception among MENGOs that they are not viewed favourably by government. In some instances, they face administrative restrictions, such as not being invited to government meetings, being viewed as antiestablishment and, in more serious instances, having their liberties curtailed.

Despite these constraints, MENGOs generally agree that, over the last few years, there appears to have been an increasing perception within the government that MENGOs play a constructive role in the country's environmental protection efforts. This perceived shift in attitudes has been attributed largely to the growing awareness resulting from processes such as the Rio Summit and the conclusions of Agenda 21 and other international UN forums that the participation and role of civil society in decision making has significant value in contributing to society's overall well-being (IUCN, 2000).

Environmental NGOs' approach to the government

MENGOs are willing to become more closely involved in partnerships with government, thereby contributing to policy formulation and provision of services, provided these activities are consistent with their mission and provided their organisational integrity and independence are not compromised.

A working group for NGO interventions, the Danish agency DANCED's NGO Programme Appraisal Mission to Malaysia on support for environmental NGOs, identified four cross-sectoral issues as core problems that must be addressed in order to achieve sustainable development in Malaysia. Among these issues were:

- institutional weaknesses and problems within the government arising from a lack of capacity to address environmental issues, insufficient understanding of certain environmental issues and lack of opportunities for members of the public and NGOs to provide input;
- poor public awareness of and participation in environmental programmes;
- lack of public involvement in government decision-making processes and lack of transparency in the government's development planning; and
- little opportunity for the public to get involved in monitoring and enforcement activities and insufficient use of economic instruments.

The need for transparency, accountability and good governance in government decision-making processes is a key call in many MENGO forums in order to ensure the attainment of genuine sustainable development and environmental protection (*New Straits Times* 1999). In this regard, MENGOs believe that it is of immense importance to environmental management that civil society plays a critical role in decision making and project implementation.

Economic constraints

Given that MENGOs are diverse in their approaches and positions, not all of them have easy access to funding sources. Some of them have strong positions against receiving money from the corporate sector for fear of having their mission compromised. Similarly, others also express reluctance to receive government money for fear that they will lose their independence and autonomy to speak out. In any case, government support to MENGOs in terms of financial assistance is minimal and constrained. Moreover, while members of the general public are somewhat concerned about the environment, they are not yet ready to give money to support MENGO activities. Faced with such constraints, most MENGOs have had to seek donor support to undertake and sustain their activities. Hence, by and large, they face financial constraints. These affect MENGOs' capacity to carry out their activities effectively. In particular, smaller MENGOs and CBOs are most constrained.

Capacity constraints

Despite having increased their activities, MENGOs, especially smaller ones, face a number of severe capacity constraints in carrying out their work effectively. These MENGOs, and even some bigger ones, appreciate assistance in some technical fields where specific knowledge is needed and especially in fundraising activities. Several Malaysian NGOs discussed the need for capacity building during a Malaysian–Danish environmental NGO workshop (see DANCED 2000a). These discussions emphasised the need for capacity building in the fields of:

- working with a logical framework approach (lfa);
- fundraising;
- staff training;
- technical assistance (for instance, in wildlife management);
- information technology and communications ;
- accounting;
- project management;
- developing leadership ;
- facilitation skills (how to stimulate people to discus issues and participate in debates);
- public relations ;
- information management;
- holding dialogues with authorities;
- laws;
- staff exchange programmes among NGOs (Malaysian and Danish or just Malaysian) ;
- identifying and approaching donors;
- increasing membership;
- advocacy and campaign methodology;
- implementing Agenda 21 at the local level;
- public participatory tools;

The environmental movement in Malaysia 131

- discussion forums;
- solving conflicts; and
- identifying an organisational strategy.

Most of these capacity-building needs were relevant for most of MENGOs, regardless of sector (DANCED 2000b).

Foreign donor support to MENGOs

Malaysian society has increasingly come to understand that MENGOs[2] can make valuable contributions to development, being able to offer skills, experiences and perspectives on a variety of issues which cannot come through government channels alone. The joint efforts of MENGOs, local governments and the private sector (including the rest of civil society) in carrying out local initiatives and participatory processes contribute to achieving national environmental policy objectives and improving Malaysians' quality of life. MENGOs express a need to participate in vital projects in order to represent public interests and increase public awareness on environmental development. However, they frequently act on an ad hoc basis rather than developing structured and planned programmes aimed at long-term impacts. In Malaysia, there seems to be need for a model that clearly illustrates the advantages of working on long-term plans, including co-operation with donor organisations if appropriate. MENGOs need to be strategic and priority-driven and to develop their strategic plans.

Both small and large MENGOs, together with other local voluntary societies that strive to develop public awareness of environmental issues, conservation and governance issues at the local planning level, require support. Donor support has not been sufficiently strategic, however. For example, support from Danish Cooperation for Environment and Development (DANCED) to Malaysian NGOs has not been guided sufficiently by a strategic and programmatic approach (DANCED 1999). In its support of MENGOs' activities, the Malaysian–Danish Country Programme has yet to come up with identified areas and modalities of significant strategic importance. Still, DANCED recognises the role and contribution of NGOs in the promotion of public awareness of environmental issues and the provision of technical support. As, in general, DANCED puts emphasis on 'demand-driven' environmental assistance, NGOs with grassroots foundations, dedication and 'hands on' experience have a comparative advantage in obtaining DANCED support (DANCED 1999).

Government support to MENGOs

Many agencies within the Malaysian government now acknowledge MENGOs' contribution to society, especially in promoting environmental awareness and developing a more caring and sustainable society. Recognising the need and opportunity to involve MENGOs more and better in environmental initiatives, especially in areas in which governmental capacity is lacking, the government increasingly supports NGO-linked programmes. Although there is no consensus yet on the exact mode of involvement of NGOs, various forms of engagement ought to be supported.

Comparing NGOs and CBOs

NGOs and CBOs in Malaysia have played and continue to play a pivotal role in raising environmental awareness, initiating environmental action and pursuing environmental advocacy at various national, regional and international fora. Their aim is to protect and promote sounder environmental policies and environmental practices, particularly with regard to environmental monitoring and management. Environmental groups in Malaysia come from diverse backgrounds, with diverse missions, mandates and methods of working on environmental issues and initiatives.

Little data are readily available on the structure and activities of environmental NGOs in Malaysia, aside from on a handful of well-established, larger and better-known environmental NGOs such as WWFM, MNS, WIMP and the Environmental Protection Society of Malaysia (EPSM). Most well-established environmental NGOs are the country offices of organisations that have branches in many countries worldwide and were set up quite differently from more locally based environmental NGOs. WWF, WIMP and TRAFFIC (Trade Record Analysis of Flora and Fauna in Commerce) fall into the category of transnational NGOs. To some degree these NGOs are reliant on foreign funding and expertise to carry out ecosystems and wildlife protection management, with probably much greater freedom to operate in Malaysia than other transnational NGOs (such as for human rights or gender issues) enjoy.

The better-established environmental NGOs are known to focus their attention essentially on green, brown or blue issues and initiatives, be it at the local, state, national, sub-regional, regional or international level, depending on their respective missions, mandates, resources, capacities and opportunities. The core concerns of these NGOs are the conservation and sustainable use of biodiversity. They also work to a lesser extent on climate change, and even less on international waters. The bulk of their interventions are aimed at the national, regional or international level instead of at the state, local or community level. Also, most of the environmental NGOs and CBOs in Malaysia, especially those working on environmental issues and initiatives at the national or state level, tend to be primarily concentrated in peninsular Malaysia rather than East Malaysia (Sabah and Sarawak).

However, poorer, grassroots-based environment groups also exist, along with some one-man-show NGOs. Among these organisations are the Centre for Environment, Technology and Development, Malaysia (CETDEM); the Sustainable Development Network Malaysia (SUSDEN); and the Environmental Management and Research Association of Malaysia (ENSEARCH). These very local NGOs have played a crucial part in environmental activism because they were founded and led by powerful, outspoken and strongly committed individuals. To a large extent these groups continue to work single-handedly to advocate sustainable development and improving environmental quality. CBOs and local communities do work on environmental issues and initiatives at the community or village level in rural areas. According to various formal and informal sources,[3] a variety of NGOs, CBOs and local communities are known to be working on a wide range of environmental issues and initiatives, including activities linked in one way or another to areas of biodiversity, climate change and international waters.

A number of issue-oriented environmental NGO networks or coalitions have emerged over the years in response to specific environmental concerns and considerations. Among these are the Pesticide Action Network, Sustainable Development Network, Biodiversity Action Network, Climate Action Network, Dams Action Network, Malaysian Climate Change Group, and others. However, there does not yet exist any officially designated umbrella coalition or network of environmental NGOs in Malaysia along the lines of the Federation of Malaysian Consumer Associations (FOMCA), which links state-level consumer associations in Malaysia.

In terms of organisation and operations, the majority of well-established NGOs generally use the English language in their daily management and activities. Bahasa Malaysia is used in formal correspondence to government agencies and at formal meetings between state or federal agencies and with local communities. The majority of NGOs dealing with environmental issues and sustainable development are made up of people of Indian ethnicity, followed by Chinese and, lastly, other races. Some community-based NGOs in Sabah and Sarawak are led by individuals who come from indigenous groups and tribes. Having had more education than most, they are well placed to help strengthen their own indigenous groups in terms of human rights issues, land rights and women's development.

Strengths of MENGOs

Environmental awareness

MENGOs have contributed a great deal in the area of environmental awareness and education. The many books, brochures, guide books, manuals and posters they have produced are a testament to those contributions (Saari 2000). Lots of fun activities, nature clubs and environmental events and campaigns organised by MENGOs have attracted many youngsters. Nature camps, jungle trekking, bird watching, canoeing, mountain biking, caving and fishing are some of the exciting activities promoted by MENGOs that involve both the young and the old. There has been a tremendous increase in such nature-based activities in Malaysia through the organisational efforts of local environmental NGOs. Aside from actively taking part in these activities, some participants become members of environmental organisations or contribute valuable services in other ways. Moreover, the mass media have shown an increasing awareness of the importance of environmental issues. This trend should continue and intensify even more. Environmental journalists keep abreast of current local environmental issues, problems and activities, and engage and involve NGOs in their discussions and in formulating their views.

Management of ecosystems

Management plans for areas protected by federal or state legislation have been mostly drawn up and written by local NGO experts. These individuals have a wealth of experience and knowledge of special protected ecosystems, including wetlands, montane forests, lowland dipterocarp, limestone forests, and peat swamp forests. Protected areas are legally established sites to provide lasting conservation of ecosystems, species and genetic resources. Parks and reserves must be managed to ensure that their objectives are effectively achieved. This requirement calls for management plans and appropriate institutions to implement them.

Many state parks and nature reserves, including Endau-Rompin in

Johor, Perlis State Park, Kinabatangan Floodplain in Sabah, and Tasek Bera and Tasek Chini in Pahang, have been studied thoroughly by environmental NGOs that were eventually responsible for the task of producing a comprehensive management plan encompassing legislation, natural resources information, basic ecological information, watershed management issues, genetic resources, zoning, protection, tourism, education, local participation, research, personnel and training. These management plans have been used and implemented by state agencies like the Forestry Department and the Department of National Parks and Wildlife. Although expert scientific knowledge lies in the hands of academics at institutions of higher learning, universities and research organisations, such individuals are not necessarily the most appropriate people to produce management plans. Management plans require more applied ecological work and sound answers to local problems of fishermen, plantation workers, villagers and indigenous tribes, mandating thorough consultation with local communities.

Weaknesses of MENGOs

Inadequate power – a weak voice

NGOs in Malaysia are not hard-core radical groups who will give up everything they own to demonstrate publicly for a good cause. Very few street demonstrations or public protests have ever been organised by environmental NGOs. NGOs usually promote conservation or sustainable livelihoods through very peaceful means and methods, such as active dialogue and creating awareness about an issue or problem – not marching to confront an official or demonstrate on a particular issue. This strategy is partly attributable to Malaysia's multiculturalism and general preference for politeness, peace and tolerance. The more aggressive, noisy street demonstrations and marches of, for instance, Korean, Japanese and Taiwanese NGOs and environmental activists would thus be out of place in Malaysia. Partly, though, NGOs' choice of non-confrontational strategies is due to state-imposed constraints on hard-core environmental activists. Malaysian NGOs have to engage in dialogues and consultations, normally through particular politicians or fora, if they want to bring about change or stop a particular activity or project. In the end, while more strident environmental activists elsewhere get things done quickly and effectively, their Malaysian counterparts bring about change slowly or not at all.

Lack of local partnerships and synergies

Most environmental NGOs prefer to work on their own without fostering partnerships within the NGO community. Each NGO tends to work independently and carry out its mission within its own sphere of influence, according to the resources available. If each of the environmental NGOs contributed members to form a partnership or nationwide NGO committee on the environment, much could be achieved at the national level. This NGO committee would be an integral part of the environmental decision-making process, having frequent dialogues with ministry and government officials on environmental issues. It might even become a member of the National Committee on Environment, thus providing feedback to the government and speaking as a single voice on behalf of the MENGO community.

While Malaysian NGOs are actively involved in a number of activities associated with biodiversity conservation, intellectual property rights, climate change, energy efficiency, recycling, international waters and sustainability of natural resources, such activities seldom focus directly on local initiatives at the community level and involving the meaningful participation of local communities, on low-cost solutions and innovations appropriate for and readily acceptable to local communities, or promotion of sustainable livelihoods by linking poverty eradication with environmental improvement. It is in these directions that environmental NGOs in Malaysia should move in the future. The NGOs or CBOs that do link up with local communities act as an interface to enable local communities to act locally while thinking globally – that is, to achieve global benefits by undertaking local actions. Such a strategy facilitates the twinning of local initiatives with larger-scale interactions via local community-level or local community-oriented interactions.

The Way Forward

Partnership with Government

MENGOs acknowledge that they currently enjoy several formal and informal mechanisms to participate in processes that allow their views to be heard in relation to government policy formulation on environmental protection. These opportunities include annual dialogues with the Minister of Environment, budget dialogues with the Minister of Finance, involvement with the environmental impact assessment process directed by the Department of Environment, and the formulation of structure plans and local plans at the state and local government levels. Apart from these occasions, the government has from time to time involved some MENGOs in policy formulation, drafting legislation or project implementation. Some examples include the role of WWF in drafting the National Conservation Strategy and National Biodiversity Policy, of WIMP in the National Wetlands Policy, of MNS in the development of management plans for Endau Rompin National Park and the Kuala Selangor Nature Park, and of TWN in relation to activities concerning biosafety, biodiversity and implementation of international environmental conventions.

Where MENGOs have been involved in large-scale projects, they have so far come into the projects as contracted consultants to government agencies, assisting these agencies to implement projects. These projects are all in natural resource management sectors, whereas the strength of these MENGOs is in biodiversity conservation and nature education. Normally, there is very little if any advocacy linked to this kind of service delivery.

A partnership approach could bring about a situation in which wider national environmental policy issues are debated in an open and frank manner. Such an order has to emerge primarily based on the interaction between the government and MENGOs, assisted, where appropriate, by foreign bilateral donor organisations. For the current Malaysian decision-making process to evolve into a more contemporary national modality, all partners have to develop their mental assumptions and approaches.

As discussed earlier, the division of powers and roles between the various layers of government in relation to environmental protection makes the need for integrated planning somewhat of a challenge. This oft-cited institutional weakness in adopting an integrated approach to environmental management and in enforcement of environment-related laws may be overcome at least in part if all layers of government take an open-minded approach to other stakeholders, especially MENGOs as the representatives of civil society on environmental issues. Given the present perception among MENGOs of the way the government interacts with them, there still appears to be room for improvement. One may hope that the increasing perception in government circles that MENGOs do play a constructive role in Malaysia's environmental protection efforts will only strengthen in years to come. Further, it would be advantageous to the government to engage MENGOs in policy dialogues that can advance the realisation of Malaysian citizens' fundamental right to a healthy and pollution-free environment. Such an approach would be mutually beneficial to all parties for the common good.

Such a dialogue process could lead to the development of co-operation projects, which may be defined as projects mutually initiated by government and MENGOs, focused mainly on wider policy issues and involving the active participation of MENGOs. Such co-operation projects would help overcome the limited opportunities for civil society, and particularly MENGOs, to provide valuable inputs. By enabling the preparation and implementation of co-operation projects, the government will have an opportunity, if the MENGOs are willing, to involve civil society representatives more systematically in their environmental protection efforts.

Conclusion

Comparative advantages of MENGOs

The MENGO community in Malaysia is very diverse, and different MENGOs boast varying capacities and strengths. This variety is in itself highly valuable. The 'grassroots' type of MENGO and some of MENGOs that are involved in community-mobilising activities are well placed to embark on projects that involve education and awareness raising at the community level, community-mobilising activities, carrying out innovative pilot projects at the community level, and so on. For those MENGOs that have had much experience in advocacy activities, their strength is in the area of having a role in policy advocacy and implementation. Some MENGOs with technical skills or with consultants on board are better placed to assist the government in projects requiring such skills, as in the management of nature parks and conservation areas, and other such activities. Those with strong public education and awareness-raising capabilities are natural partners in such activities. There are a few MENGOs that work at the regional level on environmental initiatives; they will, of course, be able to pursue projects at this level with ease. Some MENGOs are very familiar with international environmental conventions and have been assisting the government at international fora in forging some of these initiatives. These groups will remain valuable in activities related to capacity building for and implementation of these conventions. In sum, the MENGO community has great potential to play an ever larger role in policy dialogue, formulation and implementation.

Still, NGOs alone cannot safeguard and protect the environment. Malaysia needs progressive legislation, enlightened citizens and NGOs to ensure protection of the environment. A combination of good legislation, vigilant NGOs and an enlightened judiciary can go a long way in returning some peace and respite to Mother Earth. Environmental NGOs need to build a mass social movement of people who put their ethics into practice. Many people are concerned that their lifestyles impact on livelihoods elsewhere in the world, but do not really feel that they know enough about it. NGOs need to reach more people so that they can shape the future of society.

6 The Malaysian human rights movement
Meredith L. Weiss

Introduction

Though recent calls for greater justice and democracy have lent prominence to the human rights movement in Malaysia, this movement is not new. Rather, demands for improved human rights have been a centrepiece of civil society agitation since the early 1970s. Broad-based and rather amorphous, the human rights movement operates on several fronts, spanning both secular and religious non-governmental organisations (NGOs). These NGOs have engaged in a wide range of campaigns, the most prominent of them to abolish the Internal Security Act (ISA). The progress of this effort and other campaigns demonstrates the enthusiasm and coalition-building abilities of human rights NGOs, but also their weakness at sustaining momentum, long-term strategising and manoeuvring in the face of a strong and antagonistic regime.

Aims and underpinnings

The goals of Malaysia's human rights movement are diffuse. Broadly speaking, the movement strives to realise the ideal envisioned in the Malaysian Charter on Human Rights (MCHR). This document enumerates a broad range of civil and political rights due Malaysians, premising its claims on the Universal Declaration of Human Rights (UDHR) and the Asian Human Rights Charter, which was endorsed by various Malaysian NGOs. The MCHR was the outcome of feedback from NGOs and consultations in 1993 and 1994 among representatives of 50 human rights organisations, trade unions, consumer groups, women's groups, environmental protection organisations, academic bodies and other groups. It had been endorsed by 49 Malaysian NGOs as of May 1999, but significantly, the only Islamic groups among these signatories were the Persatuan Kebangsaan Pelajar Islam Malaysia (National Union of Malaysian Muslim Students, PKPIM) and the feminist group Sisters in Islam (Malaysian NGOs 1994; SUARAM 1998: 1–2).

According to the initial plan, the MCHR would be a living document, with various NGOs completing periodic status reports. However, follow-up has so far been sporadic. Suara Rakyat Malaysia (SUARAM), a human rights NGO, did release a comprehensive *Malaysian Human Rights Report* in December 1998 based on data extending through 1996. This document includes extensive information on human rights issues and violations within eight sectors: development, labour, women, indigenous peoples, children, people with disabilities, inequality and non-discrimination, and civil and political rights. As the editors assert, 'the preparation and coordination of this report has been one of the most meaningful and significant cooperative efforts among Malaysian NGOs so far' (SUARAM 1998: 2). In May 1999, not long after the release of the report, several amendments to the MCHR were tabled at a review and consultation session. The proposed amendments touched on the need to ratify international covenants on migrant workers; to prohibit forced evictions of settlers except after negotiations with all affected parties, payment of adequate compensation and provision of suitable alternative housing; to decry the arbitrary deprivation of life by state security forces; to abolish the death penalty or at least restrict its application and prohibit public executions; and to create a national mechanism for the promotion and protection of human rights.

Not all NGOs involved in human rights activism in Malaysia agree on the premises for these human rights. Broadly speaking, human rights NGOs rely either on liberal humanistic explanations or on religious justifications in asserting a claim to particular rights. Secular explanations are premised on a Lockean notion of inalienable rights, bolstered by reference to international pacts such as the UDHR and Malaysia's own constitution, while religious justifications cite the teachings either of a particular religion or common to most religious traditions. For instance, Islamic groups seeking a more firmly Islamic sociopolitical order may support the standards of justice and individual freedom upheld in the MCHR, but because these rights are enshrined in the Qur'ān and *Hadith*, not in the UDHR. Moreover, as political scientist Sheila Nair insists, 'Both secular and religious movements take for granted that citizens have a moral obligation to question the public effects of state policies' (Nair 1999: 97).

At the same time that NGOs have been making pronouncements about universal rights and liberties, from whatever perspective, the government has maintained its own discourse on human rights, spearheading an 'Asian values'-based critique of western-oriented definitions of human rights. The state has labelled advocacy-oriented NGOs, together with the organised left (less salient now than previously), dissident student movements, labour groups and opposition political parties an 'internal Other' against whom society must struggle to remain peaceful, unified and secure. In this way, 'alternative political ideas were rendered subversive and deviant' (Nair 1999: 92). Before, NGOs and other dissident groups were labelled 'communist'; now they are lambasted as 'western' or 'non-national'. For instance, Federal Territory Minister Abu Hassan Omar declared in December 1986 that seven groups – two opposition parties and five NGOs – were out to destroy 'the country's political and social fabric' (Tan and Bishan 1994: 25).

The Malaysian government, especially outspoken long-time Prime Minister Mahathir Mohamad, insists on the inappropriateness of applying either 'western' or 'fundamentalist' Islamic definitions of human rights to non-western, multiracial, under-developed Malaysia. Discourse on Asian values and concomitant human rights stresses community priorities rather than individual liberties, deference to authority and acceptance of relatively strict government control, and non-interference by one nation in the internal affairs of other nations. Prioritising economic development above civil and political rights provides justification for repressive laws that allow the government to maintain 'stability' by stifling competing views or criticism. The Barisan Nasional (BN) government asserts that such a system of 'democracy according to our own mould' will allow Malaysia to maintain ethnic harmony, political and social stability, and internal security without compromising economic resilience or being – in Mahathir's words – 'over-zealous about the democratic system' (quoted in Saliha 1997: 10, 20). Part of the reason for the current anti-BN uproar is simply that this formula – strict control and a quiescent population in exchange for economic growth – failed to protect Malaysia from falling prey to the recent Asian economic crisis.

The organisations involved

The human rights movement operates on several fronts, spanning a wide range of NGOs. Like other sorts of Malaysian NGO, many of the groups dealing with human rights have scant resources or members, sometimes being centred around just a few key individuals, and not all are fully democratic or grassroots-oriented in structure and methods.[1] Relatively few NGOs have human rights *per se* as their primary purpose.[2] These NGOs include:

- Suara Rakyat Malaysia (Voice of the Malaysian People, SUARAM). Formed in the wake of 1987's Operasi Lalang, a massive crackdown on political opposition, SUARAM is mainly involved with monitoring and reporting human rights violations in Malaysia and the region. The NGO also maintains a resource centre and has hosted the secretariats of various coalitions, including Gagasan Demokrasi Rakyat (Coalition for People's Democracy), Solidaritas Timor Timur Malaysia (Malaysian Solidarity for East Timor), and the coalition against the Bakun Dam. Based in Petaling Jaya, SUARAM launched a Johor Baru office in April 1999 and has plans for further expansion.
- Aliran Kesedaran Negara (National Consciousness Movement, Aliran). A linchpin of Penang's NGO community since its formation in 1977 (despite a threat of deregistration in 1980), Aliran claims to have been Malaysia's first non-partisan, multi-ethnic reform movement. The organisation promotes social justice, political reform and multi-religious, multi-ethnic dialogue, primarily through its magazine, the *Aliran Monthly*, but also through occasional books and forums.
- The National Human Rights Society of Malaysia (HAKAM). An offshoot of the Bar Council's Human Rights Subcommittee registered in 1991, HAKAM is a small, completely volunteer-based NGO in Kuala Lumpur comprised mostly of lawyers. The NGO offers statements and promotes human rights awareness and advocacy in coalition with other groups.
- Pergerakan Keadilan Sosial (Movement for Social Justice, Adil). Launched in December 1998 in the wake of Deputy Prime Minister Anwar Ibrahim's detention, Adil quickly attracted massive support as the vanguard of the Reformasi movement. Calling for broad-based social, political and economic reform, the group was closely linked with Anwar and his wife, Wan Azizah Wan Ismail, but faded from the scene with the launch by Wan Azizah of Parti Keadilan Nasional in April 1999.

Other secular groups deal with human rights issues in conjunction with less abstract concerns. Labelling a sector-specific issue a 'human rights' issue may aid in coalition building and conscientisation, attracting more broad-based support and perhaps also facilitating fundraising efforts. However, branding too wide a range of issues as 'human rights' concerns may also mean glossing over details so that the issue is understandable to everyone and not too clearly in the interests of only a specific group of people. In the process, NGOs feel obliged to spend much energy and effort reciprocating with support for campaigns for 'human rights' issues that are actually far from their areas of concern and expertise, and the campaign is left vulnerable to the government's pronouncements on the corruption of Asian values by western human rights rhetoric. NGOs that frame their demands in terms of human rights discourse at times and build campaigns accordingly include:

- Women's groups. Groups such as the All Women's Action Society, Women's Aid Organisation, Women's Crisis Centre, Women's Development Collective, Persatuan Sahabat Wanita (Friends of Women Association) and Tenganita (Women's Force) have used human rights discourse in lobbying for women's economic and social rights, domestic violence legislation, reform of laws on rape and divorce, regulation of the traffic in women, and so on. They have also regularly endorsed campaigns on other human rights issues.
- Labour unions. Contemporary unions have seldom organised broad-based campaigns around their own demands, largely because of the restrictive laws governing their activities and disincentives to workers' organisation.[3] Nonetheless, a range of labour unions – among others, the Federation of Textile-Garment Workers' Union, Harris Solid-State Workers' Union, the All Malaysian Estate Staff Union, the Transport Workers' Union, and the Electrical Industries Workers' Union, as well as the Malaysian Trade Unions Congress – have consistently signed on to human rights-related NGO coalitions. NGOs working with plantation, factory and migrant workers, such as Alaigal, Tholilaliyin Tholar and Tenaganita, also deal with human rights.
- Consumers' groups. The Federation of Malaysian Consumers' Associations, its affiliates, and unaffiliated groups such as the Consumers' Association of Penang and the Education and Research Association for Consumers include among their core issues humans rights concerns, both by labelling consumers' rights 'human rights' and by joining in other rights-related coalitions.
- Environmental groups. The Environmental Protection Society of Malaysia, Sahabat Alam Malaysia (Friends of the Earth Malaysia), the Penang Organic Farm Club and other environmental groups have long been active in human rights work both in peninsular Malaysia and in Sabah and Sarawak, particularly in terms of 'environmental human rights' such as the right to a clean environment or to resist deforestation of traditional tribal lands. Environmental groups often work closely with consumers' and indigenous people's groups in particular in their campaigns.

- Students' groups. University students were more active in protest activities in the 1970s than now, primarily due to the government's crackdown with the University and University Colleges Act (UUCA) after mass student protests in support of a peasant movement in the mid-1970s. The Reformasi movement, however, has regenerated student activism to some extent, partly through long-standing NGOs such as PKPIM and partly through new associations such as the mostly-non-Malay Gerakan Demokratik Belia dan Pelajar Malaysia (Malaysian Youth and Students' Democratic Movement).
- Chinese associations. Groups such as the Selangor Chinese Assembly Hall (particularly its Civil Rights Committee), the United Chinese School Committees' Association of Malaysia, and the United Chinese School Teachers' Association have been actively involved in a range of human rights coalitions. In addition, it is Chinese associations that have taken the lead in championing minority rights issues, particularly relating to mother-tongue education. Many of these groups were also energised recently in support of Lim Guan Eng, an opposition Member of Parliament convicted in a politically charged trial of sedition and malicious publication of false news.
- Professional organisations. Groups representing the health professions, attorneys, teachers and university staff have been particularly forthcoming in their support for a variety of human rights campaigns both on issues within their specific domains (as with doctors' and nurses' support for the Citizens' Health Initiative) and on more wide-ranging issues. Among these groups, the Bar Council has the highest profile as an advocacy organisation, attracting the ire of the government at times for its stance on civil and political rights. Some of these professional associations have specific religious affiliations, such as the Persatuan Perubatan Islam Malaysia (Islamic Medical Association of Malaysia).
- HIV/AIDS groups. NGOs working in the HIV/AIDS field under the aegis of the Malaysian AIDS Council have developed a Malaysian AIDS Charter defining the rights of people with HIV/AIDS. One of these NGOs in particular, Pink Triangle, has also consistently asserted the rights of gay men, lesbians, bisexuals and transgendered or transsexual individuals, generally with scant support from other NGOs.
- Other advocacy organisations. NGOs fighting for indigenous peoples' rights, such as the Centre for Orang Asli Concerns and the Indigenous People's Development Centre, often define their

projects in terms of human rights. *Peneroka bandar* (urban squatters or settlers) and urban development groups have also joined in broad human rights coalitions and define their core issues in terms of the right to housing and sustainable development. Such NGOs include the Jawatankuasa Sokongan Peneroka Bandar (Urban Pioneers' Support Office), the Urban Resource Unit, Suara Warga Pertiwi and the Sustainable Transportation Network.

A number of religious bodies also address human rights issues, particularly Muslim and Christian organisations. Among Muslim NGOs involved with human rights work are the massive Angkatan Belia Islam Malaysia (Malaysian Islamic Youth Movement), Jamaah Islah Malaysia (Malaysian Community Reform Movement), Persuatuan Ulama Malaysia (Malaysian Islamic Scholars' Association), and Ikatan Siswazah Muslim Malaysia (Malaysian Muslim Graduates' Association). Many of these groups have been revitalised by recent Reformasi mobilisation against the ISA and in favour of democracy and individual rights and freedoms; new Islamic groups have also sprung up among Reformasi activists. Islamic NGOs were at the core of a significant coalition for social justice and particularly the repeal of the ISA formed upon Anwar's ISA detention: Majlis Gerakan Keadilan Rakyat Malaysia (Malaysian People's Movement for Justice, Gerak). Though Islamic and secular NGOs have recently collaborated closely, particularly in Gerak and the similarly oriented Gagasan Demokrasi Rakyat (Coalition for People's Democracy, Gagasan), this co-operative ethos could prove transient. With attention increasingly focused on the upcoming elections (held in November 1999) rather than civil society campaigns, both Gerak and Gagasan became largely defunct after about six months of frenetic activity. Also, NGOs are increasingly openly taking sides with opposition political parties. While these parties allied in the Barisan Alternatif (Alternative Front) ahead of the 1999 elections, Islamic NGOs are still more likely to associate themselves with Parti Islam Se-Malaysia (Malaysian Islamic Party, PAS), while secular human rights NGOs (which tend to be predominantly non-Malay, non-Muslim in membership) are more prone to associate with Parti Rakyat Malaysia (Malaysian People's Party, PRM), the Democratic Action Party (DAP), or the fledgling Parti Sosialis Malaysia (Malaysian Socialist Party, PSM). Support for the new Parti Keadilan Nasional (National Justice Party, Keadilan) is mixed.

It is not only Islamic groups that engage with human rights issues in Malaysia. Christian groups have also been active in human rights education and advocacy. These NGOs include the Council of Churches

Malaysia, the Catholic Research Centre and new networks such as Christians for Adil. Catholic activists – missionaries and church workers allegedly linked with liberation theology – were among the detainees in the last major ISA crackdown, 1987's Operation Lalang, and certain churches, such as St Francis Xavier Church in Petaling Jaya, are known for cultivating awareness of human rights. Hindu and Buddhist groups (for instance, under the aegis of the Consultative Committee of Buddhist, Christian, Hindu and Sikh Religions of Malaysia) have lent their support to rights coalitions at times, too, but infrequently and with only minimal involvement.

Major campaigns and strategies

One of the mainstays of the human rights movement is campaigning for the repeal of repressive laws. While the Malaysian Constitution guarantees equality for all and a range of individual liberties, including freedom of assembly, speech and organisation, a growing body of legislation sharply curtails these rights. Among the most controversial laws are those permitting detention without trial, in particular the Internal Security Act 1968 (ISA). The campaign against the ISA is discussed in detail below. Other laws (or amendments to them) against which human rights groups and their compatriots have aggressively lobbied include the Official Secrets Act 1972 (OSA, amended 1986), the Printing Presses and Publications Act 1984 (PPPA, amended 1987), the Universities and University Colleges Act 1971 (UUCA, amended 1975), the Societies Act 1966 (amended 1983) and the Police Act 1967 (amended 1988).

Controversial laws

Malaysia's OSA is 'one of the most restrictive legislations on the dissemination of state information in the world' (Tan and Bishan 1994: 24–5). The law prevents the dissemination of any documents or information deemed prejudicial to national security, with stiff penalties (mandatory prison terms and fines) for offenders. A wide range of information has been labelled 'secret' and thus off-limits, not just defence-related material. For instance, in November 1997, academics were barred from speaking to the public or the media about the severe haze blanketing much of Malaysia (SUARAM 1998: 37–9); in May 1998, no information was released to the public on the dangerous pollution levels in the Gombak River indicated by nine tons of decaying fish discovered in a high-density residential area of Kuala Lumpur

(Ramdas 1998: n.p.); and rumours of scandals can rarely be investigated due to lack of access to relevant documents. In the same vein, the Sedition Act 1969 provides for severe penalties for any act deemed designed to create hatred, contempt or disaffection towards the king, the government or the administration of justice, or among people of various races or classes. Moerover, no one is allowed to question the system of Malay special rights or the equal citizenship of non-Malays granted in the 1948 Constitution of the Federation of Malaya and the 1956 *Merdeka* (Independence) Constitution.

The PPPA seriously curtails freedom of the press. All publications and printing presses must obtain a renewable annual licence and may be suspended, as happened to three newspapers in 1987's Operation Lalang, if seen to be 'anti-government'. Amendments in December 1987 made it easier for the government to ban publications, reduced the recourse to court challenges, and criminalised the malicious publication of false news. These provisions have been used recently in high-profile cases against opposition Member of Parliament Lim Guan Eng and NGO activist Irene Fernandez of Tenaganita. Together with the OSA and Sedition Act, the PPPA clearly impairs the free flow of information.

Compounding these legal issues is the fact that all the major mass media (print, television and radio) are controlled by interests linked with the ruling BN and are staunchly pro-government in perspective. Furthermore, Radio and Television Malaysia (RTM) is under the direct control of the Ministry of Information – enabling the government to announce in July 1999, for instance, that the opposition would be granted no airtime at all during the forthcoming general elections. Some NGOs and opposition parties offer alternative media, but with government-imposed restrictions: party organs may legally be sold only to party members, though this requirement is routinely ignored, especially for PAS's popular *Harakah* during the Reformasi period; and the long-standing *Aliran Monthly* was denied permission to publish in Malay, limiting its audience and impact.[4] After the 1999 elections, the government began to crack down on these alternative media. In March 2000, *Harakah*'s permit was restricted to allow publication only fortnightly instead of twice a week, and the publishing permits of magazines *Detik* and *Eksklusif* were suspended shortly thereafter. Rapidly increasing internet usage and access to international print and television media are mitigating the impact of these regulations and conditions, with even *Harakah* able to broadcast information daily over the internet, but most rural Malaysians in particular lack access to these media. In addition, a recent trend towards pressing libel suits for tens of millions of ringgit may put an additional damper on information flows.[5]

Students and academic staff are particularly restricted. The UUCA and related enactments prohibit most forms of political activism among students and faculty on or off campus. Under the terms of the UUCA, all campus organisations, publications and demonstrations must be approved by the vice-chancellor; students are prohibited from joining any society, political party, or trade union; and students are to be automatically suspended or dismissed if charged with any criminal offense. Professors and lecturers, too, are prohibited to hold office in any political party and discouraged by other staff guidelines from engaging in most forms of overt activism. The UUCA has been used as a weapon against Reformasi protesters, many of whom are students. The government has promised that any students caught participating in demonstrations, distributing anti-government materials or otherwise engaging in movement activities will face expulsion, and Mahathir has castigated Malay students especially for behaving like *kacang melupakan kulit*: that is, for being ungrateful to the government that gave them the opportunity to gain an education.[6] At least two students have been suspended so far for Reformasi activism (Elizabeth Wong, personal communication, 26 July 1999).

By requiring that any association of seven or more members register as a society, the Societies Act accords the government enormous control over NGOs. Registration, with or without conditions, and forced deregistration are at the discretion of the government. Once registered, the NGO must submit yearly reports to the Registrar of Societies, including the roster of officers for that year, financial accounting and the proceedings of the group's Annual General Meeting. Moreover, the approval process may take years. Many NGOs register as businesses or companies to avoid the tribulations of dealing with the Registrar of Societies. Even so, they may be threatened with deregistration or actually deregistered.

The Police Act infringes on freedom of assembly by requiring a police permit fourteen days before any public assembly of more than five people. The police frequently refuse permits to NGOs and opposition parties. If the organisations proceed regardless, the police can declare the gathering illegal and order the participants to disperse or face arrest. The 1988 amendments allowed anyone 'found at' an illegal assembly, regardless of whether they claimed innocence, to be detained, and extended the conditions under which the police may break up a meeting or gathering, including if it is on private property. Also, the law prohibits public rallies for electoral campaigns, leaving parties only able to present *ceramah* (public lectures), for which they still require a permit. The Police Act has been used to break up protests against the

ISA detention of Shia Muslims in November 1997, by the Penan in Sarawak against land surveyors in March 1997, against the arrival of the Israeli cricket team in April 1997, against the haze in September 1997, by Reformasi street protesters in late 1998 and early 1999, and more.

Aside from these enactments, other legislation further infringes upon civil liberties. For instance, laws prohibiting Muslims from converting effectively deny these citizens freedom of religion. These restrictions, however, are more often condemned by non-Muslims than Muslims as they are in line with Islam's position on *murtad* (conversion and the consequent obligation of fellow Muslims to bring that person back to the fold). Also, the Darul Arqam (Abode of Arqam) movement was banned in 1994 and a number of its leaders and members were detained under the ISA in 1994 and 1996 for spreading 'deviationist' Islam, and ten other individuals were detained in November 1997 for being Shia Muslims. At the same time, state policies preferential to Muslims (for Islamic religious education in public schools, ease of obtaining permits for construction of mosques and *surau*, and the like) aggravate followers of other religions.[7]

Freedom of movement is also restricted. Several activists, particularly in East Malaysia, have been prevented from travelling outside Malaysia or into either Sabah or Sarawak in response to their participation in advocacy activities. Moreover, the Restricted Residence Act of 1933 permits renewable 'banishment' orders for criminal suspects, granted without a judicial hearing, forcing the suspects to live far from home for up to two years at a time and restricting their movement. Also, once released from custody, former ISA detainees may not be allowed full movement but may be restricted to Malaysia or a particular area within the country.

Notably, too, Malaysia is technically still under a state of emergency. Article 150 of the federal constitution allows proclamation of a state of emergency, including suspension of Parliament and rule by executive decree in the name of the king and on the advice of the Prime Minister. Article 150 has been used four times (most famously in 1969), with none of these orders being subsequently revoked. Furthermore, in 1981, the Constitution was amended to prevent anyone from posing a legal challenge to the validity of a state of emergency or any resultant laws (SUARAM 1998: 223–4). Since the conditions under a state of emergency infringe upon individuals' human rights, the ease of declaring an emergency – not just in the case of grave national danger – contravenes international standards of human rights.

Lobbying by NGOs

Most NGOs' efforts against these laws have been basically ineffective. A rare, though limited, success was the enormous effort involving over 100 NGOs against amendments to the Societies Act in 1981. The amendments divided NGOs into 'political' and non-political (dubbed 'friendly') organisations and added tough new restrictions for 'political' organisations. However, while that part of the amendments was rescinded in 1983, limitations on societies' right to appeal decisions of the relevant authorities for their (de-)registration and other restrictive provisions were retained.[8] A similarly enormous campaign against amendments to the OSA and for the enactment of a Freedom of Information Act was waged in the mid-1980s by journalists allied with NGOs. This aggressive lobbying effort basically failed, though the final version of the amended law was slightly less restrictive, probably as a result of the protests. That the anti-OSA campaign was not more successful is remarkable: the coalition boasted a number of prominent Malaysians, including two ex-Premiers and one former Lord President and sultan, and the National Union of Journalists submitted a petition with 36,000 signatures to the government (Saravanamuttu 1997: 6; Tan and Bishan 1994: 24–5). As for the other laws, despite cycles of heightened and diminished protest against the legislation, virtually no progress has been made. For instance, remonstrations against the UUCA increased with the Reformasi movement, especially since many students were involved in street demonstrations (and a number of them arrested for illegal assembly) and student organisations were formed anew or revivified. However, the government has consistently maintained that since students should be studying, not agitating, there is no need to review the UUCA.

In the meantime, periodic enforcement of these laws by the government or its supporters maintains a culture of fear and encourages a high degree of self-censorship. For instance, in November 1996, hecklers from the BN youth wing violently broke up an international conference in Kuala Lumpur on the East Timor conflict. While 59 NGO activists and conference organisers were jailed for up to six days, the BN Youth leaders were released on bail that day, with government leaders' issuing statements in their support (Kua 1998a; SUARAM 1998: 230–4). Similarly, the government threatened to use the ISA against NGO organisers of a 1996 NGO Tribunal on Police Abuses, and in October 1998 the police disbanded a SUARAM-organised forum on the ISA. In terms of printed materials, NGO activist Irene Fernandez has been charged under the PPPA for a report issued by her

NGO entitled 'Abuse, Torture and Dehumanised Treatment of Migrant Workers at Detention Camps'. After several years, her case is still pending (Tenaganita 1997; SUARAM 1998: 83–4).

It is not just a few hardened activists who are targeted. In the months after Anwar's arrest, approximately 500 Reformasi activists were detained during street protests for illegal assembly and/or rioting (Elizabeth Wong, personal communication, 26 July 1999). These *orang kena tahanan* (detainees) not only have to endure the indignity and inconvenience of up to several days' initial remand – often after being sprayed with high-pressure acid-laced water, or kicked, dragged or beaten by the police – but if found guilty, can be sentenced to jail terms and fines of several thousand ringgit. Accorded much publicity in alternative (NGO and opposition party, plus foreign) print and electronic media, such incidents do rile up large numbers of people against the government, perhaps furthering NGOs' cause. However, these incidents also up the ante by reasserting that NGO activism is not risk-free, such that individuals concerned about their jobs or families may be reluctant to participate in future campaigns.

International covenants and the NHRC

At another level of legislation are international covenants or treaties on human rights. Malaysia is a signatory to some of these documents, often with reservations, but has failed to sign others, even if Malaysia initially voted in favour of the covenant in the UN (see Table 1). Such treaties are significant to human rights groups, particularly those with a secular universalist justification for their claims, since they set a standard that the government is technically required to meet. Ratifying, for instance, the International Covenant on Civil and Political Rights would mean that the government acknowledges those rights and is bound to study and revise any offending national laws to bring them in accordance with the treaty.

Likewise, ratification gives further credence to NGOs' attempts to link domestic human rights demands with a global discourse that counters the government's arguments of 'Asian exceptionalism'. At the moment, the government's Asian values defence can be crippling. Most obviously, NGOs are too easily discredited by being labelled 'western'. At the same time these NGOs expend unnecessary time and effort making sometimes-contradictory arguments either that they *have* defined a uniquely Malaysian set of standards (as with referring to the MCHR rather than to the UDHR) or, conversely, that Malaysians really should be subject to the same standards as everyone else (i.e., that

Table 1 Malaysia's response to international human rights covenants

---

Conventions signed and ratified
- Universal Declaration of Human Rights*
- Convention on the Elimination of All Forms of Discrimination against Women**
- Convention on the Rights of the Child**
- Convention on the Abolition of Slavery
- Convention on the Nationality of Married Women**
- Convention on the Prevention of the Crime of Genocide
- ILO Convention 98 on Principles of the Right to Organise and to Bargain Collectively

Conventions not signed or ratified
- International Covenant on Economic, Social and Cultural Rights
- International Covenant on Civil and Political Rights
- International Covenant against Torture and Other Forms of Cruel, Inhuman or Degrading Treatment or Punishment
- Convention on the Protection of the Rights of All Migrant Workers and Members of Their Families
- Convention Relating to the Status of Refugees
- Convention on the Elimination of All Forms of Racial Discrimination
- ILO Convention 87 on the Freedom of Association and Protection of the Right to Organise

---

* Accepted by dint of Malaysia's membership in the UN (non-binding document not requiring ratification).
** With reservations.
Sources: SUARAM (1998), Malaysian NGOs (1994) (and 1999 draft amendments), Kua (1998b), Elizabeth Wong (personal communication, 26 July 1999).

the UDHR is not just an artifact of western cultural imperialism). In other words, the force of the government's discourse may back activists into a corner such that they grasp at any defense of their stance, however inconsistent with their other statements or approaches.

Part of the project of reforming the legal framework for human rights is the establishment of an effective body for monitoring, investigation and prevention of abuses or legal irregularities. NGOs have been clamouring for such a commission for years. In early 1999, the Ministry of Foreign Affairs announced that it would soon table a bill for a National Human Rights Commission (NHRC). This bill was passed in July 1999. Prior to its passage, a group of NGOs formed a coalition to lobby for a better Act and to make the progress of the bill more transparent. Specifically, the Gabungan NGO Hak Asasi Manusia Prihatin Terhadap Penubuhan NHRC (Coalition of Human Rights NGOs Concerned with the Formation of the NHRC) protested the government's secrecy in tabling the bill – no draft was released for discussion and comment prior to its consideration in Parliament. It also recommended that to be legitimate and influential, the NHRC must be clearly independent from the government, with between seven and eleven commissioners serving terms of at least five years, their tenure and salaries out of the government's reach, and with a clear mandate and full powers of subpoena of individuals and documents for investigation (HAKAM *et al.* n.d.; Gabungan n.d.; Ramdas 1999).

The government's final version of the bill provides for a greater number of commissioners appointed by the king (on the advice of the prime minister) to serve two-year terms. Also, given that establishment of the NHRC was not accompanied by abrogation of the OSA and other legislation, the Commission apparently will have only limited access to potentially relevant information. Furthermore, NGOs fear that the activities of the NHRC will be no more open and transparent than the process of its formation, that its commissioners will be compliant to the will of the government, that it will not have adequate power to convince the government to repeal laws inimical to the protection of human rights or to ratify outstanding international human rights covenants, and that it will simply lack the resources and political will for active identification and investigation of abuses or unacceptable laws together with effective public education. Nonetheless, Musa Hitam, chair of the inaugural Commission, has expressed his openness to working with a range of social actors, including from NGOs, to ensure that the NHRC carries out its tasks as well and as impartially as possible.[9]

Establishment of a Malaysian NHRC is in line with the desire among ASEAN governments and NGOs to develop an ASEAN Human Rights Mechanism. This project, though, is still in the works, with NGOs and diplomats holding parallel consultations. It is not clear what effect, if any, NGOs' input will have on the final result either within Malaysia or regionally.

Other campaigns

Aside from legal reform, human rights NGOs also focus on specific injustices such as police brutality. Not only are complaints of physical and psychological mistreatment by police at the time of arrest and in lockups rife, but the police have been known to take the side of developers in evicting either urban squatters or indigenous peoples on Native Customary Rights land and of employers or management against industrial and plantation workers. Also, more than 50 suspects in criminal cases have been shot dead by police in the past few years, including at least 23 in 1998, prompting calls for restraint. An additional 151 prisoners died in remand between 1980 and 1990 (Kua 1998b: 4; SUARAM 1998: 244–52; Ramdas 1998: n.p.).

The ongoing campaign against police abuses has included monitoring abuse as reported in the media or by victims, holding forums for members of NGOs and the general public (one such forum was forestalled by the government's warning that organisers would be detained under the ISA), pursuing dialogue with police officers on problems and possible solutions, and disseminating leaflets on what to do in case of arrest as part of a 'know your rights' initiative. Reformasi activities also heightened public awareness of police brutality and lent momentum to calls for change. Not only was Anwar severely beaten by the then-Inspector General of Police while in custody, but thousands of street protesters were subjected to tear gas, water cannon, swinging batons and verbal threats as the police broke up demonstrations.

Judicial reform, too, has long been an aim of NGOs. The most egregious example of the lack of judicial independence was Mahathir's 1987–8 attack on the judiciary. With UMNO facing a split, then-Lord President Tun Salleh Abbas decided that the full bench of the Supreme Court would hear a case challenging the legality of the party. The court also agreed to hear an appeal of opposition politician Karpal Singh's ISA detention, possibly meaning a challenge to the legality of the ISA itself. In response, the Lord President and five other judges were impeached. A closed-door, government-appointed tribunal found the Lord President and two of the other justices guilty of 'gross misbehaviour' and removed them from office. Both UMNO's and Karpal's cases were subsequently dismissed. Amid international condemnation of such an encroachment on judicial independence, the Malaysian Bar refused to recognise the next Lord President (SUARAM 1998: 240–2; Means 1996: 112). Now, the corruption and sodomy trials of Anwar Ibrahim have renewed public suspicion and rumours that the courts are subservient to the executive or that cronyistic ties prejudice the court in favour of particular wealthy or powerful individuals. A range of other incidents of questionable non-prosecution of cases or unusually stringent or mild verdicts further these suspicions (SUARAM 1998: 240–2).

The Attorney-General (AG) is a frequent target of NGO attacks, given that it is the AG who determines which cases to bring to trial. NGOs have alleged that the AG practised selective prosecution in the cases of police officers found responsible for the death of a mechanic in police custody in 1995; that a High Court judge authored a 'poison pen letter' alleging corruption among several senior judges but was not prosecuted; and that former Malacca Chief Minister Rahim Tamby Chik was not charged with statutory rape of a fifteen-year-old girl, despite her implicating him and although fourteen other men were charged on the basis of her statements. Moreover, the government has frequently had individuals who were released on *habeas corpus* applications rearrested: nearly half the people arrested under the ISA, Dangerous Drugs Act, and Public Order and Prevention of Crime Ordinance from 1989 to 1996 who were released by the courts were then rearrested (Kua 1998b: 5).

NGO coalitions have also developed around various environmental concerns, with human rights discourse being used to motivate a wide range of NGOs to lend their support. Such campaigns include the Bakun Dam coalition, the Asian Rare Earth case, ongoing protests against logging in Sarawak, the Friends of Penang Hill coalition and, most recently, a campaign against the proposed damming of the Selangor River. The rights discussed in the context of these coalitions are not only the right to a safe, clean environment, but also indigenous peoples' rights to their lands and livelihoods. Such campaigns have had only limited success, mainly because they so clearly pit rights against development, at least as defined by the country's political and business elite. Andrew Harding (1996: 229–32) suggests that, while taking an 'environmental human rights' approach to the resolution of environmental problems can be useful in mustering support, 'In Malaysia the concept of human rights is not regarded as ideologically correct, and therefore an overt linkage between human rights and the environment may have undesirable consequences.'

Key tactics

Most of these campaigns use similar methods for public education, mobilisation and lobbying. A common tactic is the signature campaign, supplemented by postcard or letter-writing campaigns. Members or supporters of the NGOs involved collect names, signatures and identity card (IC) numbers from as many individuals as possible. These petitions are then delivered to the relevant government ministry, generally against the backdrop of a small rally or press conference. While signature campaigns can facilitate public education and show the government just how many people have reservations about a particular policy, the tactic does not seem very efficacious. For instance, NGOs submitted over 70,000 signatures in 1981 in opposition to the amendments to the Societies Act. While the fact that the bill was withdrawn twice and underwent substantial changes shows that the campaign as a whole (whether due to the petition or not) had some effect, in the end only the most controversial clauses were removed (Tan and Bishan 1994: 23). Similarly, the coalition opposed to the Bakun Dam has garnered reams of signatures condemning the project, yet probably the only factor postponing and scaling-down construction is the economic non-viability of the massive dam in the wake of the Asian financial crisis.

NGOs are also increasingly using the internet as well as mass faxing and distribution of handouts at events to encourage local and foreign supporters to send postcards or form-letters to government officials in support of particular campaigns. For instance, SUARAM spearheaded a postcard campaign in commemoration of the fiftieth anniversary of the UDHR in 1998 to pressure the government to bring Malaysian laws more in line with the provisions of the UDHR. SUARAM, the Urban Resource Unit and other NGOs, together with opposition parties (mainly PRM and PSM) use the internet to encourage letter-writing campaigns condemning evictions from plantations or squatter villages. Also, Artis Pro Activ (Proactive Artists, APA), a group of concerned individuals from the arts community, distributed distinctive yellow and black postcards addressed to the Prime Minister with a question mark on the front and the query, 'What's up, doc?' on the reverse at Reformasi street demonstrations. Unfortunately, while willing to wave the cards around and perhaps mail them in, most protesters did not understand that the message of the cards is asserting the right to ask questions. It is not known how many individuals have sent in letters and postcards in response to these requests and with what specific results.

The government is aware that signature and letter-writing campaigns constitute very low-risk behaviour, representing breadth but not depth of mobilisation. While putting one's name and IC number on a petition technically enables the government to track one down, such drastic crackdowns have never yet happened in Malaysia. Indeed, the vast majority of individuals who sign a petition stop there. While they may continue to observe, support and tell their friends and associates about the significance of the campaign, they take no further action.

The only exception – when large numbers of people do play a more active role – is in rare times of mass public demonstrations, as in the pro-rights Reformasi movement. Even so, since participating in a street demonstration carries a higher level of risk than signing a petition, many (especially older) individuals who sign petitions (such as the range of anti-ISA and other Reformasi petitions) remain reluctant to go so far as to join the crowds on the streets. Of course, most street demonstrators get off scot-free, too. Of tens of thousands mobilised in Kuala

Lumpur and other cities for Reformasi demonstrations and anti-BN *ceramah*, only a few hundred were arrested, whether or not they were eventually charged – enough people to scare off the faint-hearted, but a small proportion of the total.

Other common tactics in NGO campaigns are monitoring and fact-finding, public or restricted forums, and publications. SUARAM is the main NGO involved with general human rights monitoring, though other NGOs monitor violations within their sector, such as violence against women, unfair labour practices or encroachments on indigenous peoples' land. A number of NGOs conduct research on relevant issues, such as a May 1999 fact-finding mission to Sarawak to reassess the Bakun Dam situation or a large-scale study of rape in Malaysia by a group of women's organisations. The results of these investigations are generally presented in forums or publications – monographs or items in regular NGO newsletters or magazines. Some of these forums take the form of training sessions, for instance to teach NGO activists the details of individuals' rights vis-à-vis the police and what to do in case of arrest. However, with a few exceptions (such as through NGOs' working with victims of domestic violence, who help other women deal with the police and legal system), this information rarely trickles down to the public through follow-up public training sessions or forums.

In general, then, the reach of NGOs' research, publications and forums is limited. It is generally the same core group of activists who attend the forums or read the newsletters. The mass public hears of few NGO campaigns, let alone findings, given that the government-controlled mainstream mass media carry minimal (and seldom positive) coverage of advocacy-related NGO activities and that police permits for large forums are hard to get – let alone large audiences, since many Malaysians would be afraid to attend such 'subversive' activities. NGOs still routinely hold press conferences and issue endless press statements, though, to publicise their findings or complaints. However, coverage by opposition parties', NGOs' or other alternative publications, or even foreign media, is often more comprehensive than that of the mainstream local media.

The campaign to abolish the ISA

Probably the most prominent and persistent human rights campaign among NGOs has been the effort to abolish the Internal Security Act (ISA) and other laws permitting detention without trial. The anti-ISA campaign has persisted for years, though recently it has gained momentum and a higher profile through the use of the ISA against former Deputy Prime Minister Anwar Ibrahim and other Reformasi figures, including at least eighteen friends or supporters of Anwar in 1998. Other much-publicised applications of the ISA in 1998 were the use of the law against three individuals charged with spreading rumours over the internet of rioting in the Chow Kit area of Kuala Lumpur and the detention of a lorry driver for allegedly smuggling in and harbouring illegal immigrants. While NGOs' slogans specify the ISA, the campaign actually lumps together a set of laws, including the Emergency (Public Order and Prevention of Crime) Ordinance 1969 (POPO) and the Dangerous Drugs (Special Preventive Measures) Act 1985 (DDA).[10]

The ISA, promulgated in 1960 on the model of a prior colonial law, was initially designed as an anti-communist tool. Despite the demise of the Malaysian Communist Party – the last vestigial forces surrendered in the early 1980s – the ISA has never been repealed and is now used against a range of political and social dissidents and wrongdoers even when other, less controversial laws apply to the act in question. The law 'allows up to sixty days of solitary confinement, during which detainees are subjected to interminable interrogation and mental torture'. Several detainees over the years have also alleged physical torture by the police, though none of the officers involved has been tried (Kua 1998b: 2). The ISA was used extensively in the 1960s against opposition politicians, especially from the Labour Party and PRM, then in the 1970s onwards to deflect attention from crises within UMNO with the spectre of 'racial antagonism'. By July 1993, the ISA had been used in 9,542 arrests and detentions, the DDA in 3,195 and POPO in 797 (Kua 1998b: 2). As of 31 December 1997, 223 individuals were still detained under the ISA, 171 of them for criminal offences such as forging passports or identity cards (SUARAM 1998: 219–20).

POPO was enacted after the May 1969 racial riots and subsequent declaration of emergency. The law allows the Minister of Home Affairs to detain any individual for up to two years without trial to protect public order or to suppress or prevent violence. Used routinely against people suspected of criminal activity (447 times in 1995 and 56 times in 1996), POPO was also applied in 1994 against two men assisting workers in a plantation labour dispute (SUARAM 1998: 220–1).

As for the DDA, this law was passed in 1985 to allow the detention of alleged drug traffickers whom the police had insufficient evidence to convict under existing legislation. Thousands have been detained under the DDA so far; 1,081 were arrested in 1997 alone. That the law is ineffective even as a deterrent is implied by the fact that drug use and trafficking have continued to rise in recent years (SUARAM 1998: 221–2).

The coalitions formed over the years against detention without trial have been basically reactive, coming in the wake of the ISA's sporadic enforcement and with only low-level activism in between outbursts. The most recent spate of activism (late 1998 to mid-1999) was no exception, having been sparked by the September 1998 ISA detention of Anwar Ibrahim and a number of his supporters. NGOs have provided any number of reasons to oppose the ISA: it violates all major religions' standards of justice, it contravenes a range of international conventions, and it is used when other laws more supportive of the rights of the accused could be used instead. The other Acts also allowing incarceration without trial are equally condemnable but draw less attention. The campaigns that form are around the ISA, with repeal of these other Acts as tangential demands.

The anti-ISA campaigns merit attention because they highlight the inefficacy of so much human rights agitation in Malaysia. A broad array of groups come together for a short time, draw up some demands, issue some press statements and maybe hold a few forums or workshops. Soon, interest and motivation wane and the campaign tapers off. Given that the groups involved have disparate primary goals and very different philosophical bases, sustaining momentum and cooperation is difficult, despite the (often disorganised) efforts of a few dedicated human rights groups, particularly SUARAM.

In short, the government has not responded to the demands of all these groups to abolish the ISA because it does not really need to do so. The ISA attracts widespread ire only when it is used against a broad spectrum of individuals – so that people from a range of racial and other communities feel at risk – and then only for a relatively short time.[11] Furthermore, the use of the ISA seems to evoke more fear than anger. Worried that the Act will be used against them, most people avoid getting involved or getting too deeply and openly entangled in anti-ISA activism just at the times when popular indignation may be easiest to rally. Indeed, activist and former ISA detainee Kua Kia Soong alleges (1997: 9), 'Judging by the marked decrease in the number of activists in human rights work compared to the pre-Operasi Lalang days, it is clear that the ISA has played a part in deterring Malaysian dissidents.' In light of Reformasi activism, two UMNO backbenchers plus BN component party Gerakan indicated that the ISA merits review – a process potentially facilitated by the new NHRC, however flawed – but the Act remains unaffected to date.

While intimidation of protesters and the lack of positive response to popular activism are key components of the government's campaign against anti-ISA activists, ideological manipulation plays an equally significant role. Warnings that, without the ISA, the government may not be able to quell racial antagonism or the nefarious activities of various groups remain highly effective – the spectre of the May 1969 race riots still carries a lot of clout, convincing many would-be activists that the government should not eliminate all its strong enforcement powers in case they are needed again someday. Given this perception that a strong government is necessary in a multiracial society, popular support for the ISA remains quite high, even despite recent anti-ISA propaganda from Reformasi activists. If the government does decide eventually to repeal or at least review the ISA and/or POPO and the DDA, it will be on its own schedule and probably for its own advantage, whether to rally electoral support or to gain the approbation of the often-condemnatory international community.

Strengths and weaknesses of the human rights movement

The progress of the campaigns against the ISA suggests the strengths of human rights groups' short-term networking and collaboration but also the fundamental weakness of civil society vis-à-vis the state. Despite protracted, broad-based advocacy efforts, the ISA and other repressive legislation remain in force. In fact, NGOs can claim very few victories from the past 25 years of human rights activism: domestic violence legislation and amendments or additions to other laws regarding rape, prostitution and the like, though these issues are still popularly discussed in terms of 'women's issues' rather than as 'human rights'; retraction of the most atrocious clauses in the 1981 amendments to the Societies Act and the toning down of the 1986 amendments to the OSA; the eventual condemnation and withdrawal of a dangerous polluter in the Asian Rare Earth case (treated more as an 'environmental' than a 'human rights' issue); and a few other relatively small gains.

On the contrary, periods of heightened activism often achieve the opposite of what NGOs sought, with the government toughening the laws (the Societies Act, Police Act, UUCA, OSA, laws relating to the *orang asli* and indigenous peoples of Sabah and Sarawak, etc.) to forestall future campaigns. At the same time, the mass media portray NGOs in a consistently negative light, despite the fact that a fair number of those much-maligned groups, especially consumers', environmental and women's groups, work with several government ministries in designing environmental policy, consumer protection guidelines, occupational health and safety regulations, and so on.

The human rights movement's strength lies in component NGOs' ability to define an objective in terms of human rights discourse and then organise a broad coalition to tackle the issue at hand. A secretariat may form, small groups of concerned individuals from different groups may hold strategy sessions and delegate tasks then report back to their organisations, and some follow-up – whether a forum, a petition, a research project or a grant proposal – may result. Eventually, though, despite initial enthusiasm from various quarters, these coalitions invariably result in a small core group of individuals doing all the work. Attendance at planning or work sessions for these coalitions is rarely high, even for high-profile campaigns. The formation of more 'official' networks such as Gerak or Gagasan facilitates more sustained cooperation, but those alliances could not sustain their momentum. While the ties among NGOs involved in Gerak and Gagasan were undoubtedly fortified by the experience, especially between Islamic and secular organisations, the process of negotiations and planning soon mostly settled back into the usual small-group format.

Fundamentally, these coalitions are designed to be shallow, ad hoc and short term. Hence, while some lessons may be drawn from past experiences and some key activists may grow accustomed to working with one another, long-term vision is lacking. Each campaign is treated as a discrete entity rather than as part of a long-range, multifaceted project for radical alteration of the status quo. As long-time social activist Nasir Hashim argues, while Malaysian NGOs have sometimes been successful in raising people's consciousness of rights and working with them to face challenges, these NGOs are addressing the symptoms rather than the root causes of the people's problems in not considering the sociopolitical order as a whole (Mohd. Nasir 1997: 17).

Moreover, at the root of the weakness of the more extensive coalitions, in particular – ones including both religious and secular organisations – is the lack of any convincing attempt to forge a common understanding of the justification for human rights or to develop a long-term joint plan. Those groups who join in are welcomed, but insufficient effort is made to encourage new voices to engage in the coalition, meaning that Islamic NGOs form their own coalitions while the secular NGOs form theirs and seldom do the twain meet. Collaboration between these two sectors encourages supporters of the diverse groups to trust one another, promotes multiracial understanding on various levels and adds legitimacy to the campaign; the Islamic NGOs involved cannot be attacked as too exclusive or Malay-centric, while the secular NGOs cannot be dismissed as overly academic or just non-representative groups of western-educated, middle-class non-Malays. Regardless, issues of language, religion and habit, as well as the fact that collaborative long-term strategising simply has not yet occurred, continue to prevent maintenance of this sort of enduring, extensive coalition.

These organisational and motivational weaknesses are not unique to Malaysian human rights organisations but are common to many social movements, particularly in places where the personal costs and risks of organising and activism are high. The lack of success of campaigns so far, scant and generally negative media coverage of NGOs, and legal structures that discourage involvement in NGO activities render the lack of mass-based, sustainable support for human rights activism unsurprising. This final factor should not be under-estimated. Fear dissuades even genuinely committed individuals from taking action and particularly from assuming visible positions of leadership within campaigns. So do the government's periodic entrées towards greater co-operation (read, co-optation) of particular NGOs or activists. While working *with* the government for social reform seems a tempting option, under the current political order such collaboration may complement but cannot substitute for civil society agitation and advocacy work.

Considering the odds, then, it is remarkable that Malaysian human rights organisations have come as far as they have. Importantly, particularly with Reformasi, a new generation of younger activists, primarily students or recent graduates, is getting involved. Many of these individuals may lose their motivation as time passes and the excitement of Anwar's case and the maiden contest of the opposition Barisan Alternatif dies down. Those who remain, though, can rejuvenate the movement. Furthermore, over the course of events, a much larger segment of the general population has been exposed to NGOs' perspectives through the internet, proliferating alternative media, opposition politics or personal experience in Reformasi events, and has become sympathetic to NGOs' demands. Though generally dormant, these mass supporters may be more easily mobilised for the next big campaign – basic lack of public awareness of human rights issues and NGOs' efforts has been a key reason for the limited impact of NGOs' campaigns to date. These conscientised individuals will no doubt remain critical of what they read and hear, requiring that the government pay attention, as even critics are voters.

In short, the Malaysian human rights movement has few substantial, concrete gains to show for its efforts, but it has made small advances and holds promise for the future. To be more effective, activists within the movement need to spend more time on self-assessment, evaluating past campaigns to see which tactics made an impact and which expended resources with little effect. With long-term vision and creative strategising, a highly sympathetic international regime, plus a new crop of young activists hopefully sufficiently motivated to join the fray, the human rights movement could strengthen itself for greater success in years to come. However, restrictive legislation, a cowed mass media and the perhaps over-stated personal risks of participation will continue to present hurdles for NGOs in their attempts to strengthen and protect human rights in Malaysia.

7 Non-governmental organisations in Sarawak[1]

Fadzilah Majid Cooke

Because of recently enhanced interest in good governance and civil society, as well as disenchantment with states in general and particularly with developing states and those in transition (Bresser Pereira 1993), non-governmental organisations (NGOs) have been given centre stage. Often the strength of civil society is measured in terms of the depth and breadth of the NGO movement. In Malaysia, in conjunction with the perceived authoritarian tendencies of the state, the space for civil society (and the room for NGOs to manouevre) is considered limited, especially when compared to developments currently taking place in other Southeast Asian states such as Indonesia (Eldridge 1996; Eccleston 1996; Jesudason 1996). This view is from a state-centred perspective and suggests that the formation of civil society is a result of path-dependent historical legacies linked to the nature of the formation of colonial or post-colonial states. It is also a view that accords strength to civil society only when there is a dense network of formal organisations that interact with or have an impact on state behaviour but at the same time remain separate from the state (Chazan 1991: 235, cited in Hirschmann 1998: 235). This paper argues that NGO activism does not become politically relevant only when it intersects with state behaviour. Rather, its political character consists in the ability to use the cultural, social and economic networks within and beyond nation-states to alter and shape widespread behaviour and expand the political imagination (Wapner 1996: 6–10). The paper draws attention to political strategy and leadership and gives emphasis to consciousness, action and socially constructed collective identities to explain how people overcome the obstacles to joint action.

In conjunction with the interest in NGOs, and following from the work of Robert Putnam, recent work on social capital leads to optimistic expectations about the potential for democratisation from below (Bebbington 1996; Evans 1996; Fox 1996). One major issue that emanates from the interest in social capital is the possibility that civil society could be strengthened through the efforts of non-state actors due to their involvement in a dense network of civic engagement even in less than democratic regimes (Fox 1996; but see Leach, Mearns and Scoones 1999). This development has led to interest in evaluating NGO capacity, scaling up efforts of organisations and enhancing state–society synergy over time. Very often, scaling up efforts are made through contingent factors, through NGOs' attempts to link up with 'reformist' elements in the state bureaucracy (Fox 1996) or the creation of political opportunity structures (Tarrow 1989). Stemming from an assumption that multiple involvement necessarily promotes mutual assistance, scaling up and state–society links appear largely unproblematic. By contrast, we argue that pluralism in civil society does not necessarily promote democracy. Civil society is as much riddled with class interests and gender and ethnic divisions as the state sector, so the 'civic community' that Putnam maintains is essential for the strengthening of civil society may not emerge despite its plurality (Fatton 1995).

However, drawing from recent interest in Albert Hirschman's work on political cycles (Fox 1996; Bresser Pereira 1993), this chapter points to the possibility of building new initiatives based on the residual remains of past failures despite a history of retaliatory repression. It pays some attention to NGOs' scaling-up activities, but of greater interest is the process by which organisations mobilise individual and group aspirations, interact (that is co-operate, compete, conflict and build tolerance) with each other, and relate to the state over time despite repression.

Given the heterogeneity of the Sarawak NGO movement, this chapter concentrates on those groups whose main concerns are with land, livelihood and environmental issues in northern Sarawak. By nature of their orientation, these NGOs work closely with village groups. Many of their activities are, by and large, linked to grassroots concerns. However, working within the confines of the state and market, NGOs have found it more viable to push for certain agendas than others. This chapter concentrates on two major types of NGO activity: leadership training and awareness raising.[1]

The context of NGO activity in the post-logging era in Sarawak

According to the International Tropical Timber Organisation (1990), by the year 2001 most old growth forest in Sarawak would have been logged. Logging companies are well prepared for this moment as they began looking for logging opportunities in other parts of the world at least a decade ago.[2] In the 1980s, logging was basically carried out on land claimed to be state land, although this has been disputed in some areas by native peoples who claim ownership through customary rights (Lian, 1993). Native opposition to logging did not arise from their conservatism or alleged mystical attachment to the land but from conflicting interpretations of 'rights' arising from anomalies in the current mix of land and forestry legislation as well as policy (discourses and practices) that culminated in what they perceived as a disregard of their existing rights and ownership claims to the land (Majid Cooke 1999a). Nevertheless, opposition to logging was not as universal as it was made out to be (Brosius 1997; Majid Cooke 1999b).

NGOs working at the grassroots level in the post-logging era operate in the context of continued widespread socioeconomic and cultural change experienced by the Dayak[3] communities they work with, resulting from an ideology of developmentalism that equates notions of a 'modern' economy with carrying out policy practices on a large-scale. This is not a new experience; it is the continuation of the same philosophical underpinning that brought large-scale logging in earlier decades. In the 1990s and continuing into the new century, large-scale projects have been and will be given priority by the state, through renewed emphasis on agricultural (oil palm and pulp and paper) plantations and dam construction.

In the post-logging era, the *konsep baru* (new concept) of land development specifically targets native customary land. Such land, when converted into large-scale plantations, is to be managed in trust by government land development agencies in joint venture with corporations selected by the government (Ministry of Land Development Sarawak 1997: 22–33). In return for their land, Dayak groups will be awarded a 30 per cent share in the joint venture company. In addition, rural communities are to be given an upfront payment equivalent to 40 per cent of the land's value, out of which 30 per cent will be invested for them in a unit trust and 10 per cent given to them in cash (Ministry of Land Development, Sarawak 1997: 22–32). The land will form part of a land bank to be managed for 60 years by way of a provisional lease given to the joint venture company, at the end of which the communities will have the choice either to opt out of their joint venture arrangement or negotiate for its continuation. Depending on the kinds of skill they have, communities may or may not be employed on the plantations or benefit from the 'spin-off' effects anticipated in the form of contract or subcontracting opportunities that are expected to present themselves, such as in agricultural supplies, construction or maintenance.

An evaluation of *konsep baru* ought to be the subject of another paper.[4] It is useful to note, however, that although promoted as a new concept, this approach to land development actually had its beginnings in the 1980s with urban land development by the government Land Conservation and Development Authority, LCDA (Cramb and Wills 1990). When used in rural areas, the scheme had to be temporarily pushed to the background because of resistance from native populations to various ambiguities, including their status of being, on the one hand, decision-makers (in their role as shareholders) and, on the other, wage labourers on the plantations. Major uncertainty was associated with relinquishing personal and tangible links with the land in favour of an abstract one in the form of shareholding (Cramb and Wills 1990: 356).

In rural Sarawak, farmers have frequently attempted to manage engagement with the state and market through cash crop production with as minimal disruption to subsistence activities as possible and while maintaining relative autonomy. If the *konsep baru* gets into full swing, this balance may tip in new directions, requiring farmers to try new forms of engagement involving state and market. Many farmers are trying to make sense of these new relationships. Groups such as some Iban farmers in Ulu Teru (Baram) are embracing plantation agriculture wholeheartedly. However, many are also caught unprepared as their *menoa* (territorial boundaries) are zoned for development (*sudah kena projek* – hit by development projects – in the local parlance). Old anxieties over ownership and stewardship have resurfaced and new additional anxieties have developed. In response to these anxieties, there are government plans to provide certificates of ownership (not titles) to landowning individuals or families. The granting of certificates is seen as a positive step by some communities but is viewed by those experiencing intra-family or intra-longhouse disputes over land ownership as a catalyst for even greater discord if the certificates are issued prior to resolution of pre-existing conflicting claims within communities (field notes, May 2000). Underlying these anxieties, of course, is angst brought about by the developmentalist agenda.

Inserting the social in development

Development in Sarawak, as in the peninsula, is designed not only towards physical or structural change, but towards cultural transformation as well. Seen in this perspective, the *konsep baru* is one aspect of the larger process of converting rural populations into 'modern', competitive groups with industrial values and greater direct involvement in wage labour (which formerly was primarily through participation in the timber industry) and land and share ownership.

Development narratives in Sarawak emphasise the conservatism of rural Dayak towards change. Officials and planners attribute Dayak selectiveness in embracing development projects to traditionalism or anti-developmentalism. Under the *konsep baru*, native peoples are urged to become 'modern'. Modernity is contrasted with conservatism and this duality is seen as seeping through every level of social life. But it is the mental attitudes of that life that officials want to change. 'A radical mental revolution is required to effect a paradigm shift in the attitudes and perceptions of landowners towards developing NCR [native customary rights land]' (Ministry of Land Development, Sarawak, 1997: 17). Thus, for Dayak to become 'modern', they must see land as a commodity or an economic asset to be traded, not treated as an heirloom or the only form of wealth. Individuals must be prepared to take risks, share the cost of development (against being overly dependent on government assistance), and choose better alternatives for land use instead of keeping land in its 'original' state (Ministry of Land Development, Sarawak, 1997: 17–18).

Nevertheless, because development is aimed at the cultural realm (not only the physical or economic level), contestation is possible. Careful field research by agricultural and social scientists suggests Dayak willingness to experiment in the cash economy with or without government assistance, balancing issues of land, labour power and concomitant returns with the need to maintain the means of subsistence. But they also point out that what rural farmers value most is ownership of land and work autonomy (Cramb 1989a and 1989b; Lian 1987; Chin 1985). A careful analysis of land tenure arrangements of the communities he worked with led Cramb to conclude that Iban land tenure institutions, far from being primitive or backward, have been successful in ensuring orderly household and community access rights without sacrificing productive efficiency.

There is an affinity between the claims of agricultural and social scientists and those of NGOs. Unlike their international counterparts, who essentialise images of native peoples (Brosius 1999), at times with instrumental support from the latter, Sarawak NGOs tend to emphasise their diversity and complexity (Majid Cooke 1999a: 148–57). Precisely because of the diversity and complexity of Dayak identity/ies, NGOs' efforts at emphasising the commonality of experience across communities have their limits, as do efforts at scaling up in general. Because of well-defined ethnic identities (Welyne 1999), maintenance of local solidarities may not be an easy task and could be made more difficult by the mediation of class interests. Scaling up of horizontal associations may be necessary to offset the power of elites, but these are precisely the processes that are often targeted for repression.

Tan Chee Beng (1997) captures well the effects of ethnicity, class and gender on 'communal associations'. Dayak communal associations were formed from as early as before the Second World War and many more during the logging decades of the 1970s and 1980s. Most were formed with the expressed aim of securing a fairer share of the country's wealth as well as to ensure that rural communities are not left behind in political and economic development. However, the effectiveness of these associations varies depending not only on leadership qualities, but more importantly on the viability of their approach in their dealings with the state. For example, associations that were concerned mainly with issues of education and 'cultural' promotion (for example, of dance or handicrafts) were more likely to be heard than those that were critical of the government logging policy (Tan 1997: 272–77). Associations that have survived in the long run are ones that are patronised by political elites and have received government and non-governmental financial backing. Some associations formed along ethnic lines were often internally divided, reflecting differences in occupational and other forms of inherited social standing. Thus, in the 1980s among the Kayan, the groups of *maren* (aristocrat) and *panyin* (commoners) were opposed to each other in their approaches to logging and in their dealings with the state (Tan 1997: 272).

This form of opposition remains today, but with some added complexity. The state and market have provided new avenues for *maren*. Groups of *maren* are actively involved in urban economic activities and in politics beyond the village. Most no longer rely for their status on *panyin* support or labour, but remain in control because of ideology. Many *maren* have become political or administrative leaders, either through the election process or by state appointment. Those who remain in rural economies are often elected or appointed to local leadership positions but are not necessarily completely trusted (field notes, May 2000). *Panyin* groups have attempted to form associations of their own and take pains to prove that they, too, can lead and survive (field interviews, June 2000). This strategy is because electing *maren* to leadership positions may prove to many *panyin* to be a familiar way of doing things, reinforced by the former as 'custom'.

Beyond the Kayan and in general, urban-based associations were often patronised by prominent officials. Because they were supported largely by middle class professionals, especially teachers and public servants, these groups were unable to represent rural interests successfully.

On the other hand, associations based in very small rural towns, like the Persatuan Kelabit Baram and the Sarawak Berawan Association, were not successful in attracting support or funding from influential leaders (Tan 1997: 276). Clearly, although there is no shortage of formal associations in Sarawak's civil society, the formation of a 'civic community' is not automatic.

Similarly, in the late 1980s and early 1990s, some NGO-linked individuals aligned themselves with opposition political parties under the Parti Bansa Dayak Sarawak (PBDS) umbrella. PBDS brought together a range of different interests, including large segments who wanted to have a better share of the power and wealth of the existing regimes and who were disenchanted with the Sarawak National Party (SNAP). There were also those who were concerned with the issues of land and disproportionate distribution of wealth affecting the Dayak (Jayum Jawan 1993). Needing to mobilise civil society, these segments drew some members from the non-governmental sector but were uncomfortable when threatened with withdrawal of state sources of patronage (Tan 1997). When the party did not perform well in the 1991 elections, many elements in PBDS retreated from their positions and were not averse to sharing power once again with political parties in government by returning to the government fold. This was another moment when scaling up did not strengthen civil society.

Other avenues for scaling up were explored in the 1980s. Some NGOs working at the grassroots developed both national and international ties. For developing international links, individuals risk the prospect of being labelled 'traitors' to the nation (*New Straits Times*, 25 February 1992; *Japan Times*, 21 November 1990) or even 'communists' or 'terrorists' (*Sarawak Tribune*, 16 June 1991). Similarly, links with national NGOs, if too overt, may draw unnecessary attention to the project at hand and the actual severing of ties, as Sarawak exercises surveillance over entry from the peninsula. Nationally, within the NGO community itself there was tension over priorities and strategies. In the case of controversy over the Bakun Dam, fearing the very real possibility of displacement (a process that will be discussed later), NGOs in Sarawak and from the peninsula differed over the best avenue to pursue (field interviews, October 1999). The Sarawak NGOs, with backing from a few others in the peninsula, wanted to mount legal proceedings over the legality of the companies and government's proceeding with the dam. The Coalition of Concerned NGOs Against the Bakun Dam (comprised mostly of peninsula-based groups) preferred direct action, contesting the findings of the Environmental Impact Assessment in court and generally drawing attention to the abuses incurred during the relocation process

(Coalition of Concerned NGOs 1999). Both strategies were pursued with limited results. Relocation of native communities proceeded despite plans being made to reduce the capacity of the dam.

Weiss in Chapter 6 points out that Operation Lalang of 1987 marked a massive crackdown on civil protest with the passage of the Internal Security Act, characterised by the arrest of social activists, opposition party politicians, environmentalists and other concerned groups. That arrests during Operation Lalang included social activists and others from East Malaysia, including Sarawak, is not well known, or even if noted at the time, was soon forgotten.

In Sarawak, the 1987 arrests were followed by amendments to forest and land legislation that made it difficult for native peoples to register protest (Majid Cooke 1999b). The 1980s also saw a well-orchestrated governmental campaign of countering opposition through discursive displacement. Broadening the concern over destructive (largely unsupervised) large-scale logging to issues of forest destruction in forests other than tropical ones (such as temperate ones in northern countries), while simultaneously narrowing the issue of sustainability by excluding concerns over cultural diversity (e.g. of Dayak peoples in general and the Penan in particular), also caused the agenda of forest destruction and native rights to lose momentum overseas (Brosius 1999). Such displacement blunts the moral claims of native peoples to environmental and livelihood security.

The process of displacement, while subtle, was accompanied by more overt means of economic marginalisation. In accordance with the generalised policy of giving priority to industry over local subsistence needs, stemming from an ideology of conceiving of native cultural practices as 'primitive', native opposition to logging was met with increased police power (Majid Cooke 1999b). The 1987 amendment (90B) to the Sarawak Forest Ordinance made blockading of logging roads illegal and entitled the state to use police power against such activity. A further amendment in 1993 presumed guilty anyone found or arrested in an area where barricades have been set up, even if he or she does not participate in the blockade. The option to appeal for federal government intervention is not a viable one, because in the context of Malaysia's federalism, Sarawak has effective control over land issues (Majid Cooke 1999a).

It might be understandable, therefore, if the NGO movement in Sarawak is seen as having lost momentum. Most Sarawak NGOs today run on a shoestring budget and have only four or five employees. However, they take on contract staff as the occasion demands and can rely on 'contact persons' and volunteers in the villages with which they work. What activists are doing now corresponds with what has been described of activism elsewhere, suggesting that repression does not totally extinguish 'social energy' (Hirschmann 1984: 42–3, cited in Fox 1996: 1090–1).

NGOs and social capital

That civil society can strengthen despite repression has led to interest in the phenomenon of social capital. Important for mapping the potential of civil society in these instances is the key issue of how much societal political residue is left after each window of opportunity closes, and how it can be sustained until the next one opens. Given the perception among many rural groups that avenues for redress might be closed to them (interviews, October 1999), they need to rely on their own organisational activities. NGOs respond to this need and carry it further. The process is incomplete but it is far from dead. We will focus on two major forms of NGO activities: leadership training and the conscientisation of communities.

Many individuals involved in the NGO movement have direct experience of environmental degradation and are aware of the state's real capacity to deliver or withhold development goods at the whim of those in power. It is not that native rights advocates are unaware of the heavy hand of the state machinery, as maintained by Leigh (1998), but it is that very awareness that propels them. 'We know the government machinery is powerful, but we have to do something. We win sometimes, no matter how small, at least it is something. Otherwise the government can do anything it wants' (field interview, October 1999). Indeed, Sawarak NGOs have made a truly significant impact in terms of consciousness raising and grassroots capacity building, despite their more limited influence on state policy making.

Given the confines of strict surveillance, NGO leadership must devise ways of leading people beyond the fear threshold. The quality of this leadership varies but its overall effect lies in building confidence, as is seen in the statement of an NGO worker from one organisation:

> We only go where we are invited, mostly where people have problems with land. The leaders in this organisation inspire me. They have worked on these issues for a long time, despite persecution. They told me that we must treat those who are against us in the same way as those who seek our help. They say that in the long term, if we are careful about our aims, language and behaviour, even our enemies will know who we are.
>
> (field interview, September 1999)

Contrary to popular belief about the middle class make-up of NGOs, since the late 1990s, many who provide crucial support for urban organisations have actually been young rural villagers who experienced earlier repression. The life histories of four workers provide an illustration.[5] Three of the four NGO members, like most NGO community development workers, are relatively young (between 20 and 35 years old) and are from longhouses that have a history of contact with the state through 'development' projects.

John

John, a Kayan, came from one of the many longhouses that blockaded logging roads during the tumultuous period of the 1980s (Brosius 1999, 1997; Majid Cooke 1999b). At that time, 42 people from his longhouse were imprisoned. The imprisonment was made against a background of environmental degradation, internal splits within the longhouse community, confusion and frustration, with signs of leaders' being persuaded to side with the logging companies. In the post-logging era, the divisions within longhouse communities have intensified, as history repeats itself with the introduction of new development schemes, this time of oil palm plantations on NCR land. Because the land is hemmed in by plantations so that it now provides fewer opportunities for involvement in the cash economy, and partly because of the lure of city life, many young people have left John's longhouse. However, John feels he cannot go away. He was inspired by the strength of the older people who went to jail, one of whom was his own father. He also feels that he has a responsibility towards the young. He is actively involved in his longhouse's reforestation and livelihood project.

> I have been working with my community all this while, and I feel I cannot stop now. I hope that by replanting native species, such as *engkabang* or *kapur*, 30 per cent or more of the forest will grow back, so that we can have room for our farms and also room for the forest . . . We also want to expand our efforts to assist other communities. It is important to have work for the youth, so they will come back. Many young people are influenced by modern lifestyles. Farming is often very hard for them. If they don't want to farm, then who will take over the farming when the older people pass on? That is why we try so hard to modernise the farming methods . . ., so it can be easier and more profitable.

John works in town but has an arrangement for returning to his longhouse for several months of the year to work on his farm. He was, among other things, deeply engrossed in writing his understanding of the struggle that his longhouse has been involved in, first against logging and now against oil palm plantation companies.

Christina

A woman in her early twenties, Christina is new to the non-government movement. By the standards of her community, she is relatively well educated, having graduated from a technical college, the Institute Teknologi Mara (now a university). Her decision to work with the NGO movement was influenced by many factors. Working with a company that was using her community's land for a pulp and paper plantation, she experienced tremendous stress when the community became engaged in the process of negotiating appropriate compensation from the company for using its land without permission. She could not understand what she summarised as the company's reluctance to attend to the claims and grievances of the affected longhouses in her area because, after all, it is 'our land' that has been encroached upon.

As the negotiations for compensation intensified, she was torn between wanting to be the eyes and ears of her people, and being pressured by the company to convince her people to co-operate. When negotiations with the company broke down in 1998 and over 200 longhouse residents in her area decided to stage a blockade, things became unbearable for her. She resigned from her job but could not find employment for many months. She found a way out by working for the NGO that her longhouse community had contacted, helping them with their court case against the company and the government, which had given the company a provisional lease that covered part of their land.

Saweng

As an Iban who left high school to work as a labourer in the construction industry, Saweng witnessed police brutality exercised on fellow villagers when he was home visiting his family at the end of 1997. He came from a longhouse about 100 miles inland from Miri which was trying to negotiate with the plantation company that was trying to clear their land for oil palm. Most neighbouring longhouses had already given their permission to the company because they were scared to take action. According to Saweng: 'Mereka kata kalau kamu lawan, sampai kelapa sawit berbuah baru kamu keluar jel. It sebab mereka semua takut'. ('They say if we resist, you will all be sent to jail and will be released only when the oil palm bear fruit. That is why they were all afraid.') With that kind of intimidation, some households in his own longhouse wanted to allow the companies in. However, the Tuai Rumah (headman) of Saweng's longhouse was adamant about not allowing any company to work on their land.

At the time of this interview, Saweng's anger at the brutal treatment of his longhouse by the authorities still simmered. One man had been killed and three others wounded in an encounter with the police. Previously, the longhouse residents had made several attempts to report their problem to the police, but each time they were either ignored or sent away (field interviews, October 1999). On the other hand, the plantation company was under the impression that because it had been granted a provisional lease by the Land and Survey Department, it had the right of way. Moreover, since neighbouring longhouses had agreed to have their land converted to plantations, the company did not pay heed to the complaints of one longhouse about damage to its crops and livelihood. Longhouse residents became more despairing as clearing work came closer and finally encroached on their farms and gardens. When their many attempts to file police reports and to seek meetings with company representatives failed, they confiscated three bulldozers as a way of preventing further encroachment and as a negotiation strategy. One fatal afternoon, police were sent in and bloodshed ensued. That was the turning point for Saweng; he left his village and joined an NGO. His father had, in any case, volunteered for him to work with the organisation. For the first three months he was not paid for his effort. He observed and learned:

> I was inexperienced and scared to do this kind of work, I did not know how to communicate well with village people. But the senior people encouraged me to try. We are not against development, it is just that this particular model for developing native land is not good for the people. Some people think they get shares in the joint venture and they can get rich. But we can see who benefits... I have learnt a lot about our land laws. Now I am not afraid.

Saweng's longhouse has filed an application in court to stop the oil palm plantation companies (most of which are from peninsular Malaysia) from working within the boundaries of their customary land. Also named as defendants were the state government and the land development authority. After an initial hearing in 1998, the Tuai Rumah was arrested. When arrested he sought legal help through NGOs.

Joseph

Joseph is one of those senior people referred to by Saweng who had not stopped their community development work since the 1980s. During the government crackdown in 1987, he escaped arrest because he was in hospital with an illness. He feels that the court system is used by native peoples because they have tried many avenues, from direct action to writing memoranda to elected and government officials, but have received very little response.[6] Joseph sees the challenge facing the people as twofold. First, it is about expanding legal inferences regarding territorial boundaries. Given that the Sarawak Land Code provides for six different ways of native customary ownership, one of which is through occupation, the idea is to work on expanding the notion of 'occupation' to include land left fallow or previously used by ancestors or the communities in question as burial sites and as collecting and hunting grounds. This is a long, drawn-out process. Second, when people make the case in court that rights have been breached, they are challenging the basis on which the state has the authority to do so. For Joseph, an important task lies in linking communities together, to provide moral support and to lead people through the fear threshold. According to Joseph, 'John, Christina and Saweng are employed partly as a way of keeping the spirits of their longhouses up.'

Since the 1990s, in view of past experiences of state repression, much NGO work has centred on building community confidence and self-reliance through socioeconomic development programmes, especially education. Educational activities target pre-school education in remote rural communities, such as in Penan areas, and adult paralegal education, especially on land issues (field notes, October 1999). An awareness of the law is regarded as a first step to understanding a person's rights and responsibilities as a Dayak and as a citizen. Indirectly, rudimentary awareness of land legislation has also promoted a burgeoning interest in land boundaries and territories, which has led to much of the community energy's being put into community mapping.

According to Peluso (1995), the value of 'counter-mapping' undertaken by communities lies in the objective of providing alternative maps to contest official ones which, in the context of the political economy of forest resource use, have consistently succeeded in excluding many local claims to resources. I discuss elsewhere my contention that maps mean a whole lot more in terms of culture and identity.[7] In brief, those who are involved in counter-mapping may find new meaning through participation. 'I didn't know we could do our own mapping. I thought only the Land and Survey Department could produce maps' (Bujang, field interview, October 1999). Together with helping to overcome initial fears of repression (to be discussed later), counter-mapping marks the beginnings of a special form of political education, namely finding space for extending the political imagination. In practical terms, NGOs provide the technical assistance required in counter-mapping through the use of the Geographic Positioning System (GPS).

The resources the NGOs provide are largely moral and only to a small extent material. Nevertheless, even meagre material resources appear abundant by the standards of rural society. Operating on restricted budgets, NGOs provide assistance with processing legal cases and, when communities cannot, come up with last-minute posting of bonds to prevent or get individuals out of remand. Also, NGOs' small office spaces form informal community meeting places for planning new strategies of coping with the full impact of the law.

NGOs insist, however, that their involvement is minimal, and that communities themselves are responsible for their own decisions. To make their claims stick in the policy realm, Dayak groups will have to agree among themselves that they have a moral and political right to control their own resources. The assertion of these rights will have to be preceded by the realisation that they do indeed have such moral and political rights, followed by the exercise of practical control over their territorial boundaries. Such control has so far been discouraged because of the official policy of favouring resource extraction by more organised sectors of society, ostensibly for the development of the larger community.

The vigilance that some rural communities have shown in exercising some form of control over their territory ought to be seen in this larger context. An initial examination of the current cases filed in court suggest that self-organisation is first and foremost a defence of *menoa*. Nested in this larger defence of livelihood is the concern for damage to the environment.

One area of NGO activity that is not evident without some sensitivity for politics beyond state or institutional complexities, but which is nevertheless important for social mobilisation, lies in the efforts to change communities' perception of their problems. NGOs provide organisational skills to bring different communities together to share their individual problems and experiences, which is only a step away from viewing individual problems as generalised issues. The annual *Bujang Berani* (Warriors' Day) celebration is one way by which Dayak people get together to gain strength from one another. The arrest of 42 Kayan men and women from Uma Bawang in October 1987 is now celebrated annually on this day. The ceremony rotates among different districts and longhouses to promote community spirit through participation in an event presented as a landmark. At these celebrations, the fact that after over ten years of struggle, the Kayan were awarded compensation for illegal arrests is always highlighted (field notes, October 1999). 'We hope we can be as strong as our Kayan brothers' (an Iban, 26 October 1999). Given the existence of strong ethnic boundaries, that Iban or Bidayuh could look for strength to a Kayan group suggests the possibility of co-operative effort through an awareness of shared experience.

Aside from Warriors' Day, at numerous small longhouse gatherings in northern Sarawak (numerous by reason of having to face so many legal problems), communities often encourage each other by talking about their experiences. The themes vary but a commonality is often found as they talk about a defence of *menoa* (*mempertahankan hak kita, tanah atuk nenek kita* – defend our rights, the land of our ancestors) (field notes, October 1999). An awareness of shared experience also means that what may previously have been regarded as an individual problem, experienced by individual longhouses, can now be seen as a common social problem.

Conclusion

What this chapter has shown is that the proliferation of NGOs does not necessarily promote the formation of civic consciousness. This is because civil society itself is conflict-ridden, harbours ethnic hierarchies and conflicting class visions and identities, and is subject to repression. Repression, however, works both ways. It may retard the formation of civic consciousness, but it may also speed it along, depending on political contingencies and opportunity structures. If the formation of civic consciousness is possible, despite repression, but NGO organising has not been the key factor in this development, then we need to redirect our attention away from analysis of the number of NGOs alone or their web of organisational involvement in civic activity.

In any case, in rural Sarawak, as in other parts of the world such as South Africa (see Hirschmann 1998), poor people have neither the time nor the know-how to form formal organisations, or to keep them alive once formed. According to Hirschmann (1998: 236), culturally open-ended research that takes account of a community's customary or cultural associational propensity may have as much to say about the potential strength or weakness of civil society as efforts that rely on counting a list of registered NGOs and how they link up with one another. Furthermore, 'analysis should also take account of the manner in which those (few) organizations behave, mobilize individual and group aspirations, interact (that is, cooperate, compete, conflict, influence, resolve conflicts and build tolerance) with each other, as well as relate to the state' (Hirschmann 1998: 236).

In Sarawak, those few NGOs working at the grassroots level on land, livelihood and environmental issues are experimenting with the customary potentials of communities that otherwise tend to be regarded as insignificant or obstructive to development. Given the problems with scaling up, they have few options. With regard to the *konsep baru*, they are faced with the problem of having only meagre resources for the task at hand. At the very least, they need to be proactive in monitoring the details of promises made to communities and ensuring that they are understood by them and implemented properly by land development agencies. At most, they could find a way of promoting the development of a system of automatic scanning of legislation that touches on native interests. These NGOs' efforts so far may not have had a clear impact on government policies, but their effectiveness should be seen in their provision of leadership training and political education that would not normally be available to rural populations. Hence, we must redirect our gaze beyond the state or the dynamics in the immediate surrounds of the state. In this way, we will not be taken by surprise by collective action, as many of us have been in the development of Reformasi in the peninsula.

8 The peace movement and Malaysian foreign and domestic policy

Fan Yew Teng

A peace movement has only really taken shape in Malaysia since a cluster of Malaysian non-governmental organisations (NGOs) engaged with the government regarding the Gulf War in 1991. As it developed, the movement came to promote both international human rights and peaceful means of conflict resolution as well as human rights and democracy at home. Prior to the early 1990s, NGOs had devoted little attention to foreign affairs, though their domestic agendas had begun to take shape by the 1960s and 1970s. This chapter describes the evolution and foci of Malaysia's peace movement. It begins with an overview of Malaysian foreign policy since independence to explain the lack of an externally oriented peace movement prior to the critical events of the 1990s. A description of some of the major NGOs and coalitions affiliated with the peace movement as well as the movement's most prominent issue areas and campaigns at home and abroad follows. The chapter concludes with a critical assessment of what the future holds for these NGO-based initiatives.

The evolution of Malaysian foreign policy

From 1957, when Malaya attained formal independence from Britain, through the greater part of the 1960s, when Indonesia confronted the enlarged federation of Malaysia, to the 1970s, when Tun Abdul Razak took over as prime minister from Tunku Abdul Rahman, the founding father of the nation, the country's foreign policy was mainly western-oriented. It was of course also very anti-communist, a stance influenced largely no doubt by the communist-inspired insurrection at home between 1948 and 1960, euphemistically called 'The Emergency' (Abdullah 1985).

Although the Tunku, who was also his own foreign minister for most of his period in power, was wise enough not to get entangled in the

American-created South East Asia Treaty Organisation (SEATO), he was a fervent friend of the repressive and corrupt Ngo Dinh Diem regime in South Vietnam in the 1950s and early 1960s. Consider the Tunku's confession 1975, a few years after he had stepped down from power:

> I confess it openly now – I decided to send him all the arms, war materials and equipment we used against the Communists in Malaya. When tackled at the time I denied doing so, because it was against the terms of the Geneva Agreement. Actually we had clandestinely been giving 'aid' to Vietnam since early 1958.
>
> (*Star*, 28 April 1975)

In addition, the Tunku's so-called 'Two-Chinas Policy' pleased neither the Chinese communist rulers in Beijing nor the pretenders to the throne waiting in Taiwan. Nonetheless, the Tunku did achieve a genuine foreign policy triumph when at the 1960 Commonwealth Leaders' Conference in London, he was instrumental in getting South Africa's then-white supremacist government expelled from the Commonwealth. It was a singular achievement, based more on principles than on national or sectarian interests.

Be that as it may, the Tunku's foreign policy insulated Malaysia from vast areas of the world. Malaysia hardly had any relations with large parts of Asia, Latin America and Africa. The Arab and Muslim countries hardly knew us. It was, ironically, Sukarno's 'Confrontation' between 1963 and 1967 against the formation of Malaysia, which he deemed a neo-colonial plot, that woke us up rudely and abruptly to the dire and urgent need to mingle in the Afro-Asian milieu. Calls from the opposition inside and outside Parliament strengthened this resolve. Almost of a sudden, missions were sent to these neglected parts of the world for diplomatic support and political understanding.

On 23 September 1970, on the occasion of Tun Abdul Razak's taking over of the prime ministership from the Tunku, the *Guardian* of London described Malaysia as 'one of the very bastions of neocolonialism with its tin, rubber and palm-oil industries still largely in European hands'. The newspaper described the Tunku and Tun Razak as 'members of the Anglophile-Malay aristocracy', and went on to reassure British investors in Malaysia that 'Malaysia's new Prime Minister is unlikely to introduce dramatic changes in external and domestic policies'. To be fair to Tun Razak, he did introduce some domestic and foreign policy changes. Whether or not they were particularly dramatic is another question.

Tun Razak took advantage of the opening thrown up by the ideological rivalry between the Soviet Union and China, and established diplomatic relations with eastern European countries – of course, not without persistent urgings from opposition parties both inside and outside Parliament. In 1971, Tun Razak initiated the Kuala Lumpur Declaration which proclaimed the concept of the Zone of Peace, Freedom and Neutrality (ZOPFAN), the main objective of which was to make the Association of South East Asian Nations (ASEAN) embody these qualities. Then, just before the 1974 general elections, Tun Razak made an official visit to China and began the process of normalising relations with that country, no doubt taking the cue from the preceding visit by American president Richard Nixon. These efforts led eventually to Malaysia's establishing diplomatic ties with China and supporting the latter's admission to the United Nations.

Hussein Onn became Malaysia's third prime minister shortly after Suharto's Indonesia invaded East Timor in December 1975. While Malaysian foreign policy under Onn basically continued what his predecessor had started, during Onn's term of office ASEAN member countries shifted their primary concern from economic co-operation to political and security measures. Exchanges of military and internal security intelligence increased. ASEAN governments even began to share arguments and apologia for their respective domestic human rights violations. For instance, the repression and corruption of Ferdinand Marcos of the Philippines were never condemned by other ASEAN governments until it was quite clear that he was already on his way out of power. The so-called principle of non-interference was disgracefully followed. Accordingly, along with the other ASEAN member states, Malaysia silently condoned Suharto's annexation of and near genocide in East Timor.

The absence of a peace movement

Unfortunately, for almost 33 years after *Merdeka* (independence), there was no peace movement in Malaysia. True, forums on foreign policy issues were held occasionally at university or college campuses, organised mainly by student associations, with invited academicians and politicians as speakers. True, foreign policy issues were debated from time to time in Parliament and both the prime minister and the foreign minister were frequently made to give oral answers on such issues during Question Time. However, right up to the very eve of the Iraqi invasion of Kuwait in August 1990, there was no organised peace movement in Malaysia. Non-governmental organisations (NGOs) like the

Angkatan Belia Islam Malaysia (Malaysian Islamic Youth Movement, ABIM) and the Majlis Belia Malaysia (Malaysian Youth Council, MBM) might comment sometimes on the plight, for instance, of the Palestinians or on the situation in Kashmir. However, this engagement consisted mostly of press releases, with perhaps an occasional peaceful protest in front of a foreign embassy. Individual NGOs, in other words, did their own things separately, without any attempt to forge a coalition or common front of NGOs on issues of war, justice, peace and human rights. This state of affairs changed with the Iraqi invasion of Kuwait.

First, a brief account of Malaysia's foreign policy under Prime Minister Mahathir Mohamad between July 1981 and July 1990 is warranted. As I suggested at a March 1991 seminar at the Universiti Kebangsaan Malaysia on Malaysian politics in the 1990s, the writings of some local academicians and semi-academicians from our universities and government research centres, such as the National Institute of Public Administration (INTAN) and the Institute of Strategic and International Studies (ISIS) have to be read for one to believe the degree of sycophancy that has been peddled around with regard to the conduct of Malaysian foreign policy, especially by Mahathir and his government (see Fan 1992). Associate Professor Murugesu Pathmanathan of the University of Malaya calls Mahathir 'an outstanding spokesman on Third World issues and problems'. According to him, Mahathir has 'reflected enormous intellectual capacity in his grasp of the complexity of modern international problems' and 'has emerged today as a leading spokesman and champion of Third World causes' (Pathmanathan and Lazrus 1984). According to Mohd. Azhari Karim of INTAN, Malaysian foreign policy has been 'a very purposeful one'. It is a foreign policy which has 'a new vigour and dynamism' and 'a colour that is definitely that of the Prime Minister himself'. Dr Mohamed Nordin Sopiee, the director-general of ISIS Malaysia, is even more effusive and self-congratulatory about Malaysia's foreign policy and its conduct. He insists, for instance:

> I believe that is important to recognise that the makers of our foreign policy do have a splendid record. It is equally important to note that one might expect nothing less when there is and there has been so much talent in our foreign policy establishment. In terms of creativity and personnel strength, it has historically been *primus inter pares*.

Notwithstanding this possibly intoxicating sycophancy, let us attempt a balanced assessment of Malaysia's foreign policy under Mahathir between July 1981 and July 1990. Bouquets first. The Mahathir government's initiatives on Antarctica, drug abuse and illicit trafficking, and South–South co-operation are praise-worthy. Its more active participation in the Non-aligned Movement, the Organisation of Islamic Countries and the Commonwealth, and its technical assistance scheme for small countries in the developing world, are commendable. There is no doubt that Dr Mahathir has spoken loudly on the questions of Palestine and apartheid in South Africa. All in all, Malaysia had achieved a higher international profile under the leadership of Dr Mahathir.

Now the brickbats. The official stand of the Mahathir government on the Palestinian question was apparently firm, but the policy's implementation was riddled with flaws. Consider the report, for instance, that for nearly the whole of 1982 five important Malaysian companies – Pernas, Sime Darby Malasia, Pernas Sime Darby Holdings, Pernas Sime Darby Sdn. Bhd., and Sime Darby Bhd. – were on the Arab League's boycott list because of trading links with Israel (*Far Eastern Economic Review*, 12 January 1983). Consider also that former Israeli Defence Minister Moshe Arens stated that Israel had sold sophisticated Israeli-made Gabriel sea-to-sea missiles to Malaysia (*Business Week*, 22 October 1984). Regarding Malaysia's stand on South Africa, consider a report from London that the Malaysian Mining Corporation was linked to the Bermuda-registered Minerals and Resources Corporation, which was in turn linked to the Anglo-American Corporation of South Africa, the largest mining group in the world and the biggest company in South Africa (*Economist*, 1 May 1982).

Nearer home, the Mahathir regime quite happily supported Pol Pot's Khmer Rouge and the Cambodian government-in-exile. It condoned General Rabuka's coup against a duly elected government in Fiji and even invited Rabuka to visit Malaysia. Instead of insisting on Malaysia's principled stand on ZOPFAN for Southeast Asia, the Mahathir government helped justify an American military base in Singapore. At one time, Mahathir even suggested that Malaysian facilities could be used by US forces (*Washington Post*, 13 August 1989). Of course, this position is not so surprising in light of the fact that Mahathir had already signed a so-called secret military agreement with the Reagan administration while on a visit to Washington, D.C. in 1984.

The emergence of the peace movement

NGOs, known as voluntary associations before and just after the Second World War, have been in existence for a long time. For example, organisations like the Scout Movement, the Girl Guides, St John's Ambulance Brigade, and sports and social clubs and associations at the national, state, district and local levels have flourished since colonial times. Some, like literary and cultural groups, existed even before the coming of the Europeans. 'NGO' is a relatively recent term, in vogue for about two decades, to describe organisations that are not directly created by, managed by or linked to the government of the day. In the 1960s and 1970s many of what are now called NGOs were generally known as public interest groups, pressure groups and societies.

Over the last three decades in Malaysia, just as in many other parts of the world, there has been a mushrooming of NGOs. Most notable among these have been consumers' associations like the Consumers' Association of Penang (CAP) and the Federation of Malaysian Consumers' Associations (FOMCA); women's rights groups like the All Women's Action Society (AWAM) and Sisters in Islam; social reform and human rights groups like Aliran Kesedaran Negara (National Consciousness Movement, Aliran) and Suara Rakyat Malaysia (Voice of the Malaysian People, SUARAM); youth groups like ABIM and MBM; environmental groups like Sahabat Alam Malaysia (Friends of the Earth Malaysia, SAM), Environmental Protection Society Malaysia (EPSM), the Malaysian Nature Society and the World Wide Fund for Nature (WWF); and peace groups like Just World Trust and the Centre for Peace Initiatives (CENPEACE) (see Saliha 1992).

In 1981–2, when the Malaysian government wanted to classify registered pressure groups and public-interest societies as 'political societies', scores of NGOs campaigned jointly to fight against the plan (see Gurmit 1984). Even though on that occasion they were mainly fighting for their own survival and identity, an important precedent for co-operation and solidarity was set. Like NGOs in many other parts of the world, Malaysian NGOs were becoming more sure of themselves and more outspoken. As Eric Hobsbawm has put it succinctly:

> The minorities which went on campaigning, sometimes for specific issues of public interest, more often for some sectional interest, could interfere with the smooth processes of government just as effectively, perhaps even more effectively, than all-purpose political parties, since, unlike these, each pressure group could concentrate its energy on pursuing a single objective.
>
> (Hobsbawm 1996: 581)

The Gulf War

The invasion of Kuwait by Iraq on 2 August 1990 and the ensuing Gulf War in January 1991 saw the emergence of a peace movement among NGOs, at least in peninsular Malaysia. Days after the Iraqi invasion, the passage of trade sanctions against Iraq by the United Nations Security Council galvanised some Malaysian NGOs, opposition parties and individuals to form Gerak Damai (Movement for Peace), led by national literary laureate Datuk Usman Awang. Gerak Damai succeeded in organising a couple of public meetings and at least one candlelight vigil at Dataran Merdeka (Independence Square, in downtown Kuala Lumpur). The group called for a peaceful solution to the Iraq–Kuwait conflict by all parties and countries concerned and asked the Malaysian government to help resolve the dispute peacefully.

Although these peace vigils were not met with any violent response from the police, those of us participating were sufficiently harassed by the police and Special Branch to curtail our activities. Most of us were left cynically wondering what the authorities had against orderly, civilised calls for peace, particularly when we could see that throughout the world, including in the United States, Britain and France – the countries whose governments were making the loudest war cries against Iraq – peace marches and demonstrations were allowed. Even in South Africa, Muslims and others were allowed to hold peaceful anti-war marches, but not in Malaysia, where the Prime Minister claimed neutrality and was considered a 'hero' and 'champion' of the Third World. In Malaysia, such marches, demonstrations and vigils were strictly forbidden.

Malaysia's support of the United States-initiated Resolution 678 at the United Nations Security Council on 29 November 1990, which was to pressure Iraq 'by any means necessary' if Iraq had not withdrawn its troops from Kuwait by 15 January 1991, was a great disappointment to those of us who had so strongly urged and hoped for a peaceful, negotiated resolution of the conflict. The 43–day high-tech aerial bombardment of Iraq which began on 17 January 1991 left us deeply angry and embittered not only against the United States and the West but also against the Malaysian government. The actions of the latter during the Gulf War have left many still feeling betrayed even now.

In early September 1991, Malaysian peace activists arranged for Ramsey Clark, former US Attorney-General and initiator of the commission of inquiry for an International War Crimes Tribunal, to speak to Malaysians on his trip to Iraq during the war. Clark met up with anti-war NGO activists and individuals and also spoke to capacity-crowd audiences of students and lecturers at Universiti Malaya and

Universiti Kebangsaan Malaysia. Subsequently, some of us took part in the activities of the New York-based International War Crimes Tribunal.

In March 1992, several peace movement-affiliated NGOs launched a Campaign to Save the Children of Iraq to try to mitigate the terrible effects of the trade sanctions. The campaign received some coverage from the mainstream media and collected more than 55,000 ringgit for the cause. These funds were sent via the Malaysian Red Crescent Society to the Iraqi Red Crescent Society to help Iraqi children. Also, some NGOs, particularly the Malaysian Sociological Research Institute (MSRI) under Dr Alijah Gordon, collected and sent medicines for the children of the devastated country on their own initiative.

The formation of the MAF

In early 1992, flight and other sanctions were imposed hastily on Libya by the United Nations Security Council over the Lockerbie incident, even as the matter was being deliberated at the International Court of Justice (Would Court) at The Hague in the Netherlands. Those sanctions, and the rush of foreign troops to Somalia shortly after that year, lent credence to the perception among many Malaysian NGO activists that the United States in particular was bent on dominating the world under its 'New World Order'. This conviction, the deteriorating humanitarian crisis in Iraq, and the increasing brutality of ethnic cleansing in Bosnia and Rwanda goaded concerned NGOs to work together under a new umbrella coalition called the Malaysian Action Front (MAF).

The MAF was an improvement on Gerak Damai in that, unlike the latter, the MAF had some loose structure and a secretariat. The coalition was particularly notable for its diversity and breadth. The MAF included about 40 NGOs. Some of these affiliates, moreover, were (and still are) themselves coalitions or federations of a good number of organisations. The MBM is a case in point, comprising about 40 youth and student organisations nationwide. The MAF operated from the head office of ABIM in Petaling Jaya, Selangor. Anuar Tahir, then the secretary-general of ABIM, served as the MAF's chairman, with Saifuddin Abdullah, at that time the secretary of the MBM, and myself as joint co-ordinators.

The MAF's member organisations were hardly homogeneous. Rather, with the mission of working for a just international order, the MAF succeeded in bringing together an array of truly ideologically and politically varied governmental and non-governmental organisations. The MAF included the governing United Malays National Organisation's

(UMNO) Youth wing, the opposition Democratic Action Party (DAP) Youth, opposition Parti Islam Se-Malaysia (Pan-Malaysian Islamic Party, PAS) Youth, and the Parti Rakyat Malaysia (Malaysian People's Party, PRM) as well as religiously and culturally diverse groups like ABIM, the Society for Christian Reflection, and the Youth Section of the Selangor Chinese Assembly Hall.

Bosnia and beyond

The positions of the Malaysian government and concerned NGOs were relatively close with regard to the Bosnian conflict. The First International Conference on Bosnia was held in Kuala Lumpur. Both Malaysian government and opposition parties as well as NGOs were actively involved, protesting against Serbian ethnic cleansing of Muslims in Bosnia. The Second International Conference on Bosnia, held in Brussels in April 1994, was attended by an all-party delegation of Malaysian parliamentarians. In addition, Kassim Ahmad, Mohideen Abder Kader and I attended on behalf of our respective NGOs. Shortly after that conference, in early May 1994, a Malaysian Mass Rally was held at Merdeka Stadium. The place was filled with tens of thousands of NGO members as well as singers and artistes. The event was also covered live on radio and television. Cabinet minister Datuk Seri Anwar Ibrahim was a guest of honour.

Later, a December 1994 international conference in Kuala Lumpur on the theme of 'Rethinking Human Rights' marked what was perhaps the high point in cordiality between certain peace-related NGOs and the Malaysian government. The conference was organised by Just World Trust (JUST), led by Dr Chandra Muzaffar and S. M. Mohd Idris. Prime Minister Mahathir Mohamad delivered the keynote address at the beginning of the conference, while then-Deputy Prime Minister Anwar Ibrahim gave a special address at its close (see JUST 1996). However, the honeymoon period between concerned NGOs and the government was ending, beset by increasingly serious strains until the relationship ruptured.

The formation of CENPEACE

By mid-1994, the newly established Centre for Peace Initiatives (CENPEACE) was beginning to take over increasingly more of the co-ordination work of the MAF. It was obvious that, as time passed, the enthusiasm which had developed among NGOs just after the Gulf War for the 'grand coaliton' of the MAF was losing momentum.

Perhaps the big 'hot' issues of the Gulf War, Lockerbie and Bosnia were perceived to be cooling somewhat. Over time, the NGOs concerned became more selective, acting in accordance with their own inclinations, in deciding to become or remain involved with longstanding or new issues. Among areas of concern for these NGOs were the events in Chechnya, Korea, Palestine, Kashmir, Sri Lanka, the Punjab, East Timor and Burma, as well as issues like nuclear testing.

As far as the Malaysian government was concerned, it generally adopted a neutral, non-interventionist stance on these new crises abroad. In relation to Chechnya, the Malaysian government stated that this was an internal matter for Russia to handle. Official involvement with the civil war in Sri Lanka, problems in the Punjab and human rights violations in East Timor were avoided on similar grounds. As for Kashmir, the Malaysian government did not want to risk displeasing either India or Pakistan by taking a partisan stance. Not only was the stifling of pro-democracy activism in Burma (Myanmar) deemed an internal affair, but the military junta was welcomed into the ranks of ASEAN in 1997. Protesting in Kuala Lumpur against Burma's admission into ASEAN landed some NGO activists in a police lockup for two days. As for Palestine, by 1996 some NGOs were not too happy with the government's uncritical support of the Palestine Liberation Organisation (PLO) in the Middle East peace process. CENPEACE and other NGOs were at least giving a hearing to Yassir Arafat's Palestinian rival, HAMAS. Finally, NGO protests against French nuclear tests in the South Pacific in late 1995 attracted a great deal of media attention as well as further NGO support. On this issue too, though, the NGOs' call for the public to boycott French goods and services differed from the government's position that such boycotts were unnecessary.

The East Timor saga

East Timor was arguably the most controversial foreign policy issue with which Malaysian NGOs have contended. While East Timor had been a focus of concern for Malaysian NGOs since Indonesian troops invaded the territory in December 1975, these NGOs were particularly at odds with the Malaysian government regarding East Timor throughout the 1990s. To those NGOs most vociferous in their condemnation of human rights violations in East Timor, the persistent refusal of the Malaysian government to criticise the Suharto regime on its systematic and severe human rights violations there seemed not only infuriating but also somewhat cowardly. The Dili massacre in November 1991, in which a young Malaysian, Kamal Ahmad Bamadhaj, was killed, proved particularly disappointing for critical NGOs, as Malaysia's government chose not to speak up for its own citizen (Kua 1998a; *Star*, 8 and 9 May 2000). However, there were other NGOs which, for reasons of their own, decided to align themselves with the government's position.

Elements from UMNO Youth – linked to UMNO, the dominant party in the ruling Barisan Nasional (National Front, BN) coalition – violently broke up the Second Asia Pacific Conference on East Timor (APCET II), held in Kuala Lumpur in early November 1996. That disruption and the subsequent arrest, incarceration and deportation of conference participants dragged some NGOs' relationship with the government to a new low. On 9 November 1998, 36 participants in the foiled conference filed a joint suit in the Kuala Lumpur High Court against the Malaysian police for illegal arrest and wrongful detention (see Kua 1998a).

The peace movement at home

Any impression that the above-mentioned NGOs were primarily interested in international issues, to the extent of forgetting or neglecting local matters, would be mistaken. As a matter of fact, with the exception of NGOs like JUST and CENPEACE, which are primarily oriented around international affairs and Malaysian foreign policy, most other NGOs' day-to-day work and concerns are woven around local issues. While such NGOs' primary identity may be as domestic advocacy organisations, they may be mobilised to participate in relevant internationally oriented campaigns from time to time, as well.

For instance, in the mid-1990s, ABIM, Persatuan Kebangsaan Pelajar Islam Malaysia (National Union of Muslim Students, PKPIM), and the MBM were behind a nationwide campaign – endorsed and supported by a good number of other NGOs – against what they considered as western hedonism and nihilism: the consumption of alcohol and cigarettes at rock music concerts, especially the so-called 'Salem Cool Concerts'. Similarly, NGOs concerned with women's rights, like AWAM, Sisters in Islam and Sahabat Wanita Selangor (Friends of Women, Selangor) spent a tremendous amount of time, energy and patience in the 1990s campaigning for, among other things, the Domestic Violence Act. Also, about 50 NGOs from peninsular Malaysia as well as Sarawak and Sabah campaigned against the multibillion ringgit Bakun Dam project in Sarawak, the environmental issue most in the limelight in the 1990s. Although then-Deputy Prime Minister Anwar Ibrahim, who had been put in charge of the project by the cabinet, was fairly responsive to calls for a dialogue with the protesting NGOs on the Bakun Dam, little came of these overtures because of the very high stakes involved.

Their support of these domestic initiatives does not mean that activists in these and other NGOs, like Tenaganita (Women Force) and SUARAM, have not played active roles in international matters. Rather, in addition to encouraging Malaysia to hold foreign regimes to a higher standard with regard to human rights and democracy, these NGOs try to hold their own government to the same standard. Coupled with their disappointment over the Malaysian government's stance on various international issues over the past several years, though, some of these activists' experience with domestically focused activism may have made them even more cynical about the chances of fruitful co-operation with the government on any front.

In line with other human rights-related campaigns at home, some NGOs had announced in December 1996 that they would hold a people's tribunal on abuses of power by the police the following month in Kuala Lumpur. The reaction from the authorities was quick and predictable: anger at and intimidation of their critics. Even when the NGOs concerned decided that they would hold a public forum on the police instead of a people's tribunal if the parties concerned were too touchy about the latter, the response was still the same. A raw nerve had apparently been touched: the police must not be questioned or criticised openly.

Deputy Home Minister Ong Ka Ting said it was not right for NGOs to hold the forum, but he offered no explanation of why this was so. All he could say was 'Don't be stubborn . . . abide by the laws.' Neither did he care to tell the NGOs involved or the public which laws or sections or clauses thereof the NGOs involved had broken or were likely to break by holding the proposed forum on alleged abuse of police power. Inspector-General of Police Tan Sri Rahim Noor even said that the forum 'smacks, and has elements of marxism'. In response, I argued at that time, 'The important point in the controversy surrounding the NGO forum is: since when has the police force as a public service become sacrosanct, above public discussion, debate and criticism?' (Fan 1996).

At the same time, Megat Junid Megat Ayob, the other Deputy Home Minister, said in a public statement that forums denouncing the police could erode public confidence in the force and jeopardise national security (*New Straits Times* and *Berita Harian*, 18 December 1996). The next day Prime Minister Mahathir said that the Internal Security Act (ISA) – which grants the authorities power to detain people without trial – would be used against NGOs 'baiting' the government, as by holding the forum (*Star*, 19 December 1996). He said some NGOs were unhappy to see a prosperous and stable Malaysia, and wanted to see its relations with others strained. I replied at the time, 'it is indecent and shameless of the authorities to attempt to silence discussion on the work of the police by threatening to use the Internal Security Act. It is a cowardly way to suppress freedom of expression' (Fan 1996). Meanwhile, as expected, the obedient mainstream media took Mahathir's cue and came out with pieces to justify the government's stand.[1]

In the face of such hostility, the nine NGOs planning to hold the forum decided to postpone it, but they still insisted on having a dialogue with the police on alleged police abuse of power.[2] It was obvious, though, that other NGOs were playing it safe. For instance, Suhaimi Ibrahim, president of the MBM, said that he shared the view that the proposed tribunal would only create unrest and doubts in people's minds about the peace and security of the country (*Sun*, 20 December 1996). In light of the fact that Suhaimi Ibrahim was also an UMNO State Assemblyman from Pahang, however, this sort of parroting of the regime was perhaps understandable. Some of the other NGO leaders who chose to sit on the fence on this occasion were to have the opportunity less than two years later to experience police brutality and abuse of power firsthand when they themselves went into opposition politics upon the sacking and persecution of Deputy Prime Minister Anwar Ibrahim.

Meanwhile, though they press for democratic accountability abroad, some Malaysian NGOs and activists have found that helping to advance the same cause at home, as by fighting corruption, can be a rather frustrating experience. On 5 August 1997, Aliran, AWAM, the Community Development Centre (CDC), Centre for Orang Asli Concerns (COAC), Education and Research Association for Consumers (ERA Consumer), FOMCA, Jabatan Sokongan Peneroka Bandar (Urban Pioneers' Support Office), JUST, PAS, Perak Consumers' Association, PRM, Society for Christian Reflection, SUARAM, Suara Warga Pertiwi (SWP), Tenaganita and 78 Malaysian activists submitted a memorandum to the Director-General of the Anti-Corruption Agency in Kuala Lumpur. Entitled, 'To Urge Swift and Firm Action Against Corruption', the memorandum focused on three issues: the multi-billion ringgit Perwaja Steel scandal; the case of Tan Sri Muhammad Taib, former *menteri besar* (chief minister) of Selangor and a vice-president of UMNO; and the 213 companies in which Mahathir's three sons held interests. Copies of the memorandum were sent to the media, with a copy also dispatched to the Attorney-General urging him and the Anti-Corruption Agency to 'act speedily and firmly on the three cases' (NGOs 1997). Despite questions in Parliament on the memorandum, no concrete answer has been forthcoming with regard to investigations. So far as is known, none of the individuals or NGOs who endorsed the memorandum has even been questioned about the cases.

The future of the peace movement

Malaysian non-governmental organisations (NGOs) associated with the peace movement have had an ambivalent relationship with the Malaysian government, sometimes working in concert and other times at odds with one another. The decade of the 1990s was full of earth-shattering events on which the Malaysian government and Malaysian NGOs could interact with each other. And interact they did, in various ways and styles. Activities of various NGOs in this period gave rise to a relatively coherent peace movement promoting international human rights and peaceful means of conflict resolution as well as human rights and democracy at home. The experience of the movement so far has taught the activists involved to maintain their issue orientation, regardless of how their stance aligns with that of the government, and to be patient and persistent in the face of disappointment.

If some activists harboured illusions during the heydays of Bosnia-linked government–NGO co-operation, their subsequent experiences on foreign and domestic fronts, as with APCET II and the people's tribunal on the police, have likely disabused them or their optimism. On several international fronts and a good number of domestic ones, especially those deemed 'sensitive' or touching on vested interests, relations between NGOs affiliated to the peace movement and the government have been far from positive or smooth.

Past experience thus suggests that in Malaysia, as in many other developing countries, NGO work requires a great deal of patience and conviction. Indeed, it would perhaps be wise for Malaysian NGOs, particularly those active in the peace movement, to remember not to be pro or anti-government *per se*, but to be for or against issues in accordance with the merits of each case. That is not to say, of course, that NGOs cannot and should not work with other groups, including political parties or the government of the day, if and when worthwhile or necessary. However, as particularly well demonstrated by the experience of the peace movement, NGOs need to take a more realistic view of such collaboration. Even as they find areas of agreement with the regime, NGOs and activists must understand that, given the different aims and imperatives of civil society and the government, their interests will not always align. Moreover, NGOs remain the more vulnerable partner in the case of a falling-out. In the final analysis, the interests of the people whom NGOs claim to represent, promote and defend must come first, not some often capricious 'reason of state' of those in or seeking power. Hence, despite constraints, the struggle for justice, peace and human rights continues.

Notes

Preface

1 A partial exception is Patricia Martinez's chapter on the Women's Agenda for Change and Women's Candidacy Initiative (Chapter 3), included alongside Lai Suat Yan's chapter on the women's movement more broadly (Chapter 2). These two initiatives within the women's movement are significant enough as a possible indication of a real shift in tactics within civil society that we deemed them worth a separate chapter.

Introduction

1 Haynes labels 'non-institutionalized socioeconomic and political bodies in the developing world' thus. Action groups may lack a grassroots base but have some common trait uniting members and a real sense of agency, even if they rely to some extent on domestic and foreign allies (1997: 4).
2 Klandermans defines a social movement rather vaguely as 'a set of interacting individuals who attempt to promote, control, or prevent changes in social and cultural arrangements' (1989: 2). Diani is more specific, identifying what is common among social movements as an emphasis on networks of informal interaction, shared beliefs and solidarity, issue-oriented collective action at the systemic or non-systemic level, and action largely outside the usual institutions of social life (1992: 7–13). In the sub-category of new social movements (NSMs), the actors involved share or develop a specific collective identity and critique growth and 'tendencies to colonize the life-world'. Key NSMs include movements for the environment and women's rights, and against nuclear proliferation (Habermas 1981: 35; also Klandermans 1989, Klandermans and Tarrow 1988).
3 For instance, Yamamoto refers to 'those non-profit and non-governmental organisations that are active in the field of development issues in third world countries, such as rural development, alleviation of poverty, nutrition and health, reproductive biology, and education; and global issues such as the environment, human rights, refugees, and the population crisis' (1995: 1). See the contributions to that volume, though, for a sense of how the direction and shape of the voluntary sector in the Asia-Pacific region have changed over time.
4 See Chapter 1 for details on these laws.

5 The BN is comprised of fourteen parties, chief among them UMNO, the Malaysian Chinese Association (MCA) and the Malaysian Indian Congress (MIC).
6 See Crouch (1996), Jesudason (1996), Means (1991), Milne and Mauzy (1999), or (Tan 1990), among others, for details and valuable perspectives on the Malaysian political order.
7 See Jomo (1991) or Loh (1997) for a discussion of Malaysia's development policies and their consequences.
8 Malaya became Malaysia with the addition of Sabah, Sarawak and Singapore in 1963. Singapore left the federation in 1965.
9 The cultivation and study of *masyarakat madani* was associated in the mid-1990s particularly with the Anwar-linked think tank, Institut Kajian Dasar (Institute for Policy Studies), and several of Anwar's strong followers, such as long-time social activist and intellectual Chandra Muzaffar. The idea never really took root in popular consciousness, though, and even academic discussion of the concept virtually ceased after Anwar was sacked in 1998.
10 See the contributions to MINDS (1997), especially the chapter by Syed Muhammad Naquib Al-Attas, for a more thorough explication of the term and its roots. Indonesian scholars have written more on the topic, though most of these accounts are rather shallow or dismissive of any significant distinction between civil society and *masyarakat madani*. See for instance Adi Suryadi Culla (1999), Ahmad Baso (2000) or Muhammad Hikam (2000).
11 See Sabri (2000) for a dramatic account of these events.

1 Malaysian NGOs: history, legal framework and characteristics

1 However, a number of studies on civil society, NGOs and NSMs written as theory-building initiatives or with other cases in mind are useful for background and contrast. Studies on other Southeast Asian states, such as Clarke (1998), Eldridge (1995), Uhlin (1997) and Walker (1996), may be particularly revealing, given structural similarities.
2 For instance, Lee explains that secret societies were not 'consciously political' and actually denied having such a basis when the British wanted to proscribe them. The groups declared their intention to be maintenance of law and order and pointed out that they did not urge Chinese to cut off their queues – an anti-Manchu, and hence consciously political, act. However, the groups did sound and act political, especially when xenophobic feelings spilled over from China to Singapore and Malaya, or the Chinese felt economically or otherwise threatened by the British (Lee 1985: 135).
3 Given the difficulties in getting accurate information on underground organisations, these figures are no doubt subject to dispute.
4 Tham (1977: especially 109–17) is one of few authors not to ignore Indian associations apart from trade unions. His description of early reformist, nationalist, spiritual and cultural, business, and ethnic/caste (Sikh, Ceylonese, etc.) organisations is concise but detailed and informative.
5 Other institutions, such as *derau* among Kedah padi farmers, are of the same genre.
6 Though fundamentally a politically conservative, loyalist and welfare-oriented group (Roff 1994: 192).

7 The debate over who constituted the Malay community was especially significant, as manifested in the *Melayu Raya/Indonesia Raya* (Greater Malaysia/Greater Indonesia) concept, which linked Malays in the two colonial entities. This movement spanned participation of Malay nationalists in the Indonesian revolt against Dutch rule and combined overseas students associations, newsletters and other endeavours of varying degrees of political commitment (Firdaus 1985: 52–7).
8 *Bangsawan*, or Malay opera, and other theatrical performances were also long used for political socialisation, though 'under the guise of promoting Malay language and literature' (Firdaus 1985: 119–20).
9 Firdaus further subdivides the latter group of 'radical nationalists' into Islamic-educated teachers and writers and vernacular Malay-educated teachers and journalists (Firdaus 1985: 3). Indeed, the divide between the Malay Islamic faction and the Malay left was highly significant, with the former advocating an Islamic nation through the Pan-Malayan Islamic Party (PMIP, called Parti Islam from 1971 to 1973 and now called Parti Islam Se-Malaysia, PAS), and the latter forming the Angkatan Pemuda Insaf (banned in 1948), the Parti Kebangsaan Melayu Malaya (PKMM, Malay Nationalist Party, disbanded 1950), then the Parti Rakyat Malaysia (PRM, formed 1955). See for instance Shamsul 1996: 334–8 or Y. Mansoor 1976.
10 A contemporary example is the replacement of the NGO Pergerakan Keadilan Sosial (Adil) by a political party, Parti Keadilan Nasional (Keadilan), in 1999.
11 Exceptions include local branches of foreign organisations or groups founded and supported by the wives of British administrators, such as the Women's Service League (1946), which involved women of all races in voluntary welfare work and conducted courses for village women in a range of household and general subjects (Manderson 1980: 53).
12 The Consumers' Association of Penang (CAP), founded November 1969, is considered Malaysia's first modern NGO.
13 Clarke (1998: 2–3) defines NGOs as 'private, non-profit, professional organisations with a distinctive legal character, concerned with public welfare goals'. The term thus includes philanthropic foundations, church development agencies, academic think tanks, human rights organisations, and groups concerned with gender, health, agricultural development, social welfare, the environment and indigenous peoples.
14 Tan and Bishan (1994: 14) explain the state's perspective on the last issue: 'The state seeks to control NGOs in the interests of national security because NGOs are seen as lobbying and pressure groups which do not have to be accountable to the "public trust", whereas elected politicians are at least legitimized in periodic elections.' Clarke provides a useful definition for 'politics' among NGOs, explaining that 'to be "political", an NGO must first participate in processes designed to create social meaning, and second, on the basis of that shared social meaning, participate in the distribution of resources and in the struggle to influence that distribution' (Clarke 1998: 6).
15 In fact, the current act still makes specific reference to secret societies.
16 Under a 1970 amendment, the minister's approval is needed for registration of any local society established abroad or with affiliations outside Malaysia.
17 For a detailed account of the campaign, see Gurmit (1984). Ex-Deputy

Prime Minister Anwar Ibrahim, then of Angkatan Belia Islam Malaysia (ABIM, the Malaysian Islamic Youth Movement), chaired the SACC and SCS until March 1982, when he abruptly stepped down to join UMNO and run for office.

18 Tan and Bishan base their estimate on the number of NGOs that joined the secretariat formed to campaign against the amendments to the Societies Act from 1981 to 1983. Realistically, though, as reflected in campaigns on various human rights and environmental issues as well as recent *Reformasi* co-ordinating groups, no more than a few dozen groups are really active as advocacy NGOs. Garry Rodan (1997: 162) suggests that only groups 'involving regular attempts to advance the interests of members through overt political action' constitute civil society, while all other groups are part of civic society.

19 For instance, Persatuan Kebangsaan Hak Asasi Manusia (HAKAM, the National Human Rights Society), waited about two years for approval of its bid for registration, while Amnesty International has been trying unsuccessfully since 1990 to register a Malaysian branch. Periodically, the government threatens to weed out NGOs, such as human rights group Suara Rakyat Malaysia (SUARAM, Voice of the Malaysian People), registered as companies or businesses.

20 See my Chapter 6 in this volume for more on these and other restrictive laws.

21 Even a permit for publication may not be enough. For example, Aliran announced in October 1999 that it was unable to find a printer willing to print its monthly magazine due to alleged pressure tactics by the government directed at potential printers.

22 On student activism in the late 1960s and early 1970s, including the protests of 1974, see Fan 1988 or Hassan and Siti Nor (1984); on students' political involvement today, see Mohd. Azizuddin (n.d.).

23 Some NGOs have voluntarily limited the role of politicians in their organisations. Aliran requires that its members not belong to any political party, while the Federation of Malaysian Consumers' Associations (FOMCA) proposed that active politicians be barred from executive committee posts in the consumer movement (Tan and Bishan 1994: 23).

24 The NGOs were Aliran, CAP, Environmental Protection Society Malaysia (EPSM), Selangor Graduates Society (SGS) and the Bar Council. The parties were the DAP and PAS.

25 See CARPA (1988) or Nair (1995: 184–90).

26 FOMCA, the umbrella consumers' organisation, has the most extensive relations with the government of all Malaysian NGOs. FOMCA serves on the National Advisory Council for Consumers' Protection and the National Economic Consultative Council and represents consumers' interests on a permanent basis in the Ministries of Trade and Industry; Science, Technology and Environment; Health; Finance; Post and Telecommunication; Housing and Local Government; Information; and Agriculture (Tan and Bishan 1994: 18).

27 As Zaitun Kasim of the All Women's Action Society (AWAM) describes, 'They call it a dialogue; we call it a briefing' (interview, 1 August 1997).

28 A range of GONGOs (government or state-sponsored NGOs) also operate in various issue areas. These groups depend largely on the state for funding and training but sustain diverse structures and relationships with the

government, with varying degrees of autonomy. Some have little grassroots participation and are little more than vehicles for political support and patronage. See Tan and Bishan (1994: 2–3).
29 Rather than issue-based advocacy groups, the organisations with a large rural presence are generally GONGOs or youth, welfare, religious, or agricultural and labour-related associations.
30 For example, in the late 1980s and early 1990s, CAP, EPSM, and Sahabat Alam Malaysia, Malaysia's most vocal, active, and well-known environmental groups, claimed a total of only about 150 formal members (Nair 1999: 96).
31 For instance, Irene Fernandez explained that Tenaganita works as a collective, with separate desks dealing with women, health, migrant workers, the plantation sector and research, each with its own responsibilities and leaders. However, she conceded that the image outside Tenaganita is her name (interview, 29 July 1997).
32 For instance, the Dutch agency HIVOS, which sponsors Women's Crisis Centre (WCC), SUARAM, AWAM, Tenaganita, Partners of Community Organisations (PACOS), Jawatan Sokongan Peneroka Bandar (JSPB, Urban Pioneers' Support Office), Pink Triangle and other NGOs, announced it would pull out of Malaysia in 2000, citing Malaysia's relatively high level of development. For details of HIVOS's activities in Malaysia and their consultant's view of the NGO community, see van Naerssen (1995).
33 CAP, for example, suggests it would pose a conflict of interest for a consumers' group to accept money from either government or business and thus relies mostly on funds from European donors, grants from foundations or other organisations and proceeds from sales of the NGO's publications, handicrafts and other items (Mary Assunta, interview, 17 July 1998). Also, the government offered AWAM 10,000 ringgit per year for its programmes, but with the condition that its representative be able to sit in on the NGO's meetings (Zaitun Kasim and Wong Peck Lin, interview, 14 July 1998).
34 Aliran, for instance, only considers accepting foreign aid for certain projects and never for daily operating costs. The NGO sustains itself mostly through donations and sales of its monthly magazine (Anil Netto, interview, 18 July 1999).
35 Feedback from donors may affect organisational attributes, too. For instance, Loh Cheng Kooi explained that a HIVOS evaluation led to increased democratisation of decision-making procedures in WCC (interview, 17 July 1998).
36 For example, 47 NGOs and six political parties are listed as 'NGOs That Support Abolishment of the ISA' (SUARAM 1999); the Coalition of Concerned NGOs on Bakun, established in 1995, includes around 40 NGOs; and 1981's SACC involved over 100 groups. On the other hand, the Joint Action Group against Violence Against Women was formed in 1985 of individual women and just five organisations, though other NGOs eventually lent support to the campaign.
37 See Chapter 8 for details of externally focused NGO activities.
38 See Chandra (1984) for a detailed breakdown of the relative racial balance in political parties, trade unions, commercial associations, professional bodies, public interest societies, cultural and religious associations, and

student movements. By his account, virtually all these organisational types are largely communal, by chance or design, aggravated in some cases (such as within higher education) by religious revivalism.
39 Zaitun Kasim posits that AWAM's multiracial image and support is partly due to her presence, since before she (a Muslim) joined the staff, the group was seen as a non-Muslim organisation. AWAM has also been one of few non-Islamic groups to comment upon specific Muslim women's issues, such as provisions of Islamic *syariah* law; other groups are generally afraid to voice their opinion on these topics (interview, 1 August 1997).
40 See for instance Jomo and Ahmad Shaberry (1992), Zainah (1999), Saliha (1997) Shamsul (1997), or Milne and Mauzy (1999: 80–9) regarding the range of Islamic organisations, their development amidst the Islamic resurgence since the 1970s, and the relative political aspirations and political party ties of various organisations.
41 A widescale movement of NGOs and political parties for political reforms, social and economic justice, and the downfall of the Barisan Nasional.

2 The women's movement in peninsular Malaysia, 1900–99: a historical analysis

1 Based on Virginia Dancz's interview with Aishah Ghani, 1 March 1976 (published in Dancz 1987: 86).
2 See Cecilia Ng, Siti Nor Hamid and Syed Husin Ali (1999) for an account of the formation of a branch of AWAS in the village of Kampung Jenderam Ulu, Selangor, and its activities.
3 See reports in *The Star* from February 1989 covering the dispute, as mentioned by Ng and Yong (1990).
4 See Rohana (1997b) and Jomo and Todd (1994) for a detailed history of the labour movement and how it has been crippled over the years by deregistration of strong unions, imprisonment of its leaders, restrictive laws and labour policies.
5 The other nine affiliates were the National Association of Women's Institutes, the Women Teachers' Union, the St John's Ambulance Brigade, the University Women's Association, the Selangor Indian Association's Women's section, the Pan-Pacific South-East Asian Women's Association, the Young Women's Christian Association, the Lai Chee Women's Association and the Women's International Club (Dancz 1987: 151).
6 HAWA was upgraded from a division in 1997 and was under the Prime Minister's Department before being elevated to the Ministry of Women and Family Development in 2001.
7 The Income Tax Act still discriminates against women, as they are not allowed to deduct for spousal or child support.
8 The government's Islamisation campaign of the 1980s was an attempt to harness a process that had been proceeding on the ground since the early 1970s.
9 The case involving actress Norkumalasari is an example (Askiah 1993: 22).
10 Personal communication with Cecilia Ng, one of the founders of the JAG-VAW, 14 August 2000.
11 Women's presence was only really felt in the MTUC after 1965 (Rohana 1997b). The objectives of the Women's Section are to improve the living conditions of young women workers, to unionise women workers and to

raise awareness of women workers' legal rights. Some of the activities organised for women include talks and courses on leadership and labour legislation, and starting a hostel for factory girls. The AWL was registered in 1985 with the objectives of promoting equal rights for women under the law and safeguarding women. The seed for WAO was a donation from the late Tun Tan Siew Sin in 1979. Some of WAO's objectives are to provide temporary refuge and care to battered women and their children, to encourage these women to determine their own future and to help achieve it, and to cater to the educational and emotional needs of the children involved. The WAO offers services including refuge, face-to-face and telephone counselling, child sponsorship and child care. Younger women members have tried to inject a more feminist perspective that women have the right not to be battered under any circumstances (Ng and Chee 1996). The UWA was established in 1963. Some of its objectives are to promote social interaction between members; to sponsor cultural, educational and philanthropic activities for members and their families; to perform voluntary social services and to contribute towards the education and welfare of women and children in Malaysia.

12 Personal communication with Cecilia Ng, 14 August 2000.
13 The impetus for the formation of the WDC was the coming together of a group of young women in the early 1980s to discuss issues relating to women and feminism. The group then began to work with other organisations and individuals on legal reforms, public education and advocacy. Currently, the WDC focuses on research, education and training. Sahabat Wanita is discussed in detail later in this section.
14 Personal communication from Maria Chin Abdullah, president of the NWC prior to its being disbanded in 1995, 13 September 2000.
15 There was no formal dissolution of the coalition as they did not manage to get a quorum (personal communication from Maria Chin Abdullah, 13 September 2000).
16 SIS was formed in 1998 and was registered as an NGO three years later. The group comprised ten professional women with skills in various areas. Broadly, the objectives of SIS are to promote and develop a framework for women's rights in Islam which takes into consideration women's experiences and realities; to eliminate injustice and discrimination against women by changing practices and values that regard women as inferior to men; to create public awareness and to reform laws and policies on issues of equality, justice and democracy in Islam.
17 These women's NGOs were AWAM, the Consumers' Association of Taiping, Institute of Community Action – Women's Section, People's Service Organisation – Women's Section, SAWO, Sahabat Wanita, SWWS, Women in SUARAM, Women's Action Workforce Penang and WDC.
18 See the Election Commission's official results for the Selayang parliamentary constituency, available at http: //202.186.123.189/sybaseweb/aselangor.stm.
19 See Chapter 3 for a more in-depth discussion of these two initiatives.
20 An example of a top female politician who is not a good candidate to advance women's causes is the International Trade and Industries Minister, Rafidah Aziz. For example, at a forum in March 1999, Rafidah told women's NGOs not to politicise gender issues (*Star*, 29 March 2000).
21 Stivens (1992) notes the tension she produced at the mention of the issues

of sexuality and Islam in feminist writings in her presentation of the paper, 'Perspectives on Gender: Problems in Writing about Women in Malaysia' at the University of Malaya in 1988. The issues of dress, sexuality and Islam have since been addressed in Maznah (1994) and Norani (1993).
22 Fatimah Daud (1985) noted in her study on electronic factory workers in Petaling Jaya, Selangor, that urban living with the freedom to relate with the opposite sex left these workers conflicted. Her study found that majority of the female rural migrant workers felt ashamed of becoming factory workers. One of the reasons given was that they were perceived by the public as immoral and were called 'Minah Karan', or girls who are very excitable and full of sexual energy. See also Stivens (1996) for an account of sexuality among the villagers in Rembau, Negeri Sembilan.
23 Personal communication with Cecilia Ng, who commented on an earlier draft of this article.

3 Complex configurations: the Women's Agenda for Change and the Women's Candidacy Initiative

1 Segments of this chapter appeared in my paper, 'From Margin to Center: Theorizing Women's Political Participation from Activism on the Margins to Political Power at the Center', in the electronic conference convened by the Women's Global Network, December 2000.
2 See Chapter 2 for more on the historical evolution and current composition of the women's movement.
3 The Women's Agenda for Change may be purchased from WDC by contacting the organisation at wdc@tm.net.my. There used to be a website with the WAC but it has since been disabled.
4 I should point out that I agree, however, with Rohana Ariffin (1999), Cecilia Ng and Chee Heng Leng (1996), as well as the editors of the issue of *Kajian Malaysia* devoted to feminism in Malaysia (1994, vol. 12, nos 1 and 2), that it is fallacious and even neutralising to define the strategies and actions of women activists as 'feminist' or 'liberal' if the term maintains white, western women as normative.
5 These include the Internal Security Act (1960), the Essential (Security Cases) Regulations (1975), the Official Secrets Act (1972), the Defamation Act (1957), the Printing Presses and Publications Act (1984), the Societies Act (1966) and the Universities and University Colleges Act (1971).
6 In her paper, Fatimah Hamid Don uses the term 'equity', which is usually more acceptable than 'equality', especially in Islamic discourse on women. This is because the former has evolved to indicate the complementarity argument: men and women are equal but different, so they complement each other. Other Muslim feminists and women's activists in general find the complementarity/gender equity concept limiting and deliberately choose to use the word 'equality', which is the term and concept I employ in this chapter.
7 See Jamilah (1994) and Rashila and Saliha (1998).
8 For historical context, see Manderson (1980) or Dancz (1987).
9 For example, at a conference on Islam and tolerance convened by Institut Kefahaman Islam Malaysia (IKIM) in August 1995, the Prime Minister answered a question on the issue of polygamy by stating, 'I don't know why

some men want more than one wife, I can tell you that just one woman is a lot of trouble already . . .'

4 Islamic non-governmental organisations

1 In Malaysia, to be a Malay is to be a Muslim. Article 160 of the Federal Constitution of Malaysia reads: 'Malay means a person who professes the religion of Islam, habitually speaks the Malay language, conforms to Malay customs and has Malay parentage.'
2 Before the formation of the Federation of Malaysia in 1963, which included peninsular Malaysia, Sabah and Sarawak, peninsular Malaysia comprised the Federation of Malaya.
3 In addition, Malay is the national language (Article 152). The Constitution also addresses the issue of affirmative action for the Malays by according them special privileges in all state policies with regard to social, economic and education matters (Article 153). Since Malaysia's traumatic experience of racial riots in 1969 in Kuala Lumpur, these privileges have been gazetted under the Sedition Act as sensitive issues that are not to be the subject of public debate, even in Parliament.
4 Anwar Ibrahim's principle was that politics must 'be guided by moral precepts and faith reawakened' (Anwar 1997: 5). He seemed to have held this position consistently since his leadership of the Malaysian Islamic Youth Movement, Angkatan Belia Islam Malaysia (ABIM).
5 In the 1999 general election, PAS retained power in the east coast state of Kelantan, wrested power in Terengganu, and made major inroads into the state assemblies of the Malay-dominated northern states of Perlis and Kedah.
6 Chandra Muzaffar (1987) analysed the phenomenon of Islamic revival from a political and sociological perspective as a new assertion of indigenous identity by the Malays within the dynamics of Malaysian multi-ethnic politics. This period coincided with a general rural–urban migration of Malays which took place amidst the implementation of the New Economic Policy (NEP), 1970–90. The NEP was aimed partly at creating an urban and industrialised Malay community, part of the restructuring of the Malaysian economy introduced through the Second Malaysia Plan, 1971–75.
7 This characteristic differentiates ABIM and Al Arqam from their contemporaries, either Islamic or otherwise, that tend to be made up of a handful of middle-class, English-speaking, urban-based professionals and activists, and thus less familiar to the grassroots, at least until the *Reformasi* movement of the late 1990s, which was sparked off by the sacking of Anwar Ibrahim from the government. Since then, NGOs' political involvement has become a feature of what is now termed the 'new politics' in Malaysia.

5 The environmental movement in Malaysia

1 The Danish government funds the bilateral Malaysian–Danish Country Programme under its DANCED funding mechanism. While other foreign donors and development aid agencies also provide funds (AUSAID, the Canadian International Development Aid or CIDA, the Swiss IDA, the

UNDP, the British Embassy and so on), the Danish example is notable for the level of support they have provided for nature conservation and environmental NGOs in Malaysia since 1996. The Danish government insists that DANCED help Malaysian NGOs and not just the government.
2 The term 'MENGO' will be used here as a collective term to emphasise the role of local communities in assisting with environmental initiatives as well as in the development of society in general.
3 Among the formal sources are the WWFM Annual Reports of 1999 and 2000; the 22 June 2000 DANCED Newsletter; the *Malayan Naturalist* newsletter, which highlights the MNS's projects in the country; and the UNDP Technical Cooperation among Developing Countries Programme 1992.

6 The Malaysian human rights movement

1 For instance, since it is registered as a company, SUARAM has no actual membership. While anyone is welcome to participate as a volunteer or supporter, most decisions are made by a board of directors and small full-time staff.
2 This chapter concentrates on domestic human rights issues. Malaysia also boasts a vibrant peace movement, including groups that fight mainly for human rights issues overseas (even if they occasionally become embroiled in domestic campaigns). These groups include, among others, the International Movement for a Just World and the Centre for Peace Studies. In addition, human rights groups that focus primarily on domestic issues (such as SUARAM) may also engage in international activism, most notably campaigns related to East Timor, Aceh and Burma for the secular groups, and Muslim regions such as Kosovo and Bosnia among Islamic NGOs. See Chapter 8.
3 See, for instance, Grace (1990) or Arokia (1991).
4 To be fair, when Aliran did publish in Malay, inadequate support forced it to stop – its supporters among the progressive middle class are mostly English-readers.
5 For example, economist Jomo K. S. is currently being sued for RM250 million for defamation by businessman Vincent Tan in response to a December 1998 op-ed piece in the *Asian Wall Street Journal*, in which Jomo alleged that the government is bailing out Tan's Kuala Lumpur monorail project.
6 Malay students have benefited from New Economic Policy and New Development Policy provisions for quotas and scholarships to assist Malays in furthering their studies.
7 The Consultative Committee of Buddhist, Christian, Hindu and Sikh Religions of Malaysia organised in the 1980s against the government's Islamicisation programme, and the Major Organisations of the Chinese Guilds and Associations issued the 'Joint Declaration 1985' detailing the grievances of non-Malays pertaining to the government's economic, social, political and cultural policies (Kua 1992: 74–82).
8 Interestingly, it was Anwar Ibrahim who was the most prominent leader of the coalition until he left to join UMNO shortly before the 1982 elections.
9 For more on the commission, including its composition, tasks, prospects, and obstacles to overcome, see *Malaysiakini*'s extended interview with Musa Hitam (Gan 2000).

10 This tendency to focus on the ISA rather than the other laws is probably because it is harder to rally support against a law for 'prevention of crime' or against 'dangerous drugs' than against an acknowledged Cold War relic.
11 See CARPA (1988) for a discussion of the causes, process and impacts of Operasi Lalang, the last major ISA crackdown.

7 Non-governmental organisations in Sarawak

1 This study is made possible through fieldwork grants made available by the Resource Management in Asia and the Pacific Project of the Australian National University. Fieldwork for this paper was conducted over September and October 1999 and from April to June 2000. However, much learning took place from repeated visits and endless conversations in rural and urban communities over the years, beginning in 1991, during the author's Ph.D. fieldwork. I am grateful to all in Sarawak who have helped me in countless ways. They know who they are.
2 For a good exposé of the operations of Malaysian logging companies in Papua New Guinea, see Filer (1997).
3 The word 'Dayak' is used as an umbrella term. While not necessarily accepted by the different ethnic groups (Tan 1997), it is used in this paper as a strategy of convenience, to refer to the very diverse ethnic communities of Iban, Bidayuh (composing a number of sub-groups), Orang Ulu (among whom are the Bisaya, Berawan, Kedayan, Kenyah, Kelabit, Lun Bawang and Penan) and other non-Muslim groups forming the bulk of Sarawak's rural population. Given the complexities of their identities and process of self-ascription as well as the strength of ethnic boundaries (Welyne 1997), using the word 'Dayak' is therefore not an attempt to essentialise their experiences.
4 Refer to Majid Cooke (2000).
5 Respondents have been given fictitious names.
6 This is not a new development. The court system has been used by native peoples for many decades to solve land issues (Cramb 1989a).
7 See Majid Cooke (2000).

8 The peace movement and Malaysian foreign and domestic policy

1 See, for instance, Wong (1996).
2 See Mohd. Nasir Hashim's statement in the *Sun*, 22 December 1996.

References

Abdullah Ahmad (1985) *Tengku Abdul Rahman and Malaysian Foreign Policy 1963–1970*. Kuala Lumpur: Berita Publishing.

Adi Suryadi Culla (1999) *Masyarakat Madani: Pemikiran, Teori, dan Relevansinya dengan Cita-cita Reformasi*. Jakarta: PT RajaGrafindo Persada.

Ahmad Baso (2000) 'Islam dan "Civil Society" di Indonesia: Dari Konservatisme Menuju Kritik'. *Tashwirul Afkar* 7, pp. 4–19.

Ahmad Fauzi Abdul Hamid (1999) 'Political Dimensions of Religious Conflict in Malaysia: State Response to an Islamic Movement in the 1990s'. Paper presented at the Second International Malaysian Studies Conference, Kuala Lumpur, 2–4 August.

Aliran (1981) *Aliran Speaks*. Penang: Aliran Kesedaran Negara.

Anwar Ibrahim (1997) 'Islam dan Pembentukan Masyarakat Madani'. In MINDS (ed.), *Masyarakat Madani: Satu Tinjauan Awal*. Ampang, Selangor: MINDS.

—— (1997) 'Islamic Renaissance'. *Islamic Herald* 18(1): 4–5.

Asiah binti Abu Samah (1960) 'Emancipation of Malay Women 1945–57'. Unpublished BA (Hons) thesis, University of Malaya.

Askiah Adam (1993) 'Malay Women in Islam: Adat and Islam – Conflict or Conjunction?' In *Islam, Gender and Women's Rights: An Alternative View*. Kuala Lumpur: Sisters in Islam.

Bebbington, Anthony (1997) 'Social Capital and Rural Intensification: Local Organizations and Islands of Sustainability in the Rural Andes'. *The Geographical Journal* 163(2): 189–97.

Beng Hui (2000) 'What is the Women's Movement? What Have Been Our Achievements in Malaysia? What Are the Issues We Need to Deal with in the Future?' *AWAM Newsletter* (January).

Blythe, Wilfred (1969) *The Impact of Chinese Secret Societies in Malaya: A Historical Study*. Kuala Lumpur: Oxford University Press.

Braidotti, Rosi (1994) *Nomadic Subjects: Embodiment and Sexual Difference in Contemporary Feminist Theory*. New York: Columbia University Press.

Bresser Pereira, L. Carlos (1993) 'Economic Reforms and Cycles of State Intervention'. *World Development* 21(8): 1337–53.

Brosius, Peter (1997) 'Prior Transcripts, Divergent Paths: Resistance and Acquiescence to Logging in Sarawak, East Malaysia'. *Comparative Studies in Society and History* 39(3): 468–510.

—— (1999) 'Green Dots, Pink Hearts: Displacing Politics from the Malaysian Rain Forest'. *American Anthropologist* 101(1): 36–57.

Butler, Judith (1983) *Bodies that Matter, on the Discursive Limits of Sex*. London and New York: Routledge.

Caldwell, Malcolm (1977) 'From Emergency to Independence, 1948–57'. In Mohamad Amin and Malcolm Caldwell (eds), *Malaya: The Making of a Neocolony*. Nottingham: Spokesman Books/Bertrand Russell Peace Foundation.

CAP (1993) *Wasted Lives: Radioactive Poisoning in Bukit Merah*. Penang: Consumers' Association of Penang.

CAP (1997) 'Save the Main Range'. *Malayan Naturalist* 50(3): 14–23.

Carothers, Thomas (1999–2000) 'Civil Society'. *Foreign Policy* 117 (Winter), pp. 18–29.

CARPA (1988) *Tangled Web: Dissent, Deterrence and the 27 October 1987 Crackdown in Malaysia*. Haymarket, NSW: Committee Against Repression in the Pacific and Asia.

Chandra Muzaffar (1984) 'Has the Communal Situation Worsened over the Last Decade? Some Preliminary Thoughts'. In S. Husin Ali (ed.), *Kaum Kelas dan Pembangunan Malaysia/Ethnicity Class and Development Malaysia*. Kuala Lumpur: Persatuan Sains Sosial Malaysia.

—— (1987) *Islamic Resurgence in Malaysia*. Petaling Jaya: Penerbit Fajar Bakti.

Chee Yoke Ling (1996) 'Regional Developments: Implications for Malaysia'. In *State of the Environment in Malaysia*. Penang: Consumers' Association of Penang.

Chhachhi, Amrita (1988) 'The State, Religious Fundamentalism and Women: Trends in South Asia'. Working Paper Sub-series on *Women, History and Development: Themes and Issues*, No. 8. The Hague: Institute of Social Studies.

Chin, S. C. (1985) 'Agriculture and Resource Utilisation in a Lowland Rainforest Kenyah Community'. *The Sarawak Museum Journal* 25(56) (New Series, December). Special Monograph no. 4, Kuching, Sarawak.

Chinese Guilds and Associations (1985) 'Joint Declaration by the Chinese Guilds and Associations of Malaysia'. Published statement.

Clarke, Gerard (1998) *The Politics of NGOs in South-East Asia: Participation and Protest in the Philippines*. London and New York: Routledge.

Coalition of Concerned NGOs on Bakun (1999) *Final Report of the Fact Finding Mission*. Kuala Lumpur: Suaram Kommunikasi.

Comber, Leon (1961) *The Traditional Mysteries of Chinese Secret Societies in Malaya*. Singapore: Donald Moore for Eastern Universities Press.

Corbyn, Jeremy (1996) 'The Political Dimensions of Northern Global Domination and Its Consequences for the Rights of Five-Sixths of Humanity'. In JUST (ed.), *Human Wrongs: Reflections on Western Global Dominance and Its Impact on Human Rights*. Penang: JUST World Trust, pp. 46–58.

Cramb, Robert (1989a) 'Smallholder Agricultural Development in a Land Surplus Economy: The Case of Sarawak, Malaysia, 1963–88' (Agricultural

Economics Discussion Papers Series, 2/89). St Lucia, Queensland: Department of Agriculture, University of Queensland.

—— (1989b) 'Contradictions in State-sponsored Land Schemes for Peasant Farmers: The Case of Sarawak, Malaysia, 1963–88' (Agricultural Economics Discussion Papers Series, 3/89). St Lucia, Queensland: Department of Agriculture, University of Queensland.

Cramb, Robert and Wills, I. R. (1990) 'The Role of Traditional Institutions in Rural Development: Community-based Land Tenure and Government Land Policy in Sarawak, Malaysia'. *World Development* 18(3): 347–60.

Crouch, Harold (1996) *Government and Society in Malaysia*. Ithaca, NY: Cornell University Press.

DANCED (1999) Malaysian–Danish Country Programme for Environmental Assistance, 1999–2001. Copenhagen: Ministry of Environment and Energy (DANCED).

—— (2000a) Mission Report. Report of NGO Program Identification Mission to Malaysia, 15 September. Unpublished.

—— (2000b) A Strategy and Programme for DANCED Support to Environmental NGOs in Malaysia. NGO Program Identification Mission to Malaysia, 15 September. Unpublished.

Dancz, Virginia H. (1987) *Women and Party Politics in Peninsular Malaysia*. Singapore: Oxford University Press.

De Lue, Steven M. (1997) *Political Thinking, Political Theory, and Civil Society*. Boston: Allyn and Bacon.

Diani, Mario (1992) 'The Concept of Social Movement'. *The Sociological Review*, pp. 1–25.

Eccleston, Bernard (1996) 'Does North–South Collaboration Enhance NGO Influence on Deforestation Policies in Malaysia and Indonesia?' *Journal of Commonwealth and Comparative Politics* (Special Issue), 34(1): 66–89.

Eldridge, Philip (1995) *Non-Government Organizations and Democratic Participation in Indonesia*. Kuala Lumpur: Oxford University Press.

—— (1996) 'Human Rights and Democracy in Indonesia and Malaysia: Emerging Contexts and Discourse'. *Contemporary Southeast Asia* 18(3): 298–319.

Evans, Peter (1996) 'Government Action, Social Capital and Development: Reviewing the Evidence on Synergy'. *World Development* 24(6): 1119–32.

Faiz Ishak (ed.) (2000) *Information Malaysia, 2000 Yearbook*. Kuala Lumpur: Berita Publishing.

Fan Yew Teng (1988) [1983] *Oppressors and Apologists*. Kuala Lumpur: Egret Publications.

—— (1992) 'Malaysia's Foreign Policy in the 1990s'. In Hairany Naffis (ed.), *Politik Malaysia Dekad 1990–an: Prosiding Seminar Politik Malaysia Ke–IV*. Bangi: Jabatan Sains Politik, Universiti Kebangsaan Malaysia.

—— (1996) 'Which Law Will NGO Forum Break?' Press statement. Petaling Jaya: Centre for Peace Initiatives, 17 December.

Fatimah Daud (1985) *'Minah Karan': The Truth about Malaysian Factory Girls*. Kuala Lumpur: Berita Publishing.

210 References

Fatimah Hamid Don (1995) 'The National Policy on Women in Development: A Critique'. Paper presented at national conference on Approaching the 21st Century: Challenges Facing Malaysian Women, University of Malaya, Kuala Lumpur, April.

Fatton, Robert (1995) 'Africa in the Age of Democratization: The Civic Limitations of Civil Society'. *African Studies Review* 38(2): 67–99.

Fernandez, Irene (1992) 'Mobilizing on All Fronts: A Comprehensive Strategy to End Violence Against Women'. In Margaret Schuler (ed.), *Freedom from Violence: Women's Strategies from Around the World*. New York: UNIFEM.

Filer, Colin (ed.) (1997) *The Political Economy of Forest Management in Papua New Guinea*. Port Moresby: National Research Institute of Papua New Guinea and London: International Institute for Environment and Development.

Firdaus Abdullah (1985) *Radical Malay Politics: Its Origins and Early Development*. Petaling Jaya: Pelanduk Publications.

Foweraker, Joe (1995) *Theorising Social Movements*. London and Boulder, CO: Pluto Press.

Fox, Jonathan (1996) 'How Does Civil Society Thicken? The Political Construction of Social Capital in Rural Mexico'. *World Development* 24(6): 1089–103.

Funston, N. J. (1985) 'The Politics of Islamic Reassertion: Malaysia'. In Ahmad Ibrahim, *et al.* (eds), *Readings on Islam in Southeast Asia*. Singapore: ISEAS.

Gabungan NGO Hak Asasi Manusia (n.d.) *Mengapa Kita Perlukan Suruhanjaya Hak Asasi Manusia (NHRC) Yang Betul-Betul Melindungi Rakyat*.

Gan, Stephen (2000) 'Government has a "Credibility Problem"' (four-part interview). *Malaysiakini.com*, 3–6 May. Available on the internet at http://www.malaysiakini.com/News/2000/05/2000050301.php3 (accessed 9 April 2001).

Gellner, Ernest (1994) *Conditions of Liberty: Civil Society and Its Rivals*. London: Penguin.

Government of Malaysia (1991) *Sixth Malaysia Plan 1991–1995*. Kuala Lumpur: Government Printing Press.

Grace, Elizabeth (1990) *Shortcircuiting Labour: Unionising Electronic Workers in Malaysia*. Kuala Lumpur: INSAN.

Gurmit Singh K. S. (1984) *Malaysian Societies: Friendly or Political?* Petaling Jaya: Environmental Protection Society Malaysia and Selangor Graduates Society.

—— (ed.) (1987) *No to Secrecy: The Campaign against 1986's Amendments to the OSA*. Kuala Lumpur: Aliran *et al.*

Habermas, Jürgen (1981) 'New Social Movements'. *Telos* 49 (Fall): 33–7.

HAKAM *et al.* (n.d.) 'Memorandum on Proposed Malaysian NCHR'. Document distributed at the Forum on the National Human Rights Commission, Kuala Lumpur, 3–4 July.

Harding, Andrew (1996) 'Practical Human Rights, NGOs and the Environment in Malaysia'. In Alan E. Boyle and Michael R. Anderson (eds), *Human Rights Approaches to Environmental Protection*. Oxford: Clarendon Press.

Hassan Karim and Siti Nor Hamid (ed.) (1984) *With the People! The Malaysian Student Movement 1967–74*. Petaling Jaya: Institute for Social Analysis.

Haynes, Jeff (1997) *Democracy and Civil Society in the Third World: Politics and New Political Movements*. Cambridge: Polity Press.

—— (2000) 'Action Groups in the "Third World": Building Blocks of Democracy?' Paper presented at Workshop on Social Movements and Development, Yale University, 25 March.

Hellman, Judity Adler (1994) 'Mexican Popular Movements and the Process of Democratization'. *Latin American Perspectives* 81 (21:2): 124–43.

Heng Pek Koon (1996) 'Chinese Responses to Malay Hegemony in Peninsular Malaysia 1957–96'. *Tonan Ajia Kenkyu (Southeast Asian Studies)* 34(3) (December): 32–55.

—— (1999) 'Dawn of a "New" Wanita MCA'. *The Star*, 23 July: 12.

Heyzer, Noeleen (1995) 'Toward New Government–NGO Relations for Sustainable and People-Centred Development'. In Noeleen Heyzer, James V. Riker and Antonio B. Quizon (eds), *Government–NGO Relations in Asia: Prospects and Challenges for People-Centred Development*, Kuala Lumpur: APDC.

Hicks, George (ed.) (1996) *Chinese Organisations in Southeast Asia in the 1930s*. Singapore: Select Books.

Hirschmann, David (1998) 'Civil Society in South Africa: Learning from Gender Themes'. *World Development* 26(2): 227–38.

Hitchcock, David I. (1997) *Factors Affecting East Asian Views of the United States: The Search for Common Ground*. Washington DC: Center for Strategic and International Studies.

Hobsbawm, Eric (1996) *The Age of Extremes: A History of the World 1914–1991*. New York: Vintage.

Hooks, Bell (1984) *Feminist Theory: From Margin to Centre*. Boston: South End Press.

Ibrahim Saad Eddin (1995) 'Civil Society and Prospects of Democratization in the Arab World'. In Augustus Richard Norton (ed.), *Civil Society in the Middle East*, vol. 1. New York: E. J. Brill, pp. 27–54.

INSAN (1989) *Sucked Oranges: The Indian Poor in Malaysia*. Kuala Lumpur: Institute of Social Analysis.

International Tropical Timber Organisation (1990) *The Promotion of Sustainable Forest Management: A Case Study in Sarawak, Malaysia*. Report submitted to the International Tropical Timber Council, Eighth Session, 16–23 May, Bali, Indonesia.

IUCN (2000) *The Role of NGOs in North–South Dialogue*. Gland, Switzerland: International Union for Conservation and Nature.

Jamilah Ariffin (1994) 'Politics and Government Administration'. In Jamilah Ariffin (co-ordinator), *Reviewing Malaysian Women's Status: Country Report in Preparation for the 4th UN Conference on Women*. Kuala Lumpur: Population Studies Unit, University of Malaya.

Jayawardena, Kumari (1986) *Feminism and Nationalism in the Third World*. London: Zed Books.
Jayum Jawan (1993) *The Iban Factor in Sarawak Politics*. Serdang: Penerbit Universiti Pertanian Malaysia.
Jesudason, James V. (1995) 'Statist Democracy and the Limits to Civil Society in Malaysia'. *Journal of Commonwealth and Comparative Politics* 33(3): 335–56.
—— (1996) 'The Syncretic State and the Structuring of Oppositional Politics in Malaysia'. In Garry Rodan (ed.), *Political Oppositions in Industrialising Asia*. London: Routledge.
Johari Bin Mat (1993) 'Peranan dan Tanggungjawab Pertubuhan-pertubuhan Bukan Kerajaan (NGOs) Dalam Mewujudkan Masyarakat Penyayang'. Paper presented at Seminar Peranan Pertubuhan-pertubuhan Bukan Kerajaan (NGOs) Dalam Mewujudkan Masyarakat Penyayang, Kuala Lumpur, 12 August.
Joint Action Group Against Violence Against Women [JAG-VAW] (1986) Proceedings of a workshop-cum-exhibition on Violence Against Women.
Jomo K. S. (1991) *Masyarakat Malaysia: Cabaran Sosio-Ekonomi*. Kuala Lumpur: INSAN.
Jomo K. S. and Ahmad Shaberry Cheek (1992) 'Malaysia's Islamic Movements'. In Kahn, Joel S. and Loh, Francis Kok Wah (eds), *Fragmented Vision: Culture and Politics in Contemporary Malaysia*. North Sydney: Asian Studies Association of Australia and Allen & Unwin.
Jomo K. S. and Todd, Patricia (1994) *Trade Unions and the State in Peninsular Malaysia*. Kuala Lumpur: Oxford University Press.
Jomo K. S. and V. Kanapathy (1996) 'Economic Liberalization and Labour in Malaysia: Efficiency and Equity Considerations in Public Policy Reform'. Paper submitted to ILO, Bangkok.
Josey, Alex (1958) *Trade Unionism in Malaya*. Singapore: Donald Moore.
JUST (1996) *Human Wrongs: Reflections on Western Global Dominance and Its Impact upon Human Rights*. Penang: Just World Trust.
Kandiyoti, Deniz (1997) 'Bargaining with Patriarchy'. In Nalini Visvanathan, Lyn Duggan, Laurie Nisonoff *et al.* (eds), *The Women, Gender and Development Reader*. London: Zed Books.
Khadijah Md. Khalid (n.d.) 'Continuity and Change in Women's Political Participation in West Malaysia'. Unpublished paper.
Khong Kim Hoong (1988–89) 'The Role of Public Interest Groups in a Democratic Society'. *Ilmu Masyarakat* 14: 77–83.
Klandermans, Bert (1989) 'Introduction: Social Movement Organizations and the Study of Social Movements'. *International Social Movement Research*, vol. 2. Greenwich, CT and London: JAI Press, pp. 1–17.
Klandermans, Bert and Tarrow, Sidney (1988) 'Mobilization into Social Movements: Synthesizing European and American Approaches'. *International Social Movement Research*, vol. 1. Greenwich, CT and London: JAI Press, pp. 1–38.
Korten, David C. (1990) *Getting to the 21st Century: Voluntary Action and the Global Agenda*. West Hartford, CT: Kumarian Press.

Kua Kia Soong (1992) *Malaysian Political Realities*. Petaling Jaya: Oriengroup.
—— (1997). 'Whiff of *Déjà vu* – Ten Years After'. *Aliran Monthly* 17(10): 9–10.
—— (1998a) *Mob Rule: The East Timor Conference in Malaysia, November 9, 1996*. Petaling Jaya: Suaram Komunikasi.
—— (1998b) 'The Struggle for Human Rights in Malaysia'. Paper presented at the Asia-Pacific Peoples' Assembly Human Rights Forum, Kuala Lumpur, 9 November.
Lai Suat Yan (2000) 'The Domestic Violence Act: Current Challenges to Malaysian Women'. *Journal of Asian Women's Studies* 8: 135–8.
Lai Suat Yan, Maria Chin Abdullah, Ong, Ju Lin and Wong, Peck Lin (2002) *The Rape Report: An Overview of Rape in Malaysia*. Petaling Jaya: All Women's Action Society and Strategic Info Research Development.
Leach, Melissa, Mearns, Robin and Scoones, Ian (1999) 'Environmental Entitlements: Dynamics and Institutions in Community-based Natural Resource Management'. *World Development* 27(2): 225–47.
Lee Poh Ping (1985) 'World-view of Social Belonging among the Chinese in Malaysia and Singapore: The Case of Secret Societies, Clans and Dialect-group Associations'. In Mohd. Taib Osman (ed.), *Malaysian World-view*. Singapore: ISEAS.
Leftwich, Adrian (1993) 'Governance, Democracy and Development in the Third World'. *Third World Quarterly* 14(3): 605–24.
Leigh, Michael (1998) 'Political Economy of Logging in Sarawak, Malaysia'. In Philip Hirsch and Carol Warren (eds), *The Politics of Environment in Southeast Asia: Resources and Resistance*. London and New York: Routledge.
Leong Shown Chong (1996) 'The Other Side'. *Malayan Naturalist* 49(4): 3–5.
Li Dun Jen (1982) *British Malaya: An Economic Analysis*. Kuala Lumpur: INSAN.
Lian, Francis J. (1987) 'Farmers' Perception and Economic Change'. Ph.D. thesis, Australian National University.
Lian, Francis J. (1993) 'Blockades of Timber Roads in Sarawak: Assertion of Land Rights'. In Garth Cant, John Overton and Eric Pawson (eds), *Indigenous Land Rights in Commonwealth Countries: Dispossession, Negotiation and Community Action*. Christchurch: University of Canterbury, Department of Human Geography and the Ngai Tahu Maori Trust Board.
Lim Teck Ghee (1995) 'Nongovernmental Organisations in Malaysia and Regional Networking'. In Tadashi Yamamoto (ed.), *Emerging Civil Society in the Asia Pacific Community*. Tokyo: Japan Center for International Exchange and Singapore: ISEAS.
Lochead, James (1987) 'Retrenchment in a Malaysian Free Trade Zone'. In Noeleen Heyzer (ed.), *Daughters in Industry*. Kuala Lumpur: Asian and Pacific Development Centre.
Loh Kok Wah, Francis (1997) 'Developmentalism in Malaysia in the 1990s: Is a Shift from the Politics of Ethnicism Underway?" Paper presented at the First International Conference on Malaysian Studies, Kuala Lumpur, August.

Loh Mei Leng (1992-3) 'Dimensi Nasional Dan Antarabangsa Dalam Pembentukan Kesatuan Sekerja Bagi Pekerja-Pekerja Elektronik Di Malaysia'. Unpublished BA (Hons) thesis, Department of Anthropology and Sociology, University Kebangsaan Malaysia.

Mahathir Mohamad (1986) *The Challenge.* Petaling Jaya: Pelanduk Publications.

Mahathir Mohamad (1997) 'Menebus Maruah Bangsa'. Speech at the official opening of the UMNO's 40th General Assembly, Kuala Lumpur, 5 September.

—— (2000) [1995] 'Asian versus Western Values'. In Hashim Makaruddin (ed.), *Democracy, Human Rights, EAEC and Asian Values: Selected Speeches of Dr Mahathir Mohamad, Prime Minister of Malaysia.* Subang Jaya, Selangor: Pelanduk Publications.

Majid Cooke, Fadzilah (1999a) *The Challenge of Sustainable Forests: Forest Resource Policy in Malaysia, 1970-1995.* Sydney: Allen & Unwin and Honolulu: University of Hawaii Press.

—— (1999b, in press) 'Forests, Protest Movements and the Struggle Over Meaning and Identity in Sarawak'. *Akademika* (Bangi) 55 (July): 101-33.

Majid Cooke, Fadzilah (2002) 'Oil Palm and Vulnerable Places in Sarawak: Globalisation and a New Era?' *Development and Change* 33(2): 189-211.

Mak Lau Fong (1981) *The Sociology of Secret Societies: A Study of Chinese Secret Societies in Singapore and Peninsular Malaysia.* Kuala Lumpur: Oxford University Press.

Makmor Tumin (1998) 'NGO Dalam Sistem Demokrasi Malaysia'. *Massa*, 16 May, 62-3.

Malaysian Non-Governmental Organisations (1994, amended 1999) *Malaysian Charter on Human Rights.* Petaling Jaya: Suara Rakyat Malaysia.

Manderson, Lenore (1980) *Women, Politics and Change: The Kaum Ibu UMNO, Malaysia, 1945-1972.* Kuala Lumpur: Oxford University Press.

Marcussen, Henrik Secher (1996) 'NGOs, the State and Civil Society'. *Review of African Political Economy* 23(69) (September): 405-24.

Maznah Mohamad (1994) 'Poststructualism, Power and Third World Feminism'. *Kajian Malaysia* XII (1-2) (June-December): 119-43.

—— (1999) 'Women and Politics in Malaysia: Interview with Cecilia Ng and Zaitun Kasim'. *Aliran Monthly* 19(6): 36-7, 39.

—— (2000) 'Whither the Women's Movement?' *Aliran Monthly* 20(4): 15-17.

Means, Gordon P. (1996) 'Soft Authoritarianism in Malaysia and Singapore'. *Journal of Democracy* 7(4): (October): 103-17.

—— (1991) *Malaysian Politics: The Second Generation.* Singapore: Oxford University Press.

Milne, R. S. and Mauzy, Diane K. (1999) *Malaysian Politics under Mahathir.* London and New York: Routledge.

Milner, A. C. (1991) 'Inventing Politics: The Case of Malaysia'. *Past & Present: A Journal of Historical Studies* 132 (August): 104-29.

MINDS (1997) *Masyarakat Madani: Satu Tinjauan Awal.* Ampang, Selangor: Institut Strategi Pembangunan Malaysia.

Ministry of Land Development, Sarawak (1997) *Handbook on New Concept of Development on Native Customary Rights (NCR) Land, Policies, Benefits, Issues and Responses.* Kuching, Sarawak.
Mohanty, Chandra Talpade, et al. (ed.) (1991) *Third World Women and the Politics of Feminism.* Bloomington: Indiana University Press.
Mohd. Azizuddin Mohd Sani (n.d.) [1999] 'Mahasiswa Pasca Krisis'. Unpublished paper.
Mohd. Nasir Hashim (1997) 'Non-Government Organizations as a Vehicle of Change'. Paper presented at the Australian–Malaysian Conference, Canberra, 19–21 November.
MOSTE (1997) *Country Study on Biological Diversity: Assessment of Biological Diversity in Malaysia.* Kuala Lumpur: Ministry of Science, Technology and the Environment.
Muhammad A. S. Hikam (2000) '"Civil Society" sebagai Proyek Pencerahan'. *Tashwirul Afkar* 7: 83–87.
Muhammad Ikmal Said (1992) 'Ethnic Perspectives of the Left in Malaysia'. In Kahn, Joel S. and Loh, Francis Kok Wah (eds), *Fragmented Vision: Culture and Politics in Contemporary Malaysia.* North Sydney: Asian Studies Association of Australia and Allen & Unwin.
Muhammad Nur Manuty (1996) Keynote address as ABIM President. ABIM's 25th Muktamar Sanawi, September.
Nair, Sheila (1995) 'States, Societies and Societal Movements: Power and Resistance in Malaysia and Singapore'. Ph.D. dissertation, University of Minnesota.
—— (1999) 'Constructing Civil Society in Malaysia: Nationalism, Hegemony and Resistance'. In Jomo K. S. (ed.), *Rethinking Malaysia.* Hong Kong: Asia 2000 for Malaysian Social Science Association.
National Clearing House on Women in Development (1987) *Directory of Women's Organizations.* Kuala Lumpur: National Population and Family Development Board.
National Council of Women's Organizations [NCWO] (n.d.) *National Policy on Women: NCWO's Action Plan for NGOs Implementation.* Kuala Lumpur: NCWO.
New Straits Times (1999) 'Civil Society and Its Democratic Role'. 2 June.
Ng S. N. (1989) 'Borders and Boundaries: Communal Politics and Conflictive Gender Identities in Peninsular Malaysia'. Unpublished MA thesis. The Hague: Institute of Social Studies.
Ng, Cecilia (1999) 'Social Movements, Women's Movement and the State in Malaysia: The Politics of Engagement'. Paper presented at the DAWN Asia-Pacific Workshop on Political Restructuring and Social Transformation, Chiangmai, Thailand, 8–11 October.
Ng, Cecilia and Chee Heng Leng (1996) 'Women in Malaysia: Present Struggles and Future Directions'. *Asian Journal of Women's Studies* 2: 192–209.
Ng, Cecilia and Yong, Carol (1990) 'Malaysian Women at the Crossroads'. *Change International Reports: Women and Society.* London: Change International Reports.

Ng, Cecilia, Siti Nor Hamid and Syed Husin Ali (1999) 'Rural Development Programmes, Women's Participation and Organizations in Malaysia'. In Cecilia Ng (ed.), *Positioning Women in Malaysia: Class and Gender in an Industrializing State.* London: Macmillan.

NGOs (1997) 'Memorandum to Urge Swift and Firm Action against Corruption', Petaling Jaya, 5 August.

Nik Safiah Karim (1984) 'Women's Organizations in Malaysia'. In Hing Ai Yun, Nik Safiah Karim and Rokiah Talib (eds), *Women in Malaysia.* Petaling Jaya: Pelanduk Publications.

Norani Othman (1993) 'Aurah Dan Peraturan Pakaian Bagi Wanita Islam'. In *Islam, Gender and Women's Rights: An Alternative View.* Kuala Lumpur: Sisters in Islam.

Offe, Claus (1985) 'New Social Movements: Challenging the Boundaries of Institutional Politics'. *Social Research* 52(4) (Winter): 816–68.

Peluso, Nancy Lee (1995) 'Whose Woods Are These? Counter-mapping Forest Territories in Kalimantan, Indonesia'. *Antipode* 27(4): 383–406.

Putnam, Robert (2000) *Bowling Alone: The Collapse and Revival of American Community.* New York: Simon and Schuster.

Putnam, Robert (with Robert Leonardi and Raffaella Y. Nanetti) (1993) *Making Democracy Work: Civic Traditions in Modern Italy.* Princeton: Princeton University Press.

Rajoo, R. (1985) 'World-view of the Indians with Regard to Their Social Identity and Belonging in Malaysia'. In Mohd. Taib Osman (ed.), *Malaysian World-view.* Singapore: ISEAS.

Ramdas Tikamdas (1998) 'Human Rights Day Message 1998'. Kuala Lumpur: Persatuan Kebangsaan Hak Asasi Manusia (HAKAM).

—— (1999) 'Welcome Address'. Paper presented at the Forum on the National Human Rights Commission, Kuala Lumpur, 3–4 July.

Rashila Ramli (1998) 'Pembangunan Politik dan Gender: Cabaran dan Strategi bagi Calon-calon Wanita'. In Rokiah Talib and Shanthi Thambiah (eds), *Gender, Budaya dan Masyarakat.* Kuala Lumpur: Rancangan Pengajian Gender, Fakulti Sastera dan Sains Sosial, Universiti Malaya.

Rashila Ramli and Saliha Haji Hassan (1998) 'Trends and Forms of Women's Participation in Politics'. In Sharifah Zaleha Syed Hassan (ed.), *Malaysian Women in the Wake of Change.* Kuala Lumpur: Gender Studies Programme, University of Malaya.

Rodan, Garry (1997) 'Civil Society and Other Political Possibilities in Southeast Asia'. *Journal of Contemporary Asia* 27(2): 156–78.

Roff, William R. (1994) [1967] *The Origins of Malay Nationalism* (2nd edn). Kuala Lumpur: Oxford University Press.

Rohana Ariffin (1988) 'Malaysian Women's Participation in Trade Unions'. In Noeleen Heyzer (ed.), *Daughters in Industry.* Kuala Lumpur: Asian and Pacific Development Centre.

—— (1997a) *Shame, Secrecy and Silence: Study of Rape in Penang.* Penang: Women's Crisis Centre.

—— (1997b) *Women and Trade Unions in Peninsular Malaysia with Special*

Reference to MTUC and CUEPACS. Penang: University Sains Malaysia.
—— (1999) 'Feminism in Malaysia: A Historical and Present Perspective of Women's Struggles in Malaysia'. *Women's Studies International Forum* 22(4): 47–72.
Saari, Gail (2000) 'Rainforest Forever'. *Malaysian Naturalist* 54(2): 34–9.
Sabri Zain (2000) *Face Off: A Malaysian Reformasi Diary (1998–1999)*. Singapore: Options Publications.
Said Ramadan (1985) 'Three Major Problems Confronting the World of Islam'. In Ahmad Ibrahim *et al.* (eds), *Readings on Islam in Southeast Asia*. Singapore: ISEAS.
Saliha Hassan (1992) 'Organisasi Bukan Kerajaan dalam Politik Malaysia'. In Hairany Naffis (ed.), *Politik Malaysia Dekad 1990–an: Prosiding Seminar Politik Malaysia Ke–IV*. Bangi: Jabatan Sains Politik, Universiti Kebangsaan Malaysia.
—— (1997) 'Asian Values and Democracy: Islamic-Oriented Non-Governmental Organisations in Malaysia'. Paper presented at the Third International Workshop on Discourses and Practices of Democracy in Southeast Asia, Copenhagen, 30 September–4 October.
—— (1997) 'Islamic Revivalism and State Response to Islamic-Oriented Non-Governmental Organisations in Malaysia'. Paper presented at workshop on Islamic Revivalism and State Response: The Experiences of Malaysia, Indonesia and Brunei, Singapore: ISEAS, 2–3 June.
—— (1998) 'Non-Governmental Organisations and Political Participation in Malaysia'. Paper presented at meeting on Discourses and Practices of Democracy in Malaysia, Universiti Sains Malaysia, Penang, 18–19 July.
Saliha Hassan and Che Hamdan Che Mohd Razali (2001) 'Dakwah Etika dan Politik: Satu Pemerhatian Terhadap NGO Dakwah di Malaysia'. Paper presented at Seminar Kebangsaan Dakwah dan Etika Politk, Bangi, Malaysia, 25–26 June.
Saravanamuttu, Johan (1994) 'Beyond the Male Gaze: Seeking out New Terrains for Malaysian Feminist Practice'. *Kajian Malaysia* 12(1 and 2): 210–25.
—— (1997) 'Transforming Civil Societies in ASEAN Countries (With special focus on Malaysia and Singapore)'. CIS Working Paper 1997–8. Toronto: University of Toronto, Centre for International Studies.
Scott, James C. (1985) *Weapons of the Weak*. New Haven, CT: Yale University Press.
Shamsul A. B. (1996) 'Nations-of-Intent in Malaysia'. In Tonnesson, Stein and Antlov, Hans (eds), *Asian Forms of the Nation*. London: Curzon Press.
—— (1997) 'Identity Construction, Nation Formation, and Islamic Revivalism in Malaysia'. In Hefner, Robert W. and Horvatich, Patricia (eds), *Islam in an Era of Nation States: Politics and Religious Revival in Muslim Southeast Asia*. Honolulu: University of Hawaii Press.
Sharifah Zaleha Syed Hassan (1995) 'Islamic Revival in Malaysia: A Case Study in Al-Arqam'. Seminar paper presented at the 1st EUROSEAS Conference, Leiden, June.
Siddiq Fadil (1982) 'Garis-garis Besar Haluan Perjuangan'. Ucapan Dasar

218 References

Pemangku Presiden ABIM, ABIM's 11th Muktamar Sanawi, 3–5 September.
—— (1983) 'Menyahut Cabaran Abad Kebangunan', Ucapan Dasar Pemangku Presiden ABIM, ABIM's 12th Muktamar Sanawi, 30 July–1 August.
Spivak, Gayatri Chakravorty (1987) *In Other Worlds*. New York: Methuen.
Stenson, Michael R. (1970) *Industrial Conflict in Malaysia: Prelude to the Communist Revolt of 1948*. Kuala Lumpur: Oxford University Press.
Stivens, Maila (1992) 'Perspectives on Gender: Problems in Writing about Women in Malaysia'. In Joel S. Kahn and Francis Loh (eds), *Fragmented Vision: Culture and Politics in Contemporary Malaysia*. Sydney: Asian Studies Association of Australia in association with Allen and Unwin.
Stivens, Maila (1996) *Matriliny and Modernity: Sexual Politics and Social Change in Rural Malaysia*. St Leonards, NSW: Allen and Unwin.
SUARAM (1998) *Malaysian Human Rights Report*. Petaling Jaya: SUARAM Komunikasi.
—— (1999) *Undi Demi Hak Anda Bukan untuk ISA* [Vote for your rights, not for the ISA]. Pamphlet.
Suat Yan (1998) 'Achievements and Challenges in the Struggle against Violence against Women: The Rape Campaign in Malaysia'. *Asian Women* 6 (June).
Syamsurizal Panggabean (2000) '"Civil Society" sebagai Kawasan Kebebasan'. *Tashwirul Afkar* 7: 88–95.
Tan Boon Kean and Bishan Singh (1994) *Uneasy Relations: The State and NGOs in Malaysia*. Kuala Lumpur: Gender and Development Programme, Asian and Pacific Development Centre.
Tan Chee Beng (1997) 'Indigenous People, the State and Ethnogenesis: A Study of the Communal Associations of the "Dayak" Communities in Sarawak, Malaysia'. *Journal of Southeast Asian Studies* 28(2): 263–84.
Tan Wan Yean (1994–5) 'Freedom of Association with Particular Reference to In-house Unions in the Electronics Industry in Malaysia'. Unpublished Bachelor of Law (Hons.) thesis, Faculty of Law, University of Malaya.
Tan, Simon (1990) 'The Rise of State Authoritarianism in Malaysia', *Bulletin of Concerned Asian Scholars* 22(3): 32–42.
Tan, Thomas Tsu-Wee (1983) 'Singapore Modernization: A Study of Traditional Chinese Voluntary Associations in Social Change'. Ph.D. dissertation, Department of Sociology, University of Virginia.
Tarrow, Sidney (1989) *Struggle, Politics and Reform: Collective Action, Social Movements, and Cycles of Protest*. Ithaca, NY: Cornell University, Western Societies Program.
Tenaganita (1997) *The Real Side*. 4 (June).
Tham Seong Chee (1977) *The Role and Impact of Formal Associations on the Development of Malaysia*. Bangkok: Friedrich-Ebert-Stiftung.
Trinh T. Minh-ha (1989) *Woman, Native, Other*. Bloomington: Indiana University Press.
Uhlin, Anders (1997) *Indonesia and the 'Third Wave of Democratization': The Indonesian Pro-Democracy Movement in a Changing World*. Richmond, Surrey: Curzon Press, 1997.

References 219

van Naerssen, Ton (1995) 'Malaysian NGOs in the Context of Developments in Southeast Asia'. Report to be submitted to HIVOS.

Vargas, Virginia (1995) 'Women's Movement in Peru: Rebellion into Action'. In Saskia Wieringa (ed.), *Subversive Women: Women's Movement in Africa, Asia, Latin America and the Caribbean*. New Delhi: Kali for Women.

WAC (1999) *The Women's Agenda for Change*. Kuala Lumpur: Vinlin Press.

Walker, Millidge (1996) *NGO Participation in a Corporatist State: The Example of Indonesia* (Working Paper 678). Berkeley: Institute of Urban and Regional Development, University of California-Berkeley.

Wan Rahimi B. Salleh (1986) 'Penganalisaan Perkembangan Lembaga Kebajikan Perempuan Islam Persekutuan Tanah Melayu: Satu Kajian Kes Mengenai Organisasi Persatuan Wanita Islam di Malaysia'. Graduation Exercise, Jabatan ANSOS, Universiti Malaya.

Wapner, Paul (1996) *Environmental Activism and World Civic Politics*. Albany: State University of New York Press.

WCI (1999) 'Manifesto of the Women's Candidacy Initiative'. Document.

Weiss, Meredith L. (2000) 'Political Participation in Malaysia'. Unpublished paper.

Welyne, Jeffrey Jahom (1999) 'The Problem of Ethnic Identity in Sarawak'. *Akademika* (Bangi) 55 (July): 83–98.

Wieringa, Saskia (ed.) (1995) *Subversive Women: Women's Movements in Africa, Asia, Latin America and the Caribbean*. New Delhi: Kali for Women.

Women's Manifesto (1990) 'As Malaysians and As Women: Questions for our Politicians and a Manifesto for the '90s'. Document.

Wong Chun Wai (1996) 'Tribunal that's Open to Question'. *Sunday Star*, 22 December.

Y. Mansoor Marican (1976) 'Malay Nationalism and the Islamic Party of Malaysia'. *Islamic Studies* XVI(1) (Spring): 291–301.

Yamamoto, Tadashi (ed.) (1995) *Emerging Civil Society in the Asia Pacific Community: Nongovernmental Underpinnings of the Emerging Asia Pacific Regional Community*. Tokyo: Japan Center for International Exchange and Singapore: ISEAS.

Young, Iris Marion (1999) 'State, Civil Society, and Social Justice'. In Ian Shapiro and Casiano Hacker-Cordón (eds), *Democracy's Value*. New York: Cambridge University Press.

Zainah Anwar (1987) *Islamic Revivalism in Malaysia: Dakwah Among the Students*. Petaling Jaya: Pelanduk Publications.

—— (1999) 'What Islam, Whose Islam? The Struggle for Women's Rights Within a Religious Framework: The Experience of Sisters in Islam'. Paper presented at workshop on Southeast Asian Pluralisms: Social Resources for Civility and Participation in Malaysia, Singapore and Indonesia. Petaling Jaya, 5–6 August.

Index

ABIM *see* Angkatan Belia Islam Malaysia
Action Plan for Women in Development 75, 79; Irene Fernandez 151
Acts: Companies Act 120; Official Secret Acts 34, 36, 147; Police Act 31; Printing Presses and Publications Acts 34, 66; Progressive legislation 138; Restricted Residence Act 150; Societies Act 31, 120, 156; Universities and University Colleges Act 1971 (UUCA) 34, 35; *see also* legal framework
Al Arqam 104, 108, 204
Aliran Kesedaran Negara 33, 36, 106, 143
Aliran Monthly 43, 93
All-Malayan Council for Joint Action 51
AMCJA *see* All-Malayan Council for Joint Action
Angkatan Belia Islam Malaysia 33, 41, 103, 108, 204
Angkatan Wanita Sedar 50
apolitical associations 5
ARE *see* Asian Rare Earth
ASEAN 126; Asean Action Plan on Transboundary Pollution 126; ASEAN Human Rights Mechanism 154; Asean Senior Official on Environment 126
Asian Human Rights Charter 40, 140
Asian Rare Earth 126
Asian values 10, 81, 152; economic development 142
Aurat Muhammadiah 108
AWAM 65; *see also* Women's Agenda for Change
AWAS *see* Angkatan Wanita Sedar
AWL *see* women's NGOs

Bakun Dam 36, 125; Bakun Hydroelectric Power Project 125
Banishment Ordinance 21
Barisan Nasional 6, 76, 197; youth wing 151
Beijing Conference 81

campaigns 154; anti-ISA 160; Artis Pro Activ 157; Bakun Dam 157; detention without trial 158; Kua Kia Soong 160; management of ecosystem 134; monitoring and fact findings 158; networking 40; research, publications and forums 158; Urban Resource Unit 157
campaigns and strategies 147; *see also* key tactics
CAP *see* environmental NGOs
capacity building 130
CAR *see* Citizens Against Rape
CBOs *see* community-based organisations
CENPEACE *see* Centre for Peace Initiatives
Centre for Peace Initiatives 186, 189
Central Indian Association of Malaya 23
CETDEM *see* environmental NGOs

Index

Chinese associations 19, 20, 24, 63
Chinese Protectorate system 21
Chinese secret societies 20, 22, 31, 32
Citizens Against Rape 62
civic associations 2
civil family laws 60
civil societal associations 2, 3
civil society 2, 5, 10
Code of Conduct on the Prevention and Eradication of Sexual Harassment 65
Code of Conduct on Sexual Harassment; sexual harassment 57
community-based organisations 119, 132, 133, 136; CEDAW 79; community-based NGOs 134
Conscious Women's Front *see* Angkatan Wanita Sedar
constructive engagement 36
consumer movement; active politicians 199; FOMCA 199
Convention on Biological Diversity 122
Convention on Wetlands of International Importance 122
Council of Ulamas 51
cultural and progress associations 25
culture 9

dakwah 99, 102, 103, 105, 106, 107, 113
DANCED 131; NGO Programme Appraisal Mission 129
DAP *see* Democratic Action Party
Darul Arqam 11, 33, 107
Dasar Penerapan Nilai-nilai Islam 100; Islamisation Policies 103; *see also Kursus Pemurnian Akidah*
Dayak communal associations 170
death penalty 141
democracy, realistic 5
Democratic Action Party 35, 42, 53, 60, 76, 86, 91, 92; Women's Section 60; Zaitun Kasim 69
Department of Environment 117, 125, 128
Department of National Parks and Wildlife 135
DOE *see* Department of Environment
Domestic Violence Act 46, 61, 63, 77, 87
Domestic Violence Bill 64
donor support: donor organisations 131; European donor 200; financial assistance 130; *see also* funding
DVA *see* Domestic Violence Act

economic development 142
Economic Planning Unit 119
education 9
Emergency 35; Article 150 150
ENSEARCH 133; *see also* environmental NGOs
environmental education 134; biodiversity conservation 137
environmental groups 132
Environmental Impact Assessment 124, 128, 171
environmental movement 14, 115
environmental NGOs 115, 116, 121, 125, 132, 133, 135; Bakun Dam 124; Biodiversity Action Network 119, 133; Board of Trustees 120; Centre for Environment, Technology and Development, Malaysia (CETDEM) 133; Climate Action Network 119, 133; 'consultant' NGOs 120; Consumers' Association of Penang 116; Dams Action Network 119, 133; Environmental Management and Research Association 133; Environmental Protection Society of Malaysia 116; Federation of Malaysian Consumer Association (FOMCA) 133; 'grassroots' membership 120; hands on experience 131; Hills Network 119; Malayan Nature Society 117, 116; Malaysian Climate Change Group 119, 133; Malaysian Hills Network 124; Malaysian Nature Society 121; 'membership' NGOs 120; Nature Education Centres 121; Pesticide Action Network 119, 133; Sahabat Alam Malaysia 116; Sustainable Development Network Malaysia (SUSDEN) 119, 133;

environmental NGOs – *continued*
  varying capacities and strengths 138; Wetlands International – Malaysia Program 121; World Wide Fund for Nature Malaysia 116, 121
environmentalism 37; nature reserves 134
Equality Act 49
ethnic communities 206
ethnicity 45, 46

Federation of Malaya Women's Teachers Union 55
feminism 48
FOMCA *see* environmental NGOs
Forestry Department 135
Freedom of Information Act: anti-OSA campaign 151
Friends of Women *see* Sahabat Wanita
funding 39; *see also* donor support

Gagasan Demokrasi Rakyat 143, 146
gender politics 13
GONGO *see* government-organised NGOs
gotong royong 24
government consultations 157, 163; First International Conference on Bosnia 189; joint efforts 131; *Kursus Pemurniaan Akidah* 108; Malaysian government 17, 194; National Advisory Council for Consumers' Protection 135, 199; National Committee on Environment 136; partnership approach 137; partnership with government 136; WWF 137
government-organised NGOs 39, 99, 199; Belia 4B 102; HAWA 86, 201; Islamic Dakwah and Training Institute 111; Islamic Research Centre 111; Malaysian Dakwah Foundation 99; National Fatwa Council 111; Persatuan Kebajikan Islam Malaysia 101; Yayasan Dakwah Islamiah Malaysia 99
grassroots foundation 131

Guardianship of Infants (Amendment) Bill 48

HAKAM *see* National Human Rights Society of Malaysia; Persatuan Kebangsaan Hak Asasi Manusia
hands on experience 131
Harakah 43; *see also* Parti Islam SeMalaysia
HAWA 87; *see also* Women's Affairs Department; Women's Affairs Division
Health Ministry 62
historical antecedents 19
Hudud 108
human rights 132; advocacy organisations 145; *Aliran Monthly* 148; Chinese associations 145; consumers' group 144; *Detik* 148; *Ekslusif* 148; environmental groups 144; *Harakah* 148; HIV/AIDS groups 145; Irene Fernandez 148; judicial reform 155; Karpal Singh 155; labour unions 144; Lim Guan Eng 148; Nasir Hashim 162; police abuses 155; popular support 161; professional organisation 145; religious bodies 146; St Francis Xavier Church 147; students' group 145; Tun Salleh Abbas 155; women's groups 144; women's issues 161
human rights movements 14, 140, 141; coalitions 162; core group 162; human rights activism 161; organisational and motivational weakness 163
human rights NGOs 141; Persatuan Kebangsaan Pelajar Islam Malaysia 141; Sisters in Islam 141; Tenaganita 200; *see also* Malaysian Human Rights Commission; Suara Rakyat Malaysia

ijtihad 110
IKIM 111; *see also* government-organised NGOs
Indian associations 22, 23, 24

Indian migrants 22
Indian societies 22
Institut Dakwah dan Latihan Islam (INDAH) 111; *see also* Islamic-oriented NGOs
Institut Kefahaman Islam Malaysia 111; *see also* Islamic-oriented NGOs
Institut Pengajaran Komuniti 33
Internal Security Act 33, 37, 62, 86, 106, 109, 140, 147, 158, 159, 172
International covenants: International Covenant on Civil and Political Right 152; International human rights covenants 153
International Movement for a Just World 38; *see also* peace movement
International Women's Day 61
IONGO *see* Islamic-oriented NGOs
IPR *see* rights
ISA *see* Internal Security Act
Islah 97
Islamic Missionary Foundation 111; *see also* government-organised NGOs
Islamic movements 97, 111, 113
Islamic NGOs *see* Islamic-oriented NGOs
Islamic-oriented NGOs 9, 14, 97, 101; Council for the Welfare of Muslim Women; Darul Arqam 150; Lembaga Kebajikan Perempuan Islam 101; Pergerakan Puteri Islam 102; Persatuan Kebajikan Islam Malaysia 101; *see also* Angkatan Belia Islam Malaysia

JAGVAW *see* Joint Action Group Against Violence Against Women; women's NGOs
Jamaah Islah Malaysia 41, 76, 85, 104
Jawatankuasa Fatwa Kebangsaan *see* Malaysian National Fatwa Council
JIM *see* Jamaah Islah Malaysia

Joint Action Group Against Violence Against Women 61, 77, 200

Keadilan 91; *see also* Parti Keadilan Nasional
Kesatuan Melayu Muda 26
key tactics 156
konsep baru 167, 168, 180
Kursus Pemurnian Akidah 108

labour movement 54–8; *see also* Malaysian Trade Union Congress
Lalang Operation *see* Operation Lalang
Land Conservation and Development Authority 168
Land and Survey Department 176, 177
language 9
LCDA *see* Land Conservation and Development Authority
legal environment 18
legal framework 120; *see also* Acts

MAF *see* Malaysian Action Front
mainstream mass media 158
Majlis Gerakan Keadilan Rakyat Malaysia 146
Majlis Kebangsaan Bagi Hal Ehwal Agama Islam 110,
Malay community 103, 198; Article 152 204; Article 153 204; Article 160 204; Islamic revival 204
Malay left 198
Malay Nationalist Party 50
Malay organisations: Gabungan Pelajar Melayu Semenanjung 102; Kesatuan Melayu Muda 27; Kesatuan Melayu Singapura 26; Persaudaraan Sahabat Pena Malaya 27; Saudara 27
Malay societies 24
Malay Women's Teachers' Union 54
Malaysian Action Front 188
Malaysian activists 43
Malaysian AIDS Council 38
Malaysian Charter on Human Rights 140

Index

Malaysian Chinese Association: MCA Women's Section 59; Wanita MCA 49, 53, 59
Malaysian Ecotourism Plan 123
Malaysian Human Rights Commission 86
Malaysian Human Rights Report 141
Malaysian Islamic Welfare Organisation *see* Persatuan Kebangsaan Pelajar Islam Malaysia
Malaysian Islamic Youth Movement *see* Angkatan Belia Islam Malaysia
Malaysian National Fatwa Council 108, 111
Malaysian Royal Police 63
Malaysian Socialist People's Party *see* Parti Sosialis Rakyat Malaysia
Malaysian Trade Union Congress 57; women's section 201
masyarakat madani 9, 10, 100, 103, 197
MCA *see* Malaysian Chinese Association
MCHR *see* Malaysian Charter on Human Rights
media, women in 61
Memorandum on the National Policy on Women 75
menoa 178–9
Minister of Home Affairs 31, 159
Minister of National Unity and Community Development 59
Minister of National Unity and Social Development 11, 63, 76
Minister of Science, Technology and the Environment 122
Ministry of Culture, Arts and Tourism 123
Ministry of Education 121
Ministry of Environment 116
Ministry of Foreign Affairs 153
Ministry of Home Affairs 34
Ministry of Human Resources 65
Ministry of International Trade and Industry 93
Ministry of Justice 62
Ministry of Science, Technology and the Environment 127
Ministry of Women and Family Development 82, 83
MKI *see* Majlis Kebangsaan Bagi Hal Ehwal Agama Islam
MNP *see* Malay Nationalist Party
modern community organisations 25
MTUC *see* Malaysian Trade Union Congress
Muslim family laws 60
Muslim professional organisation 104

National Council of Women's Organisations 55, 59, 60, 73, 75, 76, 109
National Human Rights Commission 153; *see also* Malaysian Human Rights Commission
National Human Rights Society of Malaysia 143; *see also* Malaysian Human Rights Commission
National Policy on Biological Diversity 122
National Policy on Women 60, 75, 78, 79, 84, 90, 96; *see also* Women's Agenda for Change
National Union of Malaysian Muslim Students *see* Persatuan Kebangsaan Pelajar Islam Malaysia
National Union of Plantation Workers 55
National Women's Coalition 77
Native Customary Rights 154
NAWIM *see* women's NGOs
NCWO *see* National Council of Women's Organisations
NGO Tribunal on Police Abuses 151; *see also* human rights
NGO *see* non-governmental organisations
NHRC *see* National Human Rights Commission; Malaysian Human Rights Commission
non-governmental organisations 17, 44, 75, 198; 'grassroots' NGOs 120; 'membership' NGOs 120; capacities and strengths 138; third

Index

sector 3; transnational NGOs 132; *see also* environmental NGOs; government-organised NGOs; human rights NGOs; Islamic-oriented NGOs; political NGOs; Sarawak NGOs; women's NGOs

Official Security Acts 147
Operasi Lalang 109; *see also* Operation Lalang
Operation Lalang 36, 48, 109, 172
opposition parties 7, 11, 53

Pan-Malaysian Islamic Party *see* Parti Islam SeMalaysia; PAS
Parti Islam SeMalaysia 48, 86
Parti Keadilan Nasional 42, 86, 146
Parti Rakyat Malaysia 42, 86, 91; *see also* Parti Sosialis Rakyat Malaysia
Parti Sosialis Rakyat Malaysia 59; *see also* Parti Rakyat Malaysia
PAS 42, 92; Dewan Muslimat 54, 59, 91; *see also* Pan-Malaysian Islamic Party; Parti Islam SeMalaysia
peace movement 15, 181, 183, 185, 191, 194, 205; foreign regimes 192; *Gerak Damai* 187; Just World Trust 189; Malaysian Red Crescent Society 188; Malaysian Sociological Research Institute 188; MBM 193
peasant movement 35; APCET II 191; Malaysian Mass Rally 189; Second Asia Pacific Conference on East Timor 191
Persatuan Kebajikan Islam Malaysia *see* government-organised NGOs
Persatuan Kebangsaan Hak Asasi Manusia 199; *see also* human rights NGOs
Persatuan Kebangsaan Pelajar Islam Malaysia 141; *see also* Islamic-oriented NGOs
Persatuan Peguam Islam Malaysia 104; *see also* Islamic-oriented NGOs
Persatuan Ulama Malaysia 41, 104, 111
Persekutuan Indra Kayangan 26
PKPIM *see* Persatuan Kebangsaan Pelajar Islam Malaysia
Plantation Workers' Union 55; *see also* labour movement
Police Act 149
political society 31, 32
politics, new 204
political NGOs 18, 27
politics, old 9
polygamy 60
PPI *see* Islamic-oriented NGOs
PPPA *see* Printing Presses and Publication Act 148
Printing Presses and Publication Act 48, 147; *see also* Acts
PRM *see* Parti Rakyat Malaysia; *Suara PRM*
progress associations 26; Persekutuan Guru-guru Islam 26; Persekutuan Guru-guru Melayu 26; Persekutuan Indra Kayangan 26; Persekutuan Keharapan Belia 26; Persekutuan Perbahathan Orang-orang Islam 26
PSRM *see* Parti Sosialis Rakyat Malaysia
Pusat Islam Malaysia 111; *see also* government-organised NGOs
Pusat Penyelidikan Islam 111; *see also* government-organised NGOs

Reformasi 12, 149, 150, 151; conscientised individuals 163; younger activist 163
Reformasi movement 35
regional co-operation: Biodiversity Convention 126–7; North–South NGO networks 127
Registrar of Companies 120
Registrar of Societies 31, 120, 149
rights 127; civil liberties 12; human rights 6, 142, 143, 156; individuals' rights 3; intellectual property rights 127; women's rights 48, 53; workers' rights 54
Roket 43
Rukunegara 33

Sabah 61, 117, 118, 133
Sahabat Wanita 57
Sarawak 15, 61, 117, 118, 133, 165

Sarawak Forest Ordinance 172
Sarawak Land Code 177
Sarawak NGOs 171, 172, 173; Persatuan Kelabit Baram 171; Sarawak Berawan Association 171
SAWO *see* women's NGOs
SCAH *see* Selangor Chinese Assembly Hall
Second Asia Pacific Conference on East Timor 37, 191; *see also* peace movement
secret societies 19, 20, 21, 197; *see also* Chinese associations
Secretariat for the Conference of Societies (SCS) 32
Sedition Act 148; *see* also Acts
Selangor Chinese Assembly Hall 63
Selangor Dam Project 125; *see also* environmental NGOs
sexual harassment 65; Theresa Kok 96
sexuality 70; 'Lina's Dilemma' 71
SFTCA *see* women's NGOs
SIS *see* Sisters in Islam
Sisters in Islam 67, 104, 108
social movement(s) 9, 46, 70, 196
social networks 3
societal associations 3
Societies Act 31, 39, 106, 147, 151; Registrar of Societies 31, 120, 149
Societies Act Co-ordinating Committee (SACC) 32
Societies Ordinance 21
students movements *see* Angkatan Belia Islam Malaysia; Persatuan Kebangsaan Pelajar Islam Malaysia; University of Malaya Students' Union
Suara PRM 43; *see also* Parti Rakyat Malaysia
Suara Rakyat Malaysia 36, 63, 141, 143; *see also* human rights NGOs
SUARAM *see* Suara Rakyat Malaysia
SUHAKAM *see* Malaysian Human Rights Commission
SUSDEN *see* environmental NGOs

Tenaganita 57
Third World Network 127
Trade Record Analysis of Flora and Fauna in Commerce 132
TRAFFIC *see* Trade Record Analysis of Flora and Fauna in Commerce
transnational NGOs 132; WIMP 132; WWF 132
TWN *see* Third World Network

UDHR *see* Universal Declaration of Human Rights
UMNO *see* United Malay National Organisation
Unit Hal Ehwal Agama 112; *see also* government-organised NGOs
United Nations Development Fund for Women (Malaysia) 89
United Malay National Organisation (UMNO) 6; Kaum Ibu 50–2; Khadijah Sidek 52; Puteri UMNO 94; Wanita UMNO 29, 53, 55, 59, 86, 94
Universal Declaration of Human Rights 140
Universities and University Colleges Act 147
University of Malaya Students' Union 35
Utusan Komsumer 43
UUCA 149; *see also* Acts
UWA 202; *see also* women's NGOs

WAC *see* Women's Agenda for Change
WAO 65; *see also* women's NGOs
WCC 65; *see also* women's NGOs
WCI *see* Women's Candidacy Initiative
WDC 65; *see also* women's NGOs
WIMP *see* environmental NGOs
Women and Human Resource Studies Unit 63
Women Workers' Programmes 66; All Women's Action Society 62, 76; Association of Women Lawyers 61; Kesatuan Melayu Singapura 29; Malay Women Teachers' Union 58; MTUC Women's Section 61; National Association of Women's Institute

in West Malaysia (NAWIM) 58;
NCWO 59; Penang Women's
Association 58; Sabah Women's
Organisation 62; Sahabat Wanita
62, 76; Sarawak Women for
Women Society 76; Selangor and
Federal Territory Consumers'
Association 61; Selangor Graduate
Society 38; Selangor Women's
Relief Association 58; Tenaganita
38, 76; University Women's
Association 61; Wan Azizah Wan
Ismail 143
Women's Action Front 55
Women's Affairs Department 60
Women's Affairs Division 64, 76, 86
Women's Agenda for Change 14, 69, 70–75, 81, 83, 85, 86, 91, 96; All Women's Action Society 77; Sisters in Islam 77
Women's Aid Organisation (WAO) 61, 76
Women's Candidacy Initiative 14, 69, 71, 72, 75, 87, 88, 89, 91; *see also* Democratic Action Party
Women's Crisis Centre 62
Women's Day 51, 52, 59
Women's Development Collective 62, 76, 77; Malayan Reconstruction Co-operative Association 29; Malayan Welfare Association 29; Marina Chin Abdullah 202
Women's Federation 51; All-Malaya Women's Federation 50
Women's Force *see* Tenaganita
women's interest and rights 50, 54
Women's Manifesto 78
women's movement 45, 46, 47, 50
women's NGOs 58, 61, 72, 73, 75, 76, 82, 201; AWAM 66; AWL 202; Children and Young Women's Programme 66; JAG 66, 67; National Women's Coalition 66; NCWO 67; Persatuan Sahabat Wanita 66, 88; Sisters in Islam 67, 202; Tenaganita 41, 66; UWA 202; WAO 202; WDC 202
women's rights 191
women's sections 76; Malaysian Trade Union Congress 76; Pertubuhan Jamaah Islah Malaysia 76, 85, 104; Selangor Chinese Assembly Hall 63, 76

YADIM 111; *see also* government-organised NGOs

Zaitun Kasim *see* Democratic Action Party